James Sprunt

Information and statistics respecting Wilmington, North Carolina,

being a report

James Sprunt

Information and statistics respecting Wilmington, North Carolina, being a report

ISBN/EAN: 9783337306281

Printed in Europe, USA, Canada, Australia, Japan

Cover: Foto ©Andreas Hilbeck / pixelio.de

More available books at **www.hansebooks.com**

INFORMATION AND STATISTICS

RESPECTING

WILMINGTON, NORTH CAROLINA,

BEING A REPORT BY THE PRESIDENT OF THE PRODUCE EXCHANGE.

PRESENTED TO ITS MEMBERS, APRIL, 1883.

WILMINGTON, N. C.:
JACKSON & BELL, WATER-POWER PRESSES,
1883.

.

INDEX.

To the Members of the Produce Exchange :

Instead of the usual condensed annual report upon the immediate affairs of the Exchange, I have the honor of presenting a pamphlet compiled and published at my own expense, containing information and statistics with reference to our city and port, which I trust may be found interesting and acceptable to you, and also serve the purpose of bringing our business people into more intimate and profitable relations with the outside world.

This work has no literary pretensions ; it is simply a record of facts, prepared, within the past six weeks, during brief intervals of routine business duty, and at some physical disadvantage. In it there is much, however, which may interest the general reader ; especially with reference to the past of Wilmington, so little of which is known to the present generation of our citizens. The business statistics have been compiled with great care, especially for this report, and have never before been published in the same form. I have, as far as was practicable, sought the information in person, and from official, or otherwise reliable sources ; and in other instances through responsible agents, delegated for that purpose, so that the report might be accepted as good authority, accurate in detail, and reliable as to facts.

Although the past year has not been a prosperous one for the business of the South, generally, it is gratifying to note many evidences here, of substantial improvement.

Compare the number of industries of Wilmington with those of other Southern towns, as well as the yearly volume of general trade, and where will you find, in proportion to its population, a busier or more thriving community? There is, however, much room for improvement.

I have referred, in deference to the Chamber of Commerce, to the River and Harbor work, which is of such vital moment to our trade and commerce. The indications are, that unless a vigorous effort is made for an additional appropriation by the next Congress, this undertaking, already so nearly accomplished, will suffer serious prejudice by delay. Let us remember that a most important and indispensable element of local success, is that of hearty, honest co-operation. In united action we have strength and confidence; and in striving for the general good of Wilmington we also promote our combined interests and individual welfare. This I believe to be the means of success in all prosperous centres of trade.

In relinquishing the highest honor in your gift, I remember with gratefulness many courtesies on your part which have characterized my term of office; and it will probably be the proudest reflection of my business life that so many of our older merchants, whom as boy and man I honored and respected, have thus distinguished me with their esteem and confidence. It is gratifying to note that during the past year, among more than a hundred merchants connected with this Exchange, there has been no removal by death, and that the character and integrity of every house continues unimpaired.

JAMES SPRUNT.

WILMINGTON, NORTH CAROLINA.

SETTLEMENT.

The Cape Fear River, upon which Wilmington is situated, was known in the early history of our State as the river Clarendon.

The first settlement on its banks was made in the year 1659 or '60, and abandoned in 1663,—but at what particular point it was made is not well established. In 1665, Sir John Yeamans, with several hundred colonists from Barbadoes, made the second settlement at a point about two miles below the present city of Wilmington, now known as Old Town, or Town Creek, and in honor of the reigning King of England at the time, it was named Charlestown.

A few years thereafter, Sir John and most of the colonists from Barbadoes, removed first to Port Royal, and subsequently to the neck of land between the Ashley and Cooper rivers, and founded the present city of Charleston, S. C.

Whether any of the colony under Yeamans remained on the Clarendon is not certainly known, but it is asserted by some of our historians that such is the fact, and that the old town of Brunswick, about six miles below the site of Charlestown, owes its origin to such of these colonists as did not accompany Yeamans to Charleston.

Our earliest reliable knowledge of the town of Brunswick does not go further back than 1720, when it contained but few inhabitants, and it so continued for some years.

About the year 1725, quite a colony of educated gentlemen, who had become disgusted with the Blue Laws of Massachusetts, settled at that place; and it soon became a thriving town of commercial importance, and the principal port from which the products of the Southern part of the province were exported. It being found however, that the roadstead or harbor of the town of Brunswick was much exposed and very unsafe, the line of the river was explored for a more suitable harbor, or place for the delivery and deposit of the articles then constituting the principal exports from this part of the province; and the present site of the city of Wilmington was found to be the nearest point to the town of Brunswick suitable for the purposes required: and here, about the year 1730, wharves and buildings were first erected.

A plan of the village or town was soon made, with regularly defined streets and lots, and called New Liverpool, which name was retained until about 1732, when, as appears by the oldest conveyances of the lots, the name was changed to Newton.

There are deeds still in existence for the same lots or parcels of lands situated in the town formerly known as New Liverpool, afterwards called Newton, now known as Wilmington.

The lands next north and south of the tract on which New Liverpool or Newton was located, had been granted for some years prior to 1733, in which year John Watson, or Whatson, obtained a grant for 640 acres of land on the east side of the north-east branch of the Cape Fear river. Among other recitals in said grant it is stated that the village of Newton is situated on the tract described and granted.

The original settlers of New Liverpool or Newton were doubtless the factors or agents of the principal merchants of the town of Brunswick, which for many years thereafter, and up to the war of the Revolution, continued to be *port*

town, where the officials of the colonial government re-
sided, although prior to the Revolution the then town of
Wilmington was the more populous of the two.

In 1739, through the influence of Gabriel Johnston,
Colonial Governor, the name of Newton was changed to
that of Wilmington, in compliment to, or in honor of,
Spence Compton, Baron Wilmington, an influential friend
of the Governor; and in 1760, by a royal grant from George
the Second, Arthur Dobbs being Governor, Wilmington
was elected a Borough, with the right of sending a member
to the Assembly; and by a second grant from the Crown
in 1763, George the Third then being King, additional
rights were given to the Borough, its corporate name being
"The Mayor, Recorder and Aldermen of the Borough of
Wilmington."

In 1766 the corporate name was changed to that of the
"Commissioners of the Town of Wilmington," and that
name was continued for one hundred years, the present
corporate name, "The City of Wilmington," being that by
which the inhabitants of Wilmington were incorporated as
a city in the year 1866.

According to the recitals in the oldest deeds for lands on
Eagles' Island, and in its vicinity on either side, the north-
eastern and north-western branches of the Cape Fear river
commence at the *southern* point of that Island. What is
now called Brunswick river on the west side of the Island
being the north-west branch, and Wilmington on the north-
east branch, and not on the main stream of the Cape Fear.
That portion of the river which runs from the north-east
branch by Point Peter, or Negro-head Point, as it is called,
to the north-west branch at the head of Eagles' Island, is
called in the old deeds and statutes of the State "the
thoroughfare," and sometimes the "cut through" from
one branch to the other; and the land granted to John
Watson, on which Wilmington is situated, is described as
lying opposite to the mouth of this "thoroughfare."

The town of Wilmington rapidly increased in population, while the old town of Brunswick sank into decay, and was finally abandoned, and not a vestige of it now remains, save the crumbling walls of old St. Philip's Church, which marks the spot where once the hum of busy life was heard more than a century and a half ago.

Wilmington is in latitude 34° 12′, and in longitude 77° 56′.

The city limits extend from north to south 2¾ miles, and from east to west 1½ miles, comprising a total area of about 2,400 acres. The general contour of the town is that of an elevated sand-ridge, running parallel with the river, intersected with dunes and rivulets emptying into the river and adjacent streams.

The Cape Fear river flows past the western front of the city, and its branches and tributaries almost encompass it.

SANITARY.

Artificial drainage has in recent years carried the storm water from the city into the tributary streams of the Cape Fear, and if maintained in proper condition, is well designed to effectually drain a large area which was formerly the most unhealthy quarter of the settlement. As a result, malarial fever has greatly decreased in the last ten years, and it may be truly said that although stigmatized forty years ago as the sailor's grave, and shunned by the people of the up country as an unsafe place in which to tarry all night, during the summer and autumn, it has become exceptionally healthy. As an evidence of this, the death rate for several years past has been much smaller than in the surrounding country, and compares favorably with the most favored towns of its

---

NOTE :—It is supposed that the settlers at Old Town left on account of the sterility of the land, and for the further reason that Sir John Yeamans was appointed Governor of South Carolina at that time, and his administration here had been so conservative they preferred to follow his fortunes.

size on the Atlantic coast,--the annual death rate being about seventeen to the thousand.

Drainage has not and cannot, it is true, alter the malarial influence upon crews of vessels sleeping on the river in the months of July, August, September and October. This standing menace to the prosperity of our shipping, as evidenced by the scarcity of tonnage during these months, has been seriously considered for many years, and a remedy actually devised. The difficulty has been to impress the lesson of prevention learned at such a cost, upon the interested parties. The State Board of Health has done much towards inculcating important advice upon the subject as will be seen by the following extract from a report of Dr. T. F. Wood, Secretary of the N. C. Board of Health, to the Medical Society of North Carolina, 1882.

"For many years it has been known, as well by the people as by the doctors, that the fevers occurring among the vessels in our tide-water streams were preventable, in a marked degree. Observations extending over a space of time marked by four or five generations, demonstrated that the cause of sickness among sailors was due very largely to sleeping on board vessels in the Cape Fear River particularly. This fact was so firmly established in the opinion of merchants in Wilmington, that $20,000 was subscribed to build a home for seamen in which they might find a safe retreat from the effluvia of the river, and what it not exactly pertinent to the present subject, to escape also the venereal effluvia of low sailor lodgings.

In this building ample provision was made for more sailors than ever visit the port of Wilmington at one time, and by the Christian benevolence of Capt. Gilbert Potter, one of the oldest citizens of that city, who had himself been a sea-captain, a house of worship, supplied by the yearly ministrations of a preacher, was provided, to throw around these "toilers of the sea," a beneficent influence.

The Board of Health, therefore, issued a pamphlet entitled "A Guide to Shipmasters Visiting the Cape Fear River," a copy of which is herewith transmitted."

Advice to Shipmasters for the Prevention of River Fever

—The Fever Thermometer—Its Uses.

The use of the thermometer to indicate the existence of fever is now established beyond doubt. It has been shown by thousands of observations that the heat of the body in any part of the world—in the tropics or the arctic circle - varies very little from 98.4° Fahr., in a grown person, in health. Upon this settled observation is based an estimate of the amount of fever in any given case.

The fever thermometer differs from the ordinary instrument in being self-registering. In the figure a thermometer is shown with the index just below 95°. This index is a slender line of mercury separated from that in the bulb by a slight space, and in a good thermometer the index does not fall back and unite with the mercury in the bulb.

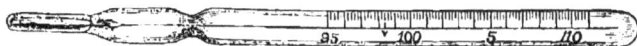

To READ THE THERMOMETER.—The instrument must be examined and the index must be below the arrow seen at 98.4°. If it is above it can be shaken down, either by holding it firmly between the finger and thumb and shaking forcibly as in flirting the ink out of a pen ; or, by taking the instrument at its upper tip, the end opposite the bulb, elevating the hand as high as the head, and, by a smart impulse downwards, thus shake the index below the arrow.

The instrument is put under the tongue, or between the teeth and the cheek, the lips closed upon it, and it is allowed to remain at least three minutes by the watch.

On removing the instrument, an examination of the index will show the temperature, which is indicated at the upper tip of the index, that is the end of the index the farthest from the bulb.

WHAT A RISE IN TEMPERATURE MEANS.—For the purposes of the instruction intended to be conveyed, it is safe to assume that every degree of heat beyond the arrow is a degree of fever.

The following table will show the relation between the pulse and the temperature of the body :

An increase of temperature of ONE DEGREE above 98° Fahrenheit, corresponds with an increase of TEN beats of the pulse per minute. (*Aitken.*)

Temperature	98°—Pulse	60.
"	99°— "	70.
"	100°— "	80.
"	101°— "	90.
"	102°— "	100.
"	103°— "	110.
"	104°— "	120.
"	105°— "	130.
"	106°— "	140.

The rule above is subject to some variation, but is a fairly good guide.

It is well known that 101° before 11 A. M. indicates an approaching fever, and that the same after 5 o'clock a declining fever; and so on with every degree above it. 103.5° is about the average of the malarial fever of the rivers. Many severe cases reach 104.5° and 105.5°. Even 106° is not surely fatal, but beyond this, in the most favorable conditions, the danger is very great. 108° to 110° is most surely fatal.

With these introductory remarks we will call the attention of shipmasters to certain precautions, which long experience in this latitude has shown necessary to be observed.

The fever occurring amongst the seamen who visit this and other Southern rivers is malarial. It is due to the exposure of sleeping on board vessels, and keeping late hours at night.

THE NATURE AND COURSE OF RIVER MALARIAL FEVER. —It commences sometimes with a chill. The chill is either a shaking ague, or sometimes the only symptoms are coldness of the fingers, blue nails, cold nose, and ears and toes. Both forms may be an essential part of similar fevers. A chill may last from half an hour to two or three hours, and is always followed by fever. Chill is only a cold stage of fever, and the thermometer will most always show from 100° to 102° even when the chill is highest. The fever comes on, the coldness of the skin gradually goes off, and the heat of fever follows, the temperature rising gradually to 103.5 to 105°.

For instance, if the chill comes on before 11 o'clock A. M., as it often does, the fever will reach its height usually by 5 o'clock P. M., and then gradually decline, either by copious sweating or an abundant discharge of urine. If the fever goes entirely off it is *intermittent*. If it merely declines it is *remittent*. In either case a person seized with fever may look for a return on the succeeding day, or the day after. These are forms of the same fever and have all been named. Thus we have them coming on *daily, twice daily, every other day, every third day*, and so on ; but the fevers are essentially the same, being practically cured by the same treatment.

THE WAY TO AVOID RIVER FEVER.—Live temperately, and do not sleep in the river on board vessel during the months of August, September and October. The air of the town is perfectly harmless to most persons, and especially those who go to bed early, and are not intemperate.

Sleeping on board during the months named does not always cause sickness, but it does nearly always. Sometimes fever does not develop until a vessel gets to sea, and then all hands may be taken down at the same time. Such cases are known.

PROPHYLACTIC.—The daily use of quinine or the preparations of peruvian bark, *will prevent fever.* It is a good practice to give to crews of vessels a daily morning dose equal to five grains of quinine. Some of the cheaper preparations of bark answer this purpose very well. None of them are equal to quinquinia, a preparation tested now during several seasons, and found to be remarkably efficient. It contains 15 per cent. of quinia and 45 per cent. of other valuable alkaloids of peruvian bark, which really gives it an advantage over the sulphate of quinine usually sold. It is recommended with great confidence.

WHAT TO DO AFTER THE VESSEL GETS TO SEA.—In every case of complaining on the part of a seaman, the Captain or an intelligent officer should take the man's temperature. If it is more than 98.4° he will be wise to conclude that there is a fever approaching. 100° or 101° is absolute evidence, apart from any other condition of the man, that he has fever, and it is tolerably certain that if it is not checked he will have more the next day.

WHAT TO DO IF THE TEMPERATURE RISES.—No amount of fever should prevent the patient from taking *quinine,* or some other preparation of bark in the proper doses. It is always best to commence quinine early in the morning because the fever increases towards noon, and with the increase of fever comes on many times such a sick stomach that the patient cannot retain the much needed medicine. But if the stomach does not reject it he ought to have his medicine in proper quantities, notwithstanding the fever for every day of its continuance unaffected by medicine, lessens the chance of recovery.

WHAT MEDICINE TO GIVE. - If the fever is detected early, medicine should be given at once. It is necessary usually to give *twenty grains of quinine* every twenty-four hours. *More* is needed sometimes, but it is not often that a less quantity will succeed. It is best to direct* five grains of *quinine* in pills every two hours, commencing as early as four o'clock in the morning, until twenty grains are given. Should pain in the head and hot skin, and unpleasant "singing" or "roaring" in the ears, trouble the patient, *bromide of potash** *should be given in ten grain doses,* dissolved in water, every two or three hours   Usually a very hot and dry skin yields to the action of the remedies above.   Should they fail, *fluid extract* of Jaborandi should be given, fifteen drops every hour until copious sweating comes on.

Constipation is sometimes an accompaniment of this fever, and should be relieved by *Calomel and Soda at night, or Epsom Salts and table salt in the morning.*

Relapses are not uncommon, and although the thermometer may not indicate fever after a few days of treatment, (and it is urged that the thermometer should be carefully applied morning and evening,) it is never safe to withdraw the quinine the day following the one on which the patient misses his fever.   At least *ten grains* should be continued daily for three or four days in succession.

RECAPITULATION.

1. The thermometer is a sure guide in the early detection of River Fever.

2. Whenever a man shows any indisposition after a stay on the river during the months of August, September and October, apply the fever thermometer, and if he has 100° or over, you may look out for more fever the next day.

3. Quinine should be given in five grain doses until twenty grains are given before noon.   No time should be lost.

4. Relapses can be prevented by continuing the medicine four days in succession after the last indications of fever.

*See formulas on the last page.

FORMULA 1.—QUININE PILLS.

Take of

Quinine, two scruples or forty grains,
Tartaric Acid, ten grains,
Glycerine, twenty to twenty-five drops.

Mix well, and make twelve pills. Roll in magnesia before putting in a box.

One pill every hour until six are taken a day.

2.—QUININE SOLUTION.

Take of

Quinine, forty grains,
Tartaric Acid, thirty grains,
Water, two ounces or four tablespoonsful.

Mix and make a solution.

A teaspoonful every hour until six doses are g ven each day.

3.—BROMIDE SOLUTION.

Take of

Bromide of Potassium, one ounce,
Sugar, two tablespoonsful.

Dissolve the bromide in the water and add the sugar until all is dissolved.

The dose for headache, and for the excitement caused by quinine is a teaspoonful every two hours.

A little lemon juice or hydrobromic acid makes the solution pleasanter to take.

4.—QUINQUINIA SOLUTION.

Prophylactic.

Take of

Quinquinia, one ounce,
Tartaric Acid, half an ounce,
Water, three pints.

Mix and make a solution.

Dose, a tablespoonful every morning.

5.--Quinquinia Solution for Fever.

Make as in the solution of quinine and in the same quantities.

6.—Quinquinia Pills.

Make the same as quinine pills and in the same quantities and doses.

7.—Calomel and Soda.

Purgative.

Take of
    Calomel, six grains,
    Bicarbonate Soda, twenty grains.
Make a powder and mix in a spoon with syrup.

8—Epsom Salts and Table Salt.

Purgative.

Take of
    Epsom Salts, one-half to one ounce,
    Table Salt, one teaspoonful.
Mix and make a solution in a cup of water. To be taken before breakfast.

The following remarks on the subject of remittent fever, kindly furnished me by the author, Dr. Fairfax Irwin, Passed Assistant Surgeon in Charge of our Marine Hospital, will be interesting in this connection. It will be observed that he agrees substantially with the other authority quoted.

"Remittent fever, or as it is popularly called on the Cape Fear, 'river fever,' is so common, and aside from its dangerous character, so expensive to ship-masters and owners that a few remarks on its character and treatment will not seem out of place, especially at this its chosen season. This article is based on the results obtained from the treatment of ninety cases of remittent fever during the past eighteen months, all of which have recovered with an average duration of treatment of about nine days per man.

These cases were all treated in the Marine Hospital in Wilmington, N. C., and were, as a result, in a very favorable situation for observation. To the treatment, followed with little variation in all cases, the favorable result is attributed. That too much is not claimed will be readily allowed by any who are acquainted with the character of the malarial fever in this region, and especially when it is remembered that this disease is clinically the same as the billious fever of thirty or forty years ago, which was itself so fatal.

The river fever is seen but in isolated cases before August and from that time increases in virulence until the kindly hand of frost is laid upon it.

The most severe cases are seen among the sailors, especially those unacclimated, and is directly traceable to exposure at night to the poisonous exhalations from the rice fields along the river. The sailors sleeping upon the vessel-decks on warm nights are soon attacked, while the captains sleeping ashore usually escape entirely. Seamen from foreign vessels fall an easy prey, and give the largest percentage of malignant cases.

It is not to be forgotten, however, that sailors in addition to exposure are usually filthy in their habits, reckless and dissipated to a degree. Before passing to a short sketch of the natural history of this fever it may be well to refer to a common idea held by seafaring men, that salt water 'brings out the fever,' a vessel after remaining for ten days or two weeks in the Cape Fear River usually drops down to Smithville at its mouth, to complete loading, and here frequently, after having been healthy all of the time spent above, the crew succumb almost suddenly to fever, hence the notion of salt water 'driving it out.' I believe this is nothing more than a coincidence, the outbreak of the disease after its regular period of incubation. Sailors have died at sea after leaving Wilmington, of the fever, though healthy on departure and with such malignant symp-

toms as to cause masters to report them as cases of yellow
fever.

Remittent fever as I have seen it here, after an incubation of from ten days to two weeks breaks out quite suddenly and with alarming symptoms from the first. Perhaps in some cases a certain lassitude and weakness for a
few days may precede, but as a rule the onset is sudden.

Contrary to the statement in most works on the subject,
there is no initial chill ; this did not occur in any of the
ninety cases treated. Many men were brought into the
hospital insensible, having been taken sick during the
day.

The prominent symptoms were a dull, stolid countenance:
weary, slouching gait ; acute lancinating pains in the head
and back, dull pains in the limbs, tenderness on pressure
over the region of the stomach with great irritability of
that organ : a characteristic tongue, large, flabby, showing
indentations of the teeth, and thickly coated with bluish
white fur, rarely dry except in protracted cases, and often
so large as apparently to fill the mouth. The coating was
often absent, but the bluish-white tint was invariably
present.

The full rapid pulse, throbbing carotids, and moist surface showed the excited circulation. The sweats were in
most cases as copious and as debilitating as in phthisis.
The temperature ranged from 100° to 105° (38° to 40.4°C.)
on the first evening, the average being 104° (40° C.)

There was a marked tendency to congestion of various
organs, especially the lungs, but an implication of the liver
to any appreciable extent was not observed ; the yellow
hue of the skin so often spoken of in books was not seen.
Albumen was not discovered in the urine in any case. De-
lirium was rarely present, severe cases were more apt to
become comatose. The irritation of the stomach was frequently most severe and difficult to manage, everything
being rejected and passed on to the vomiting of pure bile.
There was no eruption.

There is little danger of a mistake in diagnosis : the sea- son of the year, the sudden seizure, the steel-colored tongue, acute pains in the head and back, and distinctly remittent range of temperature are characteristic.

There was rarely more than one exacerbation, owing, it is believed, to the large doses of quinia used. When a second exacerbation followed, it was always found to be due to an insufficient use of quinia. In the whole number of cases treated there was little variation of symptoms, but a few interesting exceptions may be mentioned.

Epistaxis was somewhat common and one case required plugging of the nares to prevent exhaustion from loss of blood. Hemorrhages from the bowels was present in a case which lasted two weeks ; there were no other symp- toms of typhoid fever, however. One case so strongly sim- ulated cerebro-spinal fever as to leave the diagnosis in doubt for a few days ; there was well marked opisthotonos, but recovery followed in due course.

A case in private practice seen in consultation with Dr. Geo. G. Thomas, of Wilmington, had the Cheyne-Stokes' breathing perfectly, and presented the appearance of ap- proaching dissolution. Large doses of quinia were being given but the disease had advanced so far before advice was asked for that it seemed as if the nervous system would be overwhelmed by the poison before the remedy had time to act. A blister was applied to the back of the neck and atropia sulphate (0,0010 gramme) given every three hours, with good effect, and recovery followed. Atropia was given to counteract the slow spasmodic breath- ing ; the *besoin de respirer* being almost absent, as in opium poisoning.

The *treatment* used in the ninety cases to which this paper chiefly refers was based on the principle that remittent fever is caused by a poison now known as malaria, which is present in almost overwhelming degree, and to which quinia is a direct antidote if used in large doses.

Cases showing the usual evening temperature of 40° C., and upward were given from 30 to 45 grains (2 to 3 grammes) of quinia sulphate, usually in solution with dilute sulphuric acid, and largely diluted with ice water. As the stomach in many cases was so irritable as to reject this really nauseous dose, the quinia was then given in pills freshly made with glycerine; when these were rejected, as was often the case, the drug was administered hypodermically, the dose in this case being from 10 to 15 grains (0.666 to 1 gramme). The solution for hypodermic use was made with citric acid, and although many times used, no abcess ensued in any case.

This large dose almost invariably reduced the temperature from one to three degrees by morning, the quinia was then given in doses of 5 grains (0.333 gramme) thrice daily, and the large dose again repeated at night if the temperature rose. This method, with a few exceptions, cut short the fever in from three to five days, as the average duration of nine days for the whole number of cases will show. Some, especially where there was an existing organic disease, were more rebellious, and required large quantities of quinia before convalescence was established.

As much as 465 grains (30 grammes) of quinia were given in eight days in two different cases, and no ill effects were observed; in fact in no case did quinia cause any disturbance beyond deafness which soon passed away under cessation of the drug and small doses of hydrobromic acid. Dimness of vision was never complained of.

If the bowels were inactive, an enema was given at once, but no preparatory treatment was ever used. As the skin and kidneys were active, opium or diaphoretics were not called for. To moderate the heart's action fluid extract of aconite-root in one drop doses every four hours was given in most all cases; this, with ice compresses to the head, was about all the treatment.

The irritable stomach was best controlled by creasote or vin. ipecac. (5 minims) 0.333 cc. every two or three hours.

Rigid milk diet was given and no stimulants used. It is desired to insist upon the needlessness of the almost universal custom of preparing the system for the action of quinia, much valuable time is lost in an unnecessary procedure, and it is thought that opium is positively contraindicated by the symptoms.

In conclusion, the fact should not be lost sight of that remittent fever is eminently a disease to be prevented. While vessels are in the river the crews should be required to sleep ashore. Captains should be furnished with clinical thermometers, with instructions for their use, and on the first indication of fever, a dose of at least 30 grains (2 grammes) of quinia should be given.

The total number of cases observed during eighteen months was ninety, total number of days treatment four hundred and forty, average per patient nine and one-third days."

CITY GOVERNMENT,

The present government of the City is composed of the Board of Aldermen and Board of Audit and Finance.

The Board of Aldermen is composed of the following named gentlemen : Hon. E. D. Hall, Mayor, and Messrs. G. J. Boney, Samuel Bear, John L. Dudley, S. H. Fishblate, William L. DeRosset, William H. Chadbourn, Isham Sweat, Valentine Howe and John J. Guyer.

The Board of Audit and Finance is a branch of the city government created by an act of the General Assembly, 28th February, 1877, and is at present composed of the following named gentlemen : Mr. R. J. Jones, Chairman, and Messrs. William Calder, O. A. Wiggins, W. R. Kenan and John S. McEachern.

Since Wilmington was incorporated as a city by the General Assembly, 1st February, 1866, the following named have filled the office of Mayor:

Mr. A. H. VanBokkelen, elected in March, 1866.

Mr. John Dawson, elected in January, 1867.

Mr. Jos. H. Neff, appointed by the Provisional Governor of the State in July, 1868, and elected in January, 1869.

Mr. S. N. Martin, elected in January, 1870.

Mr. James Wilson, elected in May, 1872.

Mr. W. P. Canaday, elected in May, 1873.

Mr. John Dawson, elected in June, 1877, and resigned in February, 1878.

Mr. S. H. Fishblate, elected in February, 1878.

Mr. W. L. Smith, elected in March, 1881.

Mr. E. D. Hall, elected in March, 1883.

The following comprises a list of the present officers of the city, with their pay:

Hon. E. D. Hall, Mayor; salary $1,200 per annum.

Mr. R. J. Jones, Chairman of the Board of Audit and Finance, and Commissioner of the Sinking Fund, for which he receives a yearly salary of $400, and gives a bond for $5,000.

Mr. Henry Savage, Clerk and Treasurer, salary $600 per year, and also Tax Collector; estimated salary $1,500 per annum, out of which he has all clerk hire to pay; he gives a bond of $20,000.

Mr. John Cowan, Clerk of the Board of Audit and Finance; salary $600, and Clerk of the Police Department, with a salary of $600 a year.

Mr. H. C. Brock, Chief of Police; salary $1,200.

Dr. F. W. Potter, Superintendent of Health; salary $600.

Mr. Charles D. Myers, Chief of Fire Department; salary $300.

Mr. L. M. Williams, Clerk of Market; salary $400.

A. W. Wiggs, Captain of Police; pay $55.00 per month.

Three Sergeants of Police, at $1.60 per day each.

Twenty-five Privates of Police, at $1.50 per day each.

Three Health officers at $35.00 per month each.

Two Janitors, at $40.00 per month each.

One Superintendent of Street Force, at $40.00 per month.

The other employees of the city vary in numbers and are paid, say for street-cleaners, &c., 83¼ cents per day.

CITY FINANCES.

At the beginning of the fiscal year, April 1st, 1882, the net bonded debt of the city, after deducting the amount of bonds held by the Commissioners of the Sinking Fund, was $528,800, all in Coupon Bonds, interest payable January and July each year.

Of the above amount of bonds outstanding, there was of those issued for subscription to the Wilmington, Charlotte and Rutherford Railroad stock, past due and never presented for payment, though repeatedly advertised for,—$8,500.

On July 1, 1882, $60,400 of the bonds matured, and the City Government has just accomplished the payment of them by the sale of six per cent. bonds, authorized by the last General Assembly, so that the bonded debt of the City now stands, say :

$263,900, in eight per cent. Coupon Bonds, and $288,300, in six per cent. Coupon Bonds, making $552,200,—total bonded debt of the City, of which $44,400 is now held by the Commissioner of the Sinking Fund as per his last annual statement herewith, which would leave the net debt $507,800, subject to a further deduction of the amount to go to the Sinking Fund from the unexpended balances of the appropriations of the years ending March 31, 1881 and March 31, 1882.

The Commissioner of the Sinking Fund receives a semi-annual income of $1,379 from the bonds he now holds, this amount being re-invested in City bonds as fast as the same is paid, thereby increasing the fund and its income semi-annually.

There is no floating debt, all bills against the City being paid on presentation.

The City has recently purchased the two pieces of property known as the New Market Houses, for which it has issued its notes for $30,000—payable twenty years after January 1st, 1883, with interest at the rate of six per cent. per annum. Many persons are of the opinion that the property fully represents the amount of the notes, and if judiciously managed, the income from the same will pay the interest and gradually sink the principal by its maturity.

The taxable value of the Real and Personal property as per the tax book of 1882 is $5,017,983, and the rate one and three-fourths per cent.

The value of the non-taxable property within the City limits, such as Churches, Schools, Wilmington & Weldon Railroad, and Public Buildings, is estimated at $650,000, of which the City owns $105,000. The income for the year ending March 31st, 1882, from Real and Personal property tax, Merchants License and back taxes, was $111,450, which is a fair indication of what the income will be this year.

The interest for July, 1882, and January, 1883, was $40,-782. It will be for the coming year $38,410.

The appropriation for expenses for the year ending March 31st, 1883, is $63,490.

There are two items included in the expenses for this year which have never occurred before,—the Water Works $6,750, and the City Hospital $1,000, the two amounting to $7,750, which if deducted from the amount appropriated, $63,490, would leave $55,740 as the ordinary expenses of the City, by which to make a comparison with former years. It would appear that this great reduction in the value of the Real Estate made by the Assessor, was more in the interest of the tax-payers than of the City, as all the sales of Real Estate made since the new assessment have been at an advance of about thirty-three and one third per cent., making the market value of the Real Estate about $4,000,000.

In 1877 the City bonds were selling at seventy cents or less on the dollar.

Now the six per cents. are worth par, and the eight per cent. bonds cannot be bought for less than 107. In 1877 the coupons were bought up at a discount ranging from ten to twenty per cent. and paid into the Tax Collector's office for taxes at par.

Now the coupons are regularly paid as they mature.

All merchants' license taxes have been reduced since 1877, on an average, thirty-five per cent.

The current expenses for the year ending May 12th, 1877, were $79,359.57, and the same class of expenses for the present year, as stated above, will be $55,740..

I am indebted substantially for the foregoing particulars to our efficient and obliging Treasurer, Maj. Henry Savage, who, unlike many modern public officials, is always ready to furnish information with reference to his department, for reasonable purposes.

I desire also to acknowledge official courtesies from Mayor Smith, Capt. Cowan, Capt. Brock, and Chief Engineer Robinson.

AUDIT AND FINANCE.

As the establishment of the Board of Audit and Finance in 1877 brought a most gratifying and substantial change for the better in our city finances, and as the administration of this important branch of our municipal government has been characterized by a degree of efficiency and public spirit most praiseworthy to its members,—especially to the original Board, upon whom devolved in its organization a very difficult and responsible task,—I have thought it my duty, as well as a privilege, to append with a copy of the Act of Assembly creating the Board, a correspondence published last year upon the retirement of Mr. Norwood Giles, who served as the first Chairman of the Board ; and to whom, with his colleagues, Messrs. D. G. Worth, R. J. Jones, W. D. Mahn, and T. W. Player, we are indebted

in a great measure for the present highly satisfactory condition of our municipal credit.

An Act to establish a Board of Audit and Finance for the
City of Wilmington.

SECTION 1. *The General Assembly of North Carolina
do enact,* That in the month of March, A. D. one thousand
eight hundred and seventy-seven, and biennially thereafter, the Governor of this State shall appoint five discreet
and proper persons among the electors of the city of Wilmington, one from each of the five wards of said city, who
shall constitute and be styled "the Board of Audit and
Finance of the city of Wilmington," and the persons so
appointed shall continue in office for two years, and until
their successors are duly appointed and qualified. No
person holding an office or appointment under the Board
of Aldermen of said city, or under any law in reference to
said city, or who may be a contractor for any work,
materials, supplies or other things whatever for the use
of said city, shall be eligible as a member of said Board,
or qualified to act as one of its members. Any vacancy
occurring among the members of said Board during
their term of office, shall be filled by the remaining
members.

SEC. 2. Said Board shall, from their body, elect a chairman, who, with the clerk hereinafter provided for, shall
sign and certify all orders of the Board ; and in case such
chairman shall be absent at any meeting of the Board, a
temporary chairman shall be chosen, who, during such
meeting, shall exercise the powers of the regular chairman.
The chairman of said Board shall have power to administer
oaths, and issue subpoenas for witnesses to appear before
the Board, who shall be required to appear and testify,
under like pains and penalties as if summoned to any
Superior Court. Before entering on their duties, the

members of said Board shall, before some justice of the peace, take and subscribe the oath of office, prescribed in section four of article six of the constitution, and cause the same to be filed in the office of the Clerk and Treasurer of said City.

SEC. 3. The Board shall appoint a Clerk, prescribe his duties, and require him to give bond, payable to the City of Wilmington, in such sum as said Board may consider sufficient, secured by two or more good sureties, and conditioned for the faithful performance of the duties of his office. The said Clerk shall hold office at the pleasure of said Board, shall have power to administer oaths, and shall receive such compensation, not exceeding six hundred dollars *per annum*, as said Board may establish.

SEC. 4. Said Board shall hold regular meetings twice every month, and oftener if necessary, in some room in the City Hall at such times as the Board may determine, and of which due notice shall be given by advertisements to be posted at the Court House door, and ten other public places in the city. Said meetings shall be opened to the public, and the times of holding the regular semi-monthly meetings shall not be changed, unless ten days notice of such change shall be given as aforesaid. The Clerk shall, in proper books, keep a minute record of the proceedings of said meetings, recording the names of the members present, the character and amount of all claims and demands against the city, and the names of the claimants. All such claims and demands shall be made out in distinct items, verified by the affidavit of the claimant or his agent, stating that the claim is just and due, that the articles were furnished or services rendered, as the case may be, and that no part of the same has been satisfied. Notwithstanding such affidavit, the said Board may require further proof as to the validity of any claim; and any person who shall knowingly or wilfully offer or cause to be offered for audit by said Board, any false or fraudulent claim or demand against the City of Wilmington, shall be deemed guilty of a misdemeanor; and any person who shall wilfully swear to any false statement before said Board, shall be guilty of perjury.

SEC. 5. It shall be the duty of said Board to audit and pass upon the validity of all claims and demands against the City of Wilmington, and no claim or demand against said city shall be paid by the treasurer of said city, or by any other person, out of any funds belonging to said city, until the same has been duly audited and approved by said Board, and a warrant signed by the Chairman and Clerk, given for the payment of the same. All claims, demands and accounts presented to said Board to be audited, shall be treated and proceeded with in all respects as is provided in section twelve, chapter twenty-seven, of Battle's Revisal, in reference to claims or accounts against counties. Any member of said Board who shall knowingly vote to allow any false, fraudulent or untrue claim or demand against said city, shall be deemed guilty of a misdemeanor, and upon conviction, shall be punished by a fine of not less than five hundred dollars, and by imprisonment for not less than one year.

SEC. 6. No ordinance of the Board of Aldermen of said city, levying any tax whatever, shall be valid or of any effect unless an estimate and the rate of assessment of the taxes so to be levied, shall be first submitted to said Board of Audit and Finance, and approved, by at least three of its members. The estimates aforesaid shall specify the amount required during the next coming fiscal year to pay interest on the debt of said city, and to provide a sinking fund for its ultimate payment, and the amount which will be required, as nearly as can be ascertained, to meet the necessary expenditures for the several departments of the city government, and the amounts to be expended under said estimates shall be apportioned by said Board of Audit and Finance, according to the specifications accom-

panying the same, among the several departments of the
city, of which apportionment a copy shall be delivered to
the Clerk and Treasurer of said city. All warrants which
may be drawn on account of any duly audited claim or
demand, shall specify the particular fund from which the
same is to be paid, and no such warrant shall be paid from
any other fund, than the one designated therein ; and if
any such warrant shall be paid, in violation of this provision, or if any claim against said city shall be paid or be
received on account of any indebtedness to said city,
before a proper warrant for the same has been issued, the
Treasurer of said city, or any other person paying the
same out of any funds belonging to said city shall be liable
for the amount so paid, and shall be deemed guilty of a
misdemeanor.

Sec. 7. The said Board of Audit and Finance shall, once
in every three months, cause to be posted at the Court
House, and ten other public places in said city, a statement of all claims and demands against said city, audited
by said Board, giving the respective amounts claimed and
allowed, the character of said claim and the name of the
claimant.

Sec. 8. It shall be the duty of said Board of Audit and
Finance, and it shall have the exclusive power to fix the
salaries or other compensation of all officers and employees
of said city, and to pass upon and approve the official
bonds of such officers ; and no contract, even for the
necessary expenses of said city, nor any bond, note or
other obligation in behalf of said city, shall be valid or of
any effect, unless the same be approved by said Board, and
such approval be endorsed thereon. Any officer of said
city who is required to give a bond for the faithful performance of his duties, who shall enter upon the discharge
of the duties of his office, or in any way intermeddle therewith, before the official bond shall be duly approved as
aforesaid, shall be deemed guilty of a misdemeanor, and

on conviction shall be fined not less than five hundred dollars, and imprisoned not less than six months, and shall further forfeit his office.

SEC. 9. Said Board shall, at such times during each year as may be deemed judicious, and at the end of each fiscal year, audit and cause to be settled the accounts of the City Treasurer, and of all other persons holding any funds belonging to said city ; and on all such settlements, all interest, benefit, advantage received or to be received, directly or indirectly, from the use, disposal or deposit of any funds belonging to said city, by any officer or agent of the city, shall be duly accounted for. Such officers or agents upon making any such settlements shall be required to make and file with said Board an affidavit, declaring as the fact may be, whether he has or has not received, or is not to receive directly or indirectly, any interest, benefit or advantage from the use, deposit, or any disposal of said funds, and shall also be examined orally on the matters referred to. In the event that any officer of said city, upon the investigation of his accounts as aforesaid, shall be found to be in default, said Board of Audit and Finance is hereby authorized and empowered to declare his office vacant.

SEC. 10. The Board of Aldermen of the said city shall, annually, at least one month before the time of the annual assessment of taxes by said Board, and at such other times as may be necessary, advertise for proposals for all labor and for all materials required by said city for the opening, guttering, grading and cleaning or paving, or otherwise improving the streets, alleys or sidewalks of said city ; for lighting and repairing the lamps of the city ; for all labor and materials for the repair or construction of all buildings belonging to the city ; for all printing and advertising required by the city ; for all supplies of any kind required for the use of the city, or any department thereof ; and shall contract for the same with the lowest bidder, who may be considered fit and competent ; but no such contract shall be binding on the city till approved by the said Board of Audit and Finance, by which all such contractors shall be required to enter into bonds secured to its satisfaction, for the faithful performance of their several contracts.

SEC. 11. The Chairman of the Board of Audit and Finance shall be "the Commissioner of the Sinking Fund of the City of Wilmington," and shall have all the powers and perform all the duties incident to that office by any and all acts of the General Assembly authorizing or requiring the appointment of such an officer. He shall enter into bond, with two or more good and sufficient sureties, to be approved of by the Board of Aldermen of said city in such sum as said Board of Aldermen shall fix, and payable to the city of Wilmington, and conditioned for the faithful performance of all the duties incident to said office, or which may be hereafter imposed on such officers. The Chairman of said Board, as Commissioner of the Sinking Fund of the city of Wilmington, shall in the months of January and July of each year cause to be published, in one or more of the newspapers in said city, a statement showing the true condition of said Sinking Fund, giving the amount and character of the investments of the same, and the place of deposit of the securities belonging to it.

SEC. 12. The Treasurer of the said city, upon a proper warrant to be drawn on him as is hereinbefore provided, shall pay over to the said Commissioner of the Sinking Fund the amounts which may from time to time be collected from taxes assessed and levied for the Sinking Fund of said city, and also all sums which may have been assessed and collected for any other department of the city government, and which may be remaining in his hands unexpended and unappropriated at the end of any fiscal year. The sums of money which may be paid as aforesaid to the Commissioner of the Sinking Fund, shall be invested and managed as required by law; and in making investments of the same, and of all sums accruing from securities in which the same may be invested, preference shall be given to such of the bonds of said city which will yield the largest income on the amount invested; all of such bonds of the city of Wilmington which may be purchased for the purpose aforesaid and all the coupons thereto, shall be immediately and indelibly stamped with the words: "the Sinking Fund of the City of Wilmington;" and the number, amount and date of issue of every such bond shall be recorded by said Commissioner in a proper book kept by said Board of Audit and Finance for that purpose; and a duly certified copy of such record shall from time to time, as additional investments for said fund shall be made, be furnished by said Commissioner to the Board of Aldermen of said city, who shall cause the same to be filed by the clerk and treasurer of said city, and recorded in a proper book in his office. All bonds as aforesaid, and all other securities purchased as investment of any fund belonging to said sinking fund, and all interest accruing thereon, shall be held exclusively for the use of and as part of said Sinking Fund, and shall not be disposed of or transferred, or in any way used for any other purpose whatever. The chairman of said Board of Audit and Finance, as compensation for his services as Commissioner of the Sinking Fund of the City of Wilmington, shall be entitled to a salary of four hundred dollars per annum; and the Treasurer of said city, upon the proper warrant as aforesaid, signed by the Chairman and Clerk of said Board of Audit and Finance, shall pay the necessary expenses of said Board, the salary of their Clerk, and the salary as aforesaid of its Chairman.

SEC. 13. The Treasurer of the city of Wilmington shall at the end of every month, cause to be posted at the Court House and at ten other public places in said city, a statement duly verified by his oath, in which shall be set forth the names of all persons to whom he has paid any amount during that month, the amount so paid to each person, the particular fund from which such payment has been made, and the whole amount of money belonging to the city then remaining in his hands.

SEC. 14. That all laws and parts of laws in conflict with the provisions of this act are hereby repealed, and this act shall be in force from and after the ratification of the same.

Ratified the 28th day of February, A. D. 1877.

City Finances—Report of the Commissioner of the Sink-

ing Fund, and Accompanying Statement of

the City Clerk and Treasurer.

OFFICE BOARD OF AUDIT AND FINANCE,

CITY OF WILMINGTON, N. C, January 4th, 1882.

The Honorable, the Mayor and Aldermen, City of Wilmington :

GENTLEMEN:—As required by law I beg to report present status of the Sinking Fund.

SECURITIES HELD.

Of Bonds maturing February 1st, 1892, ...$ 2,500 00

"   "   "   January 1st, 1897,......... 3,300 00

"   "   "   January 1st, 1899,... ..... 1,000 00

"   "   "   January 1st, 1901,......... 10,000 00

"   "   "   January 1st, 1904,......... 25,000 00

Cash uninvested,............................. 55 00

Total,..................................$41,855 00

All of above has been accumulated since the establishment of the Board of Audit and Finance, in 1877.

The possession of a Sinking Fund of above proportion is of itself a matter of gratulation, but when it is coupled with the fact that *within the same time,* the debt of the

City has actually been reduced *more than one hundred thousand dollars*, the tax-payers cannot fail to appreciate the management of City affairs since 1877.

Not only has this immense debt reduction been accomplished, but the tax on Real Estate has been reduced one-quarter of one per cent., notwithstanding the fact that the assessed value thereof has been reduced $637,832. The license taxes have also been materially reduced.

The above concise statement of important financial items is highly gratifying, and of interest to every citizen, for not only has the municipal credit been restored, but a continuation of economical administration and proper application of revenue, must undoubtedly lead to further reduction of taxes.

All Bonds belonging to the Sinking Fund, and the Coupons thereto attached, have been indelibly stamped, "Sinking Fund, City of Wilmington, N. C.," and are deposited in the vault of the Bank of New Hanover.

Your attention is especially directed to the accompanying valuable report of Mr. Savage, your Clerk and Treasurer, wherein a comparison is instituted, and the present improved state of finances satisfactorily and clearly demonstrated.

Very Respectfully,
NORWOOD GILES,
Commissioner Sinking Fund.

OFFICE CITY CLERK AND TREASURER,

CITY OF WILMINGTON, N. C., January 3rd, 1882.

NORWOOD GILES, ESQ., *Chairman of Board of Audit and Finance, Wilmington, N. C.:*

SIR:—In answer to your request of this date, that I furnish you with a "statement of the present condition of city finances, as compared with the same when I entered

upon the duties of my office, in July 1877," I respectfully
submit the following report :

By the city tax book of 1877 I find Real Estate assessed
at $3,832,890, and the rate of taxation two per cent.

On July 1st, 1877, the debt of the City, as near as could
be ascertained was about $673,000, with not a dollar in the
Sinking Fund. Much of this debt was in past due bonds
and coupons and a floating debt of about $15,000. There
was no money of moment in the Treasury and an over-
draft at Bank of $1,200. To pay the policemen and other
expenses for June, 1877, it was necessary to borrow $2,300
from bank.

The bonds were selling for seventy cents, or less, on the
dollar, and the coupons were bought up at a discount
ranging from ten to twenty per cent., and paid into the
Tax Collector's office by the purchasers for taxes at par.

The current expenses of the City for the fiscal year ending May 12th, 1877, were $79,359.57 ; balance due Treasurer
by his account that date, $1,999.72.

I find by the tax book of 1881 real estate assessed at
$3,195,058, and the rate of taxation one and three-fourths
per cent. The present debt of the City is, all in bonds,
$572,100 ; the sinking fund is $41,800. No floating debt
or past due coupons. The six per cent. bonds are now
at par, and the eight per cent. bonds cannot be bought
at 105.

The Current Expenses for the Fiscal Year
    ending April 1st, 1881, were.............$ 54,480 67
Cash on hand at that date, ...   10,415 75
Thus we see that Real Estate was assessed in
    1877 at..... .... 3,832,890 00
The same Real Estate was assessed in 1881 at 3,195,058 00
Reduction of assessment on Real Estate...... 637,732 00
Total value of Taxable Property, Real and
    Personal, in 1881,......................$4,856,557 00

The valuation of personal property is *made by the tax-payers themselves*, and is largely in excess in 1881 of that returned by them in 1877.

The City Tax on Real Estate in 1877 was ......$ 76,657 80
The City Tax on the same Real Estate in 1881,
    with four years' improvements, is.......... 55,913 51
                                               ————————
Reduction of City Tax on Real Estate,..........$ 20,744 29

In the matter of the monthly license taxes on merchants I find that the following taxes were paid per month for the respective years :

	1877.	1881.
Auctioneers,.............................	$10 00	$ 5 00
Bar Rooms,.............................	12 50	10 00
Bakers.............................	5 00	2 50
Commercial Brokers..................	5 00	3 00
Commission Merchants, on sales of from		
$5,000 to $10,000....................	7 50	5 00
Wholesale and Retail Dealers, on sales of		
from $500 to $1,000.................	5 00	4 00

And all other license taxes have been reduced in the same proportion.

Upon the summing up I find the Sinking Fund *increased* $41,800 ; the debt *reduced* $100,000; the tax on Real Estate *reduced* 33⅓ per cent.; the Merchants' License tax *reduced* 35 per cent.; the City Bonds at and above par, an *advance* of 50 per cent.

Very Respectfully,

HENRY SAVAGE,
Clerk and Treasurer.

OFFICE BOARD OF AUDIT AND FINANCE.

WILMINGTON, N. C., January 2nd, 1883.

To the Honorable, the Mayor and Aldermen, City of Wilmington:

GENTLEMEN :—As required by law, I herewith submit statement, showing the condition of the Sinking Fund of your city :

Securities Held—

Of Matured Bonds					$ 1,700
Of Bonds Maturing February	1st, 1892,				3,000
" " "	January	1st, 1897,			3,700
" " "	January	1st, 1899,			1,000
" " "	January	1st, 1901,			10,000
" " "	January	1st, 1904,			25,000
Cash Uninvested					29

Total, ... $44,529

The value of maintaining this fund as an important factor in sustaining our city credit is fully recognized by every one who deals in our city securities, or is at all interested in the good faith of the city toward its creditors, as it forms a part of the contract under which our bonds were issued. For it must be borne in mind that the several acts of the Legislature authorizing the City to issue bonds, provided for the creation and maintenance of a Sinking Fund for their gradual payment. But it was not until the creation of the Board of Audit and Finance—whose Chairman was made *ex officio* Commissioner of the Sinking Fund—that any attention was ever given to the subject. Hence, in 1877 when the Board of Audit and Finance was organized, its chairman found no such fund in existence. While the pressing demands upon the City Treasury—which was *then* laboring under the heavy burden of over a hundred thousand dollars *past due indebtedness*, gave no encouraging prospects of establishing one—yet the law required

it should be done, and the necessary machinery was set to
work by tax assessment for that purpose. As the money
is collected and paid over to the Commissioner of the Sinking Fund, it is invested in the City Bonds, which are registered and stamped—both bonds and coupons—"Sinking
Fund, City of Wilmington," and now form a permanent
Fund, the interest of which is invested semi-annually.
That it has grown to its present proportions is certainly a
matter for congratulation, and, if prudently managed, it
will go on increasing until our bonded debt is entirely ab-
sorbed by it, while it gives assurance meanwhile to our
creditors that the City is mindful of its obligations and is
preparing to meet them.

RICHARD J. JONES,
Commissioner Sinking Fund.

CITY CONTRACTS.

The following comprise existing contracts with the City,
and their nature, for fiscal year ending March 31, 1883,
to wit:

Clarendon Water Works Co., for use of Fire Hydrants
(there are now 105) $6,750 per annum.

City Hospital, (City paying two-fifths of expenses, County
three-fifths) $1,000 per annum.

T. J. Southerland,—feeding mules, keeping carts and
harness in repair, and furnishing drivers,—$32.50 per
month for each mule and cart. There are now six mules
(and one horse at $12.50 per month) $207.50 per month, or
$2,490 per annum.

Wilmington Gas Light Co.,—furnishing gas at $2.00 per
month for each street lamp. There are now 189 street
lamps, making $378 per month, or $4,536 per annum. Geo.
W. Batson, Lamp Lighter, $1,008 per annum.

J. L. Winner, keeping City Clock in order, $120 per
annum.

J. W. Taylor, furnishing lumber, $14 per M feet.

J. A. Walker, rent of wharf and small lot opposite, $350 per annum.

CITY POLICE.

The organization of the Police Force consists of one Chief, one Captain, three Sergeants, twenty-five Privates, one Detective and one Clerk.

The appropriation for this department for the fiscal year ending March 31st, 1883, including incidental expenses and equipments for the Force—such as whistles, uniforms, over-coats and hats, as well as pay for extra policemen during, elections, holidays, and times of public excitement, is $19,440, of which sum there has been expended to date (March 1st) $15,086.83.

The number of arrests made for the past year were 479 and amount of fines collected $389.51.

There were 445 men, women and children, who applied for, and were accommodated with lodging at the Station House. Of this number many were "tramps," passing through the country, others were honestly seeking work; all without money or a home here.

A considerable quantity of stolen property has been recovered by the Force and restored to rightful owners.

The majority of arrests reported were for violations of City ordinances, yet quite a large number were for infractions of State laws; and the aid rendered to County officials in the discharge of their duties in this particular has been material.

While the Chief prefers that an exacting public should judge of the efficiency and worth of the Police Force, he desires to bear testimony to their collective merit, and to the manner in which they have discharged the duties assigned them.

The municipal strength of the Police Force of this City has always been regarded as too small. There is a large scope embraced in the corporate limits to be patrolled. In the more populated, or business parts of the city, for the proper protection of property, their stations must necessarily be close together at night, one on a block, thus leaving very few to be distributed on the outskirts, or even in the central portion of the city.

As compared with the pay of the police in other Southern towns, their remuneration is small.

The three Health Officers, who are placed under the surveillance of the Chief of Police, have also discharged their duties in a creditable manner. Not always meeting individual expectation as regards promptness in the removal of rubbish, or abating a temporary nuisance, they have been steadily on the alert, and have evinced a care and judgment in the discharge of their disagreeable duties, which has resulted in keeping the city in a cleanly and good sanitary condition.

THE FIRE DEPARTMENT.

There are at present in service three Steam Fire Engines, all in excellent order. Two of them have hydrant connections with the Water Works, which have operated satisfactorily. There is also one hand engine in good order, but which is never used. These, with a Hook and Ladder Company, two Bucket Companies, one Hose Company, 3,500 feet of good hose, and about 500 feet of old hose (not reliable), constitute the available means of protection from fire.

The Department, now in charge of Chief Engineer Charles D. Myers, has always maintained the highest character for promptness, efficiency and reliability. It is composed of vigorous, public-spirited young men (white and colored) of the best class, and can always be depended upon. The service is entirely voluntary, and although our citizens generally admit its effectiveness, it has merited, for years, a more substantial recognition at the hands of property-holders, and especially of underwriters of local fire risks.

Capt. F. G. Robinson, the recently retired chief, brought, as a guarantee of his capacity, an experience of many years as Foreman of the Little Giant Engine Co. No. 1, and his responsible duties have been performed with credit to himself and honor to the Department. For six years the duties of this office devolved upon Col. Roger Moore, whose administration was characterized by an efficiency probably equal to any paid Fire Department in the United States. A clearer, head, a better executive, or a more patriotic servant of the public has never, in the opinion of many of our citizens, been elected in this community.

The following list comprises the present Fire Department:

CHAS. D. MYERS,.. .... *Chief Engineer.*

HOWARD RELIEF FIRE ENGINE COMPANY, No. 1.

A. ADRIAN,.......................... ...Foreman.
H. HINTZE, ...First Assistant.
M. RATHGEN,........................Second Assistant.

LITTLE GIANT FIRE ENGINE COMPANY, No. 1.

E. G. PARMELEE, ...Foreman.
W. C. VONGLAHN,....................First Assistant.
M. NEWMAN, ...Second Assistant.

CAPE FEAR FIRE ENGINE COMPANY, No. 3. (COLORED.)

VALENTINE HOWE,...................Foreman.
BEN. SHEPARD,......... ....First Assistant.
J. BLAND,............................Second Assistant.

HOOK AND LADDER COMPANY, No. 1.

R. H. GRANT, ...Foreman.
N. A. QUINCE,.............. ....First Assistant.
B. G. EMPIE.......................Second Assistant.

CITY HOSPITAL.

The Wilmington City Hospital was opened for reception of patients, November 1, 1882. By an act of the Legislature, the Hospital is a joint institution of the county and city, the former bearing three-fifths of the expense, and the latter two-fifths.

Up to date, about 160 patients, afflicted with various medical and surgical diseases, have been received and cared for, and quite a number of important surgical operations have been performed successfully.

Several pay patients have availed themselves of the accommodations of the Hospital for treatment, and have paid therefore about two hundred dollars.

The Hospital rates for board and nursing, including medicines, are from 70 cents to $1.60 per day. Surgical operations are charged for extra, as agreed upon by the patients, in accordance with their means.

The Dispensary, located in the main Hospital building, furnishes all needful medical supplies to the inmates, besides giving many prescriptions to the outside county and city poor. The surgeon in charge resides on the premises, and gives the most of his time to the management of the institution and grounds.

The surgeon makes a monthly report of expenses, articles furnished, number and condition of the patients, to a Board of Managers, consisting of three members of the Board of County Commissioners, and two of the Board of Aldermen. All accounts are promptly audited, endorsed by the Chairman, and paid each month.

The Hospital greatly needs more room for patients, a well-lighted operating room, and a mortuary, or proper temporary receptacle for the dead. A report representing these wants has been made to the Board of Managers, and arrangements are being made to construct the building. The officers consist of a resident physician, a steward and a matron.

The present surgeon in charge is Dr. Wm. Walter Lane, whose capacity and fitness for this responsible duty is generally acknowledged by the profession, and whose energy and carefulness with reference to details has been repeatedly complimented by the county and city government. He desires me to say that it is his purpose to make this institution a credit and honor to the city, as well as a boon to those unfortunates who may seek its benefits. There is no more worthy object of benevolence in our community; and I take pleasure in commending it most heartily to our generous people as worthy of their support.

The present public allowance is clearly inadequate, and any private contributions will be appropriated by the surgeon in accordance with the wishes of the donor.

COUNTY GOVERNMENT.

The administration of the County Government is vested in five Commissioners, viz:

> HORACE A. BAGG, *Chairman,*
> B. G. WORTH,
> ROGER MOORE,
> JAMES A. MONTGOMERY,
> E. L. PEARCE,

who are elected by the Board of Magistrates of the county for the term of two years, and are styled The Board of Commissioners of the County of New Hanover. They hold their meetings on the first Monday in each month and are paid $2 per diem for their services.

The Sheriff of the county is S. H. Manning, who gives bonds in the sum of $95,000, with D. L. Russell, E. J. Pennypacker, E. E. Burruss, H. E. Scott, and A. W. Shaffer as his sureties. Paid by fees of his office.

The Treasurer of the county is Owen Birney, who gives bond in the sum of $40,000 with E. E. Burruss, Alfred Martin, H. M. Bowden and Wm. Larkins as his sureties. Paid by commissions.

The Coroner of the county is David Jacobs, who gives bond in the sum of $2,000, with H. E. Scott and S. H. Manning as his sureties. Paid by fees of his office.

The Register of Deeds of the county is Jos. E. Sampson, who gives bond in the sum of $5,000, with F. W. Foster and S. H. Manning as his sureties. He is also *ex officio* Clerk of the Board of Commissioners. Paid by the fees of his office and $2 per diem as said Clerk.

COURTS.

There are two terms of two weeks each of the Superior Courts of the State held in the county of New Hanover on the thirteenth Monday after the first Monday in March and September of each year. In this Court only civil actions are tried. The Judges are paid by the State.

The Clerk of this Court is Stacey Van Amringe, who gives bond in the sum of $10,000 with George Chadbourn and H. E. Scott as his sureties. Paid by fees of his office.

There are six terms of the Criminal Court of New Hanover county held on the first Monday in April, June, August, October and December, and on the second Monday in February. The Judge of this Court is Hon. O. P. Meares, who is paid a salary by the county of $2,500.

The Clerk of this Court is John W. Dunham, who gives bond in the sum of $10,000, with F. W. Kerchner, W. B. McKoy, Henry P. West and Wm. Larkins as his sureties. Paid by fees of his office.

The Solicitor of this Court is Benj. R. Moore, who is paid by the fees of his office. He is also the attorney for the Board of Commissioners, and as such is paid a salary of $500 per annum.

The attorneys residing in the City of Wilmington and practising in these Courts are

GEORGE DAVIS, ... Licensed in 1840.
MAUGER LONDON, ...   "   " 1841.
DUNCAN K. McRAE, ...   "   " 1841.

and Thos. W. Strange,...............Licensed in 1878.
constituting the firm of McRae & Strange.
John L. Holmes,......................   "   " 1849.
DuBrutz Cutlar, ...   "   " 1853.
Duncan J. DeVane,..................   "   " 1858.
Daniel L. Russell,..................   "   " 1866.
and A. G. Ricaud,...................   "   " 1879.
constituting the firm of Russell & Ricaud.
Chas. M. Stedman,.............. ......   "   " 1866.
Willian Latimer,....... ....   "   " 1877.
and Edward S. Latimer, ...   "   " 1879.
constituting the firm of Stedman & Latimer.
Marsden Bellamy,..............   "   " 1866.
Junius Davis,.........................   "   " 1868.
Eugene S. Martin,...................   "   " 1874.
Frank H. Darby,........... ....   "   " 1874.
John D. Bellamy, Jr.,... .. ..   "   " 1875.
Wm. B. McKoy........... ....   "   " 1879.
John C. Davis,......................   "   " 1882.
Ed. H. King, ...   "   " 1882.

COUNTY MAGISTRATES.

The following is the list of Magistrates recently appointed by the Legislature for New Hanover county :

WILMINGTON TOWNSHIP.

John M. Henderson, Wm. H. Strauss, John R. Melton, John Cowan, Wm. W. Harriss, Sol. Bear, E. D. Hall, John S. James, John L. Cantwell, James W. King, Lemuel H. Bowden, Walker Meares, Matthew J. Heyer, David G. Worth, Charles H. Robinson, Abram David, Owen Fennell, Jr., James Madden, John C. Millis, Charles A. Price, J. D. K. Klander.

MASONBORO TOWNSHIP.

B. S. Montford, A. J. Johnson, A. B. George.

FEDERAL POINT TOWNSHIP.

Jacob H. Horne, John Canady, Elijah Williams.

CAPE FEAR TOWNSHIP.

Oscar M. Filyaw, Wm. Cromwell, John E. St. George.

HARNETT TOWNSHIP.

Charles H. Alexander, E. W. Manning, George Harper.

RECEIPTS AND EXPENDITURE FOR THE COUNTY IN 1882.

Receipts *exclusive of School Fund* as shown in settlement of Sheriff with Treasurer, January 18th, 1883, $28,639.64.

Amount in hands of Treasurer on that date....$ 31,050.62.

Debt of County evidenced by Bonds at 6 per
    cent interest due March 1st, 1887,......... 13,000.00.

Estimated expenses of County for ensuing fiscal
    year, ending November 30th, 1883,........ 26,250.00.

Expenses for the last fiscal year,............. 26,582.55.

There is no floating debt.

Included in the $31,050.62 is $13,000 which is set aside to pay the bonds.

The Tax Levy the past year, 1882, was,

State Tax on property, on $100 valuation..........$ .40½

County " " " " " " .... .34½
                            ————

      Total,...................................$ .75

Included in the 40½ cents levied by the State is 12½ cents for the School Fund.

State Tax on each poll,.......................$ 1.21½

County " " " " 1.03½

Included in the $1.21½ levied by the State is 37½ cents for the School Fund.

ANNUAL STATEMENT

Of the Board of Commissioners for the County of New Hanover, for the

Fiscal Year Beginning the 1st day of December, 1881, and

Ending the 30th day of November, 1882.

TREASURER'S REPORT.

General Fund Account, New Hanover County in Account with ELIJAH HEWLETT,

Treasurer, from December 1st, 1881, to November 30th, 1882.

DR.

To amount transferred to Special Fund	$1,000 00	
" " " " "	1,300 00	
" " paid Warrants	25,990 03	
" " paid Commissions	765 22	$29,055 25
Balance		26,475 83
		$55,531 08

CR.

By Balance December 1st, 1881		$20,298 06
" S. H. Manning, Sheriff, General Tax	$27,631 65	
" S. H. Manning, Jury Tax	17 35	
" S. H. Manning, Schedule B Tax	6,500 00	
" J. E. Sampson, Register, Marriage License Tax	227 05	
" S. VanAmringe, C. S. C., Jury Tax	17 60	
" Delinquent Tax	781 40	
" Cronly & Morris, nett sale Stove	07	
" Amount from Columbus County	55 50	$35,233 02
		$55,531 08

Special Fund, New Hanover County, in Account with ELIJAH HEWLETT, County

Treasurer, from December 1st, 1881, to November 30th, 1882.

DR.

Paid for Bonds and Premiums	$ 7,773 60	
" for Coupons	915 00	
" Treasurer's Commissions	147 46	$8,836 06
Balance		$145 65
		$8,981 71

CR.

By Balance December 1st, 1881		$3,573 38
" Amount transferred from general fund	$1,000 00	
" " " " "	1,300 00	
" S. H. Manning, Sheriff	3,108 33	$5,408 33
		$8,981 71

County Treasurer's Report of Receipts and Disbursements of School Fund from

December 1st, 1881, to November 30th, 1882.

RECEIPTS.

Balance on hand as per last report..	$ 8,516 09
Received General State and County Poll Tax, 1882.............................	3,496 60
" " Property School Tax, 1882.............................	5,970 63
" from Fines, Forfeitures and Penalties.............................	256 61
" from Liquor License..	613 60
" from Sale of Estrays..	7 38
	$18,860 01

DISBURSEMENTS.

Paid Teachers of Schools for Whites	$3,907 25
" " " " Colored.............................	5,177 50
" for School Houses (white)..	495 17
" " " (colored)..................................	1,450 36
" County Superintendent...	408 00
" Register of Deeds..	75 00
" County Commissioners...	96 50
" Treasurer's Commissions..	274 38
Total Disbursements	$11,884 16
Balance	$ 7,006 78

RECAPITULATION.

CRIMINAL COURT.

Judge...	$2,500 00	
Clerk	1,014 39	
Solicitor..	553 50	
Sheriff..	724 05	
Jurors...	2,604 45	
Witnesses	973 31	
		$8,369 70

SUPERIOR COURT.

Clerk..	$ 199 67	
Sheriff..	22 25	
Jurors...	588 80	
Witnesses	1 60	
		812 32
Attorney..	535 00	
Commissioners...	853 60	
Coroner...	217 10	
Constables..	228 94	
Justices of Peace...	698 05	
Register of Deeds...	434 09	
Advertising...	126 00	
Roads and Bridges..	375 81	
Clerks, Auditing Committee, Janitor, Ice, &c............	1,272 08	
Elections..	618 22	
Poor House..	2,806 55	
Out Door Poor..	2,400 97	
Jail...	1,682 60	
Public Buildings...	1,166 90	
Stationery and Printing....................................	362 76	
Tax Listing...	1,039 00	
Tax Remitted...	47 52	
Old Claims..	26 74	
Clerks of other Counties..................................	29 50	
Sheriffs of other Counties................................	38 95	
Superintendent of Health.................................	900 00	
Hospital...	1,510 06	
		$26,582 55

Current Expenses proper of County...$25,042 49
County Proportionate part of Expenses of City Hospital......... 1,510 06

$26,582 55

BONDED DEBT.

Bonded debt due March, 1887...$15,800
Floating debt.. 00,000

TAX LEVY OF 1882.

State Tax on Property.. 40½
County Tax on Property... 34½

Total... 75

State Tax on Poll...$1.21½
County Tax on Poll... 1.03½

Total...$2.25

AMOUNT DUE EACH SCHOOL DISTRICT.

District No. 1, White..$ 226 26
"   "   2,   " 1,316 97
"   "   3,   " 78 63
"   "   4,   " 72 46
"   "   5,   " 249 50
"   "   6,   " 2 73

Total White..$1,976 61

District No. 1, Colored...$3,944 58
"   "   2,   " 447 81
"   "   3,   " 71 10
"   "   4,   " 255 81
"   "   5,   " 250 77
"   "   6,   " 6 04

Total Colored...$4,985 11
Total White... 1,976 61
Balance general School Fund..................................... 45 03

$7,006 78

B. G. WORTH, Chairman,
ROGER MOORE,   } Auditing Committee.
H. A. BAGG,

Treasurer's report shows on hand to General Fund $26,475.83 out of which the County is prepared to pay the Bonded debt and is anxious to do so, in fact will pay premium for Bonds of 1 per cent. and accrued interest. $2,800 of the $15,800 of indebtedness have been bought at this premium since 1st January.

POPULATION.

From the following tables, it is apparent that the increase in our population for the last decade is of a steady and healthy growth. We can therefore reasonably estimate our present population at about 19,000.

STATISTICS.—POPULATION AND SCHOOLS.

Census of 1880.

White			Colored			Population Aggregate.
Male.	Female.	Total.	Male.	Female.	Total.	
3,405	3,452	6,857	4,781	5,723	10,504	17,361

1850.			1860.			1880.		
White.	Colored.	Aggregate.	White.	Colored.	Aggregate.	White.	Colored.	Aggregate.
5,526	7,920	13,446	5,202	4,350	9,552	3,381	3,683	7,264

SCHOOL STATISTICS.

No. of School Children 6 to 21 years of age.			No. Enrolled in Common Schools.			No. Enrolled in other Schools.			No. attending no School.		
Colored.	White.	Total.	Colored.	White.	Total.	Colored.	White.	Total.	Colored.	White.	Total.
1,952	3,116	5,068	575	875	950	625	1,203	1,828	1,916	374	2,250

Percentage of attendance Common Schools.		No. of School Districts.			No.of Public School Houses.			No. of Teachers.			No. Months of Instruction.	
White.	Colored.	White.	Colored.	Total.	White.	Colored.	Total.	White.	Colored.	Total.	White.	Colored.
80	78	1	1	2	2	2	4	8	12	20	8	8

SOURCES OF INCOME.

From the State.	Poll Tax.	Liquor Tax.	Real Estate.	Auctioneers.	Fines and Penalties.	Total Fund for City.
$1,176	$2,382	$2,689	$4,875	$46	$202	$11,640

Apportionment of Income.

White Race.	Colored Race.
$4,901	$6,232

Expenses of Maintaining the Schools.

White Race.	Colored Race.	Cost per Capita both Races.
$4,261	$1,617	$8.32

PUBLIC SCHOOLS.

We have good cause to congratulate ourselves on the flourishing condition of our Public or Common Schools. Elementary education is now within the reach of every child amongst us, with no cost to the parents, and there are but few children (at least of the white population) who do not avail themselves of this privilege. These schools are provided with competent teachers, and are under the constant supervision of Mr. M. C. S. Noble, whose education, experience in teaching, and indomitable industry, in every way qualify him for this responsible position.

The management of our Common Schools is in the hands of the five County Commissioners. These Commissioners form the County Board of Education, and appoint three School Committeemen for each District, and the School Committee, in their turn, appoint teachers and oversee the general management of the schools.

The County Superintendent is appointed by the Board of Justices of the Peace.

The system, surrounded in this manner, by all the safe-guards necessary to protect both the interests of the children and those of the tax-payer, works well in this city.

Wilmington township, which is coextensive with the city of Wilmington, has two school districts, in each of which is one for the whites and one for the blacks.

District (No. 1) White, lies North of Market Street.
    "   (No. 2),   "   " South "   "   "
    "   (No. 1) Black   " North of Chestnut Street.
    "   (No. 2)   "   " South "   "   "

Hemenway Graded School, District No. 1, white race, is on Fourth Street, between Red Cross and Campbell.

Peabody Graded School, District No. 1, colored race, is on Fifth, between Red Cross and Campbell streets.

Union Graded School, District No. 2, white race, is on Sixth, between Nun and Church streets.

Williston Graded School, District No. 2, colored race, is on Seventh, between Ann and Nun streets.

Number of children of school age in District No. 1, white	1,009
Number of children of school age in District No. 2, white	943
Total	1,952
Amount apportioned	$3,904
Number of children of school age in District No. 1, colored	1,606
Number of children of school age in District No. 2, colored	1,510
Total	3,116
Amount apportioned	$6,232
Average daily attendance in white schools about	300
" " " " colored " "	425
Number of teachers in white schools	8
" " " " colored "	12

In a speech by Senator Blair, of New Hampshire, June 13, 1882, allusion was made to the disproportionate attendance of school children in North Carolina to the population, in the following language: "Wilmington, North Carolina, has an enrollment of 866, or 18 per cent., while 82 per cent, of the children of that city would appear to be without means of public education." This reflects unjustly upon our public school system.

The school laws of Massachusetts require the attendance of children between the ages of 5 and 15 years—those of North Carolina between 6 and 21 years.

It is well known that the greater number of both male and female children leave school before they reach the age of 17 years; and, as all over that age are registered as attending no school, it would appear that there is a want of proper interest in the matter of education ; whereas both sexes generally attain all the elements of an education at or about 17 years of age, at which time they are generally obliged to work for a livelihood.

The cost of each pupil per school year in Wilmington is about $8.50—in New York city it is about $30.

It may interest some of our people to know that Golds-boro' levies a special tax for its Graded School, and although a town of only 3,300 inhabitants, has an average daily attendance of 447.

Wilson, a town of 1,400 inhabitants, has an average of nearly 400 attendants, and has raised by private subscription in the past two years $6,000 for the support of its school.

Special features of the Wilmington schools consist in the fact that they are all thoroughly graded, and conducted on the same general principle. The teachers are well qualified, and many of them have made special preparation by attending the State Normal School. The Principal conducts four teachers' meetings during each month--two for the white teachers and two for the colored teachers. At these meetings, school government and methods of teaching are discussed, and work for the next two weeks is properly assigned. While the schools are in session, the Principal goes from room to room, takes notes on the teachers' manner, and the decorum of the pupils, and at times conducts the recitation himself; and while inspecting, forms, in a great measure, the subject of discussion at teachers' meetings. Occasionally, to illustrate any new method of instruction, the teachers are resolved into a model class, when the recitation is first conducted by the Principal, and afterwards by the teachers in turn. In this way the peculiarities of each teacher are brought to view, criticised, and then approved or disapproved, according as they are good or bad.

The members of the District School Committees from

time to time, either in a body or individually, visit the schools and inspect the character of the work done.

They pay particular attention to the most economical methods, and are careful to employ only thoroughly capable teachers.

In this way, and with the aid of instructors working for a reputation, they hope to make the schools under their charge, an honor and an ornament to the city, and an object of interest to visitors from abroad.

The members of the School Committee are :

District No. 1—Donald MacRae, Chairman; Wm. M. Parker, Jos. E. Sampson.

District No. 2—James H. Chadbourn, Chairman ; Walker Meares, John Norwood.

The question as to the effect of education upon the rising generation of colored people is not easy to solve. Sufficient time has not elapsed since their emancipation to determine how much, if any, benefit has resulted. For several years after the war, this field seemed to commend itself in a peculiar sense to the philanthropy of the North. The disorganized state of civil affairs, and the impoverished condition of the Southern people, prevented them from educating their own children, and no money could therefore be raised for the education of the negroes. Race prejudice, intensified by the institution of slavery, cramped subsequent efforts of our people to accomplish anything in this direction. The negroes being freed by the act of the Northern people, were therefore regarded in a special sense as their wards, and they were under obligations to meet that responsibility. Peculiar difficulties have attended the efforts of Northern philanthropists, such as a natural antagonism, aggravated by political emissaries coming in some instances in the garb of teachers, and the widespread and profound ignorance and superstition of the negroes themselves. In spite of this, there has been a steady

improvement, most marked where the efforts at real instruction have been thorough and permanent. In the first few
years of the experiment, the work was sadly marred, not
only by the political bias and aspirations of its projectors,
but by a show and parade on public occasions highly offensive to the intelligent and dignified class of our citizens.

In later years, beginning with the administration of the
Rev. Mr. Blake, careful observers in our community—gentlemen who have had good opportunity for observation—
have noted a marked improvement in the habits, the morals
and industry of many of the negro school children.

Mr. Dodge's system requiring a nominal fee for tuition,
has proved an excellent plan, insuring regular attendance
and fostering a spirit of independence perhaps surprising
to many who are familiar with the dependent nature of the
race. Whatever may be the technical details of the methods
adopted in Mr. Dodge's school, the effect is beyond question a good one, as the boys after leaving this institution
get employment more readily than others, because their
moral principles are higher, and because they are generally
better fitted for intelligent occupation than the majority of
those who profess to have received an elementary education.

The people of Wilmington have great cause for thank-
fulness that our negro population is so law-abiding and
faithful to duty ; and to take courage from the results
already accomplished in a transition so violent—from a
life of slavery to that of freedom and citizenship in the
eyes of the law. The utmost harmony has prevailed between the races for many years past, and instances of dis-
agreement between employers and employes are far more
rare than among the whites in the North. With direct
reference to this subject, I have requested the Agent of
the American Missionary Society in Wilmington to give
me a short outline of his work in our community, which
is herewith appended, and I doubt not, a large number of

our intelligent citizens who read this will be surprised at
the magnitude of the undertaking, and the efficiency of its
administration.

"DEAR SIR:—In compliance with your request for a condensed statement of the work and expenditures of the
American Missionary Association in this city, I have the
honor as their agent, of giving you the following report:

The American Missionary Association began its work
among the Freedmen in this city in the month of April,
1865. The object of this work was to impart intellectual
and moral instruction, and to teach an orderly Christian
life. To this end a corps of eight teachers opened public
free schools in different localities in the city. The number
of teachers has varied from time to time, sometimes being
more and sometimes less than at the beginning. At the
same time, afternoon schools for women and night schools
for both sexes were opened. Sunday School work was
carried on in connection with these schools from the first.

This work was sustained alone by the Association till
1869, when the School Board of Wilmington began to
co-operate with it in sustaining free schools, and continued
to do so until 1873, when the local authorities concluded to
discontinue further co-operative school work, and to
establish public schools of their own. This led to the
re-organization of the Association's work, and to the establishment of the Preparatory Departments of the present
Normal School, which were opened for the admission of
pupils October, 1873, with a small tuition fee of one dollar
per month. The various departments of our work were at
that time condensed into what we could do in the one building on the corner of Nun and Seventh streets as it then
stood ; but we soon became uncomfortably crowded. The
need of establishing regular and orderly worship became
apparent, and for a time this was conducted in the school
room. Through the representations of Mr. Woodworth, of
Boston, Mr. Gregory, of Marblehead, Mass., became interested in our wants, and gave the money to build the church

edifice which now stands on Nun street. This led to a visit from Mr. Gregory at the time of the dedication of the church. Upon examining the work done under unfavorable conditions, he was so impressed with the importance of the work itself, and the need of enlarged facilities, that he furnished the means for building the Home which the teachers now occupy, and for the renovation and enlargement of the old building for school work ; thus giving us our present appointments, which seem well adapted to the work to be done.

The entire expenditure of the Association for the work at this station, including Mr. Gregory's liberal gift, is in round numbers $90,000. $18,800 of this amount has been expended since 1879 in enlargements and improvements. At the time of the discontinuance of co-operative work with the Association, the city bought the building known as the "Williston School" of the Association, for the sum of $3,000. $500 of this purchase money was given to the city by the Association to be expended in repairing the building.

In addition to any advantage which may have come to the city from the work, more than one hundred of our pupils have gone out as teachers among their people.

Now, while I do not claim perfection for the methods, or that the workers have always been the wisest and the best, I am willing to submit the question of the usefulness of our work in this city to the decision of the good people of Wilmington, and to abide by their verdict.

Yours Respectfully,

D. D. DODGE.

Agent A. M. A.

UNION FREE SCHOOL.

It appears from reliable data, that the question of building this public school house, was brought to the attention of the citizens of Wilmington through Mr. John W. Barnes, Sr., in the summer of 1856. A meeting of citizens was held, and a subscription list opened for procuring means to pur-

chase a lot and material necessary for the construction of a building.

Mr. S. N. Martin headed the list with a subscription of $100, and Mr Miles Costin presented the lot, the estimated value of which was $290. Other subscriptions soon followed, and in a short time a sufficient amount was realized to warrant the erection of the building, which was finished during the winter, and styled the "Union Free School."

Messrs. A. H. Van Bokkelen, P. W. Fanning and B. G. Worth,—who were always identified with the best interests of Wilmington, and to whom this place is indebted in the past for numberless acts of benevolence,—gave the undertaking a hearty and steady support, and were afterwards more closely identified with the school as committeemen.

The deed for the lot was executed by Mr. Costin to James G. Green, John W. Barnes, and Thomas J. Freshwater, as Trustees, November 3rd, 1856, and recorded December 31st, of the same year. This deed empowers the County Court to appoint successors in case of death or resignation.

In April of the ensuing year (1857), a meeting of the subscribers was held in the new building, in which it was determined to start the school on the 1st of May, and to continue three months, experimentally. To this end Messrs. S. N. Martin, A. H. Van Bokkelen and P. W. Fanning were constituted a committee to receive contributions, employ a teacher and put the "Union Free School" in operation.

The committee proceeded to secure and furnish a supply of school books (which was replenished from time to time during the existence of the school) and employed Mr. John W. Barnes as teacher.

At the close of this short session, the committee being impressed with the necessity of continuing the school, the first annual session was accordingly commenced October 1st, 1857.

Owing to want of harmony between the State Common School Committee and the "Union Free School" Committee, the apportionment of the Common School Fund for this District (No. 2) could not be made available for the enterprise during this year.

In the spring of the ensuing year, however, in response to a petition from citizens, the "Board of Superintendents of Common Schools" for New Hanover County remodelled the town districts (then two in number), dividing each into two districts, and appointing new committees in the lower or southern districts (Nos. 2 and 58), in which this school was situated, whereby it would receive the benefit of the funds appropriated for both, and also the advantage of two co-operating committees—lending an influence to the enterprise which secured its continuance until July 1st, 1863—a period of six years.

The committees appointed, as above mentioned, were the original "Union Free School" Committee for District No. 2, and John W. Barnes, George M. Bishop and W. H. Biddle for District No. 58.

In consequence of the absence of Mr. Martin from the State during the year 1862, B. G. Worth, Esq , was appointed as his successor, and nobly sustained the school from his private means, in connection with the amount received from the Common School Fund during its last annual session.

The school house originally seated about one hundred pupils. During the vacation of 1859, however, the teacher succeeded in procuring money sufficient to build an additional room, capable of holding forty small scholars. Prior to this, many were refused admission for want of room. The whole number of pupils in attendance during the six years was 380. Of this number 192 were males and 188 females.

The largest number in attendance at one time was 145. The smallest number, except during the months of June and July of each year, was not less than 100, and this was before the additional room was built for primary classes.

During the winter of 1865–66, there was a free school in the Union School House, taught by the Rev. Mr Thurston, and supported by the Soldiers Memorial Society of Boston, Massachusetts.

In December 1866, Miss Amy M. Bradley came to Wilmington under the auspices of the American Unitarian Association, and the above named society, and on January 9th, 1867, opened the Union School House with a beginning of 3 pupils, which was shortly increased to 157. She was assisted the first term ending June 30, by Miss Gerrish and Miss Rush, and during the term, built a recitation room at an expense of $141.50, which 'was paid for by the private contributions of a few citizens of Wilmington. The remainder of expenses, total $1,594.07, was paid by her principals in the North.

During the second year the number of pupils was increased to 188, and the expenses to $1,731.74, of which $232 was contributed in Wilmington, and the remainder by Northern people.

The third term was divided by her charge of Union School (223 pupils), Hemenway School (157 pupils), and Pioneer School (45 pupils), at an expense of 7,328.55, during which she bought land for the site of Hemenway School, $1,000 being given by Wilmington citizens, and the remainder of expenses contributed by Northern people.

Her fourth term was classed Normal School (60 pupils), Union School (211 pupils), Hemenway School (176 pupils), expenses $4,866.59, during which she built a Normal School room, and received toward salaries of 7 assistants, $1,500 from the Peabody Fund, and the remainder from her friends in the North.

The fifth term, October 10th, 1870, to June 30th, 1871, Union and Hemenway Schools, expended $5,983.81, (of which the State provided $1,286.70, and the Peabody Fund $1,000) retaining 7 assistant teachers and enrolling 192 and 205 pupils, respectively.

In addition to their annual report, November 23rd, 1871, the School Committee of the Township of Wilmington, James H. Chadbourn being Chairman, made the following statement :

"In the first communication of the committee to your Board, you were informed that there were no school-houses within the limits of the township belonging to the State or county ; and in a subsequent communication, dated February 8, 1870, a proposition was made to you for the purchase of two school-houses (one for each race), for the sum of $3,000 each, and you were requested to levy a tax upon the property of the township, which would produce the sum of $6,000 for that purpose.

The proposition was agreed to, and a tax levied, which yielded the sum of $5,738.61.

The Committee with the approval of your Board and the Superintendent of Public Instruction, purchased the Hemenway school-house of Miss Amy M. Bradley, for $3,000, with the promise on her part, that the money she received for it should be expended in continuing her two schools then in successful operation. This understanding was carried out in good faith, and to the entire satisfaction of the committee.

The cost of sustaining the Union and Hemenway Grammar Schools for the past two years, has been $10,850.40,— $1,266.70 of this sum was received from the State, 2,500 from the Peabody Fund, $3,000 from the sale of the Hemenway school-house, – and the balance, $4,083.70, from the friends of Miss Bradley and her work.

Seven teachers have been constantly employed for a term of nine months each year. The number of scholars has been over 400, and the average attendance about 300. These schools have attracted the attention of all who feel

any interest in free schools in this city, and by good judges
who have visited them, have been compared favorably with
the best grammar schools in the country."

In October, 1871, agreeably to the foregoing understand-
ing, the advanced divisions of the Union and Hemenway
schools were united under the name of

THE TILESTON NORMAL SCHOOL,

and the session opened in the Union School House,—
the Hemenway School House having been purchased by
the county. In October, 1872, this school was moved into
the new building on Ann street, erected by that distinguished philanthropist and friend of education, Mrs. Augustus
Hemenway, of Boston, under the supervision of James
Walker, builder, of Wilmington, at a cost of $30,000. Mrs.
Hemenway subsequently appropriated annually $5,000
to the support of the school, aggregating at present the
sum of $90,000 for the benefit of the education of the white
children of Wilmington, in recognition of which, to the
shame and reproach of our city and State, no public
acknowledgement has ever been made.

In the earlier part of her work, Miss Bradley's object
was often misunderstood by our sore-hearted people; but
in recent years, hundreds of homes in our midst bear cheerful testimony to the genuine and substantial good she has
accomplished. The system and course of instruction has
been thorough, practical and comprehensive; the discipline,
by moral suasion, inflexible and effective ; and the result,
—the graduation of hundreds of our young people of
limited means, in all the essential branches of an education which compares favorably with that of any institution
in the State, fitted for any walk in life, elevated in tone and
morality, and impressed with natural feelings of gratefulness to her through whose instrumentality they were
saved from a life of comparative ignorance and obscurity.

One of the noblest and most effective aims of the institution, has been the preparatory education of boys for the mechanical professions. With unusual discernment Miss Bradley saw that the avenues of the learned professions were being crowded with mediocrity, and that our counting-houses were filled to overflowing, with little prospect of advancement, and that the mechanical trades,—degraded in public estimation by false notions of the dignity of labor,—were offering extraordinary attractions in remunerative and abundant work, with every encouragement for excellence in all departments of skilled workmanship.

With this in view, many of our boys have been prepared by her efficient instruction, for intelligent apprentices as machinists, boiler-makers, carpenters, masons, and blacksmiths ; others for matriculation at the Boston School of Technology, with higher aims as mechanical and mining engineers.

There is nothing superficial in the work of this school. An hour's visit will convince the most skeptical that the Principal is thoroughly in earnest, that her assistants are imbued with the same spirit, efficient in the highest degree, forbearing and patient, and that the good it has accomplished is simply incalculable.

The present mumber of pupils is over 300, and the government and course of study is as follows :

MISS AMY M. BRADLEY,................*Principal.*

TEACHERS :

Mrs. Mary E. Russell,	Miss Ida Farns,
Miss Atta L. Nutter,	Miss Kate L. Alderman,
Miss Marie R. Simonds,	Miss Minnie Bogart,
Miss Josephine Folger,	Miss Emma McDougall.
Miss Mary L. Alderman,	

COURSE OF STUDY.—(TILESTON NORMAL SCHOOL).

1. Self Government.	17. Physical Geography.
2. Calisthenics.	18. Mineralogy.
3. Vocal Music.	19. Geology.
4. Reading	20. Natural Philosophy.
5. Spelling,	21. Chemistry.
6. Writing.	22. Algebra.
7. Drawing.	23. Geometry.
8. Arithmetic.	24. Trigonometry.
9. Grammar.	25. Book-Keeping.
10. Geography.	26. Civil Government.
11. Botany.	27. Rhetoric,
12. Zoology.	28. English Literature.
13. History United States.	29. Latin.
14. Physiology.	30. French,
15. Psychology.	31. German.
16. General History.	32. Spanish,

CHURCHES,

There is probably no place in the State where the Sabbath is more hallowed, or the attendance upon Divine worship more general in proportion to the population than in Wilmington. There are 38 places of public worship; the principal church buildings being St. James' (Episcopal), St. John's (Episcopal), St. Paul's (Episcopal), St. Mark's (colored Episcopal), First Presbyterian, Second Presbyterian, Chestnut Street Presbyterian (colored), St. Thomas' Pro Cathedral (Roman Catholic), Front Street Methodist, Fifth Street Methodist, St. Stephens' (colored Methodist), St. Luke's (colored Methodist), First Baptist, Second Baptist, First Baptist (colored), Temple of Israel (Hebrew), Congregational and Lutheran. The average Sunday attendance of whites is estimated at 3,000, and that of the negroes 6,000. The value of church property is estimated between $265,000 and $270,000.

SECRET AND BENEVOLENT SOCIETIES.

There are twenty-eight benevolent organizations in the city of Wilmington, of which twenty-two are white, and six colored. First in order, as in age, is St. John's Lodge No. 1 F. & A. M. This was probably the first Lodge organized in North Carolina, as the register of the Grand Lodge of England, published in 1762, contains the following: "213. A Lodge at Wilmington, on Cape Fear river, in the Province of North Carolina, March 1755." In 1791 the Grand Lodge, after a full investigation of the claims of all the Lodges to priority, in the award of numbers, gave St. John's Lodge at Wilmington, the "No. 1," thus showing that it has claims to antiquity, which claims, the records sustain. It is to be regretted that we have not the record containing the names of its first members, but we know that they were among the most prominent of our citizens. For more than a century, this Lodge has been active in good works, and in its green old age, still flourishes with as much vigor as in the early days of its youth.

Cape Fear Lodge No. 2, I. O. O. F. (Independent Order of Odd Fellows) was instituted by dispensation from the Grand Lodge of the United States, in the town of Wilmington, on the 13th of May, 1842. Its first officers were :

W. S. G. Andrews, Noble Grand.
Valentine Hodgson, Vice Grand.
Wiley A. Walker, Secretary.
Alexander McRae, Treasurer.

The Lodge was organized on the second floor of a building owned by the late Aaron Lazarus, on the corner of North Water street and Ewing's alley, and had only vacated those quarters about two or three months for their new one, on Front street, now occupied by J. L. Boatwright, Esq., when the great fire of 1843 burned every building on the wharf, from Ewing's alley to the depot of the Wilmington & Weldon Railroad Company.

On the 26th of April, 1870, the Lodge commenced the erection of their new Hall, on Third street, and on the 1st of January, 1871, formally occupied the same as their permanent home. It numbers now 51 members, and the officers are :

J. W. Hawkins, Noble Grand.
E. E. Malpass, Vice Grand.
A. J. Yopp, Secretary.
W. L. Smith, Financial Secretary.
John Maunder, Treasurer.

The other societies are as follows :

MASONIC.
Wilmington Lodge No. 319.
Concord Chapter No, 1.
Wilmington Council No. 4.
Wilmington Commandery No. 1.

I. O. O. F.
Orion Lodge No. 67.
Oriana Lodge, Daughters of Rebecca, No. 3.
Wilmington Degree No. 1.
Campbell Encampment No. 1.

KNIGHTS OF PYTHIAS.
Stonewall Lodge No. 1.
Germania Lodge No. 4.

AMERICAN LEGION OF HONOR.
Clarendon Council No. 67.

KNIGHTS AND LADIES OF HONOR.
R. H. Cowan Lodge No. 549.

I. O. RED MEN.
Wyoming Tribe No. 4.

I. O. B. B. (Hebrew).
North State Lodge No. 222.

K. S. B. (Hebrew).

Manhattan Lodge No. 158.

ROYAL ARCANUM.

Cornelius Harnett Council No. 231.

KNIGHTS OF HONOR.

Carolina Lodge No. 434.

The colored associations are:

Giblem Lodge, Mt. Nebo Lodge No. 14, Free Love Lodge, Golden Lyre Lodge, Good Samaritans, Love and Charity Benevolent Association.

LADIES' BENEVOLENT SOCIETY.

One of the chief, and probably the oldest of the charitable institutions of Wilmington, is the "Ladies' Benevolent Society." This Society was organized early in 1845, chiefly through the efforts of Mrs. M. M. Martin, Mrs. William B. Meares, Mrs. John Walker, Mrs. J. A. Taylor, and other benevolent ladies, and had for its primary object furnishing food to the destitute poor ; but it was always the desire of its originators to extend the usefulness of the organization by providing a home for widows and orphans. In 1852 Mr. Miles Costin, a wealthy and charitable citizen, presented the Society with a lot in the southeastern portion of the city, upon which such a Home was to be erected. This made it necessary for the Society to become incorporated, and in 1852 it received a charter as "The Ladies' Benevolent Society of Wilmington, North Carolina."

About the same time Mr. P. K. Dickinson, a friend of every benevolent enterprise, donated to the Society ten shares of Wilmington & Weldon Railroad stock, to be used for the same purpose.

The dividends from this stock were carefully saved, until they amounted to $1,200, when the entire amount was lost by the failure of the bank in which it was deposited.

During the war, the operations of the Society were entirely suspended, but in 1863 a reorganization was effected, and Mrs. C. G. Kennedy elected President. This lady has been successively re-elected, and to her, more than to any one else in Wilmington, is the success of the Society due, almost her whole time being devoted to its work. In 1872 the lot which had been donated to the Society was sold, and one-half the proceeds given to the family of the donor, who were left much impoverished by the war. The remaining half, together with the proceeds of the railroad stock, was used to purchase a more suitable place for the Home which the Society wished to organize, and in 1881 was established the "Old Ladies' House of Rest." The President, in her annual report for 1881 says: "The House is rather small, and is now occupied, almost to its full extent, by respectable and worthy ladies, to whom, as yet, we can only give a comfortable shelter, not having funds for the support of those who are received, but hope to be sustained in our efforts to make it altogether what its name imports. It is even now a harmonious and peaceful home—not denominational, but guarded by Christian principles."

The Society is supported entirely by voluntary contributions of money, wood and provisions, from benevolent citizens, and the dues of its members, which are one dollar a year.

It is noticeable that of late years the contributions have fallen far below those of previous years, while the demands upon the Society for aid have increased, and it has been with the utmost difficulty that the calls of absolute want have been supplied.

ST. GEORGE AND ST. ANDREW SOCIETY, OF WILMINGTON.

This is a charitable society, and was instituted in 1871. Its object is to relieve and aid sick and distressed Englishmen and Scotsmen. The members of this society wish to alleviate all suffering amongst their fellow countrymen. The Treasurer has expended about $1,500 in such charities since the society was founded. The present membership numbers 34. None but Englishmen, Scotsmen, or the sons or grandsons of native English or Scots are admitted as resident members.

OFFICERS:

ALEX. SPRUNT,...........................President.
ROBT. SWEET,.............................Vice President.
JOHN COLVILLE,........................Treasurer.
H. G. SMALLBONES,.....................Secretary.
T. F. WOOD,.............................Physician.

The regular meetings are held on the second Monday of each month, and the annual meeting on the 21st of March. The fees are 50 cents per month, and the life members are required to pay $50, which relieves them from all other dues.

THE HIBERNIAN ASSOCIATION, OF WILMINGTON

was organized in 1866 for the purpose of relieving sickness and distress among its members, and also to assist strangers, their fellow-countrymen, who would otherwise be a burthen to the community. The present membership is about 50.

The Society is not a secret organization, but purely benevolent, and includes in a bond of good fellowship nearly all of the most respectable Irishmen of our community: many having risen to wealth and honor, and not a few of whom have been identified in the past with the material progress of our city.

The officers are elected yearly, and are at present as follows:

FRANK H. DARBY,.......... ....President.
JAMES REILLY,. ....Vice President.
T. DONLAN,...........................Treasurer.
JAMES CORBETT,................... .....Secretary.

THE SEAMAN'S FRIEND SOCIETY.

In 1853 a number of benevolent and enterprising citizens organized a Society in Wilmington "to improve the social, moral and religious condition and character of seamen;" which appears at that time to have been most deplorable, and in recent years to have relapsed into as bad a condition.

For several years the work prospered; a Methodist minister, Rev. Mr. Langdon, was employed as a travelling agent for the Society, and collected in Wilmington and other parts of the country, money to pay for the property known as the "Seaman's Home," on Dock and Front streets, now valued at $20,000, upon which a bonded debt of $5,400 still remains.

In 1856 Capt. Gilbert Potter built a Bethel on the ground adjoining the Home, on Dock street, and owned by the Association, at an expense of about $6,000, which he presented to the Society, and for many years Divine service was regularly conducted in it to good congregations of sailors by local ministers, and by the Society's chaplain.

In those years, the Home was in charge of a most worthy man, Capt. George W. Williams, who not only wrought a good work among the crews of foreign and domestic vessels, but who kept an attractive and well-ordered house, comfortable and cleanly rooms, good substantial fare, an inviting, well-found reading-room, and by his experience of many years as a ship-master, his well-known character as an upright, honest man, and his influence as an humble Christian, accomplished so much good in this shipping community, that the Society was esteemed a boon among our business people, and supported accordingly.

In recent years, the good work of the Society has been greatly retarded by inefficient and mercenary superintendents, who rented the Home upon speculation for their own benefit as a boarding-house, and by a degree of indifference among the members most deplorable, when we consider the wide field of usefulness which is open to improvement.

Although a chaplain has been annually elected by the Board of Trustees for several years past, and his salary ($400) paid by the Seaman's Aid Society of New York, it is a lamentable fact that during the past year, the Home chapel has been closed week days and Sundays, because, as the Secretary informs me, "the chaplain could not get a congregation, and finally abandoned the effort;" although a few weeks ago, and in this Christian community, there were no less than 450 foreign and 220 American seamen in port, probably not a dozen of whom attended religious services on Sunday in Wilmington. This is a serious matter, and commends itself to our local ministers as well as to the members of the Seaman's Friend Society. In the meantime have sprung up along our wharves, those mushroom curses known as sailors' boarding-houses, with attractive bar-rooms and depraved women, who, with regularly paid runners, professing to be friends of poor Jack, entice him to these dens, entertain (?) him until his last cent is expended, and then mercilessly ship him, appropriating not only his available cash, but also his advance wages. So bold have these runners become in their nefarious work, that very frequently, and in my own business experience, an entire ship's crew has been enticed to desert immediately upon arrival; and although a State law has been passed for the relief of masters and owners of vessels, making this enticement an indictable offense, such is the ingenuity and duplicity of the runners, and the depravity of the sailors themselves, that by their perjury or false swearing, nearly every effort to prosecute has thus far been unavailing.

With reference to this great evil, Mr. Barker, a Wilmington ship agent, says: "I agree with you that this outrage should be stopped. Many ship-masters consigned to me have complained of it, and I believe that united action by ship-masters and merchants here will prevail against it."

Mr. Alexander Sprunt, British Vice Consul, says: "For many years complaints have frequently been made to me by British ship-masters of desertion among their crews, caused by boarding-house runners, who infest the harbor, and I have repeatedly advised them to prosecute suspected persons, but to no purpose. The Seaman's Friend Society should take this matter in hand."

Mr. E. Peschau, German Consul, says: "German ship-captains and ship-owners have suffered much trouble and loss in Wilmington by the enticement of their sailors by men-stealers on shore. I have tried repeatedly to bring some of these wretches to justice, but they have evaded me. I would gladly join you in an attempt to remedy the evil."

Mr. R. E. Heide, Vice Consul of Norway, Sweden and Denmark, says: "I am glad to know that you have brought this matter before the Exchange. My people suffer much from these bad influences on shore. Scandinavian sailors are known all the world over as law-abiding and capable seamen, but they are often misled here by bad influences, and suffer more from it than the owners do, as they often desert their vessels, leaving much wages due them. I agree with you in all you have said about the Seaman's Friend Society, although I am one of the Executive Council, and I am sure much more good could be done."

Mr. C. P. Mebane, ship-broker, says: "Your remarks upon the desertion of sailors are timely. For some years past it has been a growing evil, encouraged by the failure of prosecutors and the boldness of boarding-house runners. It seems to me that this trouble might be stopped by the city authorities, or by the influence of the Seaman's Friend Society, which is now doing so little for the avowed object of its organization."

The Society formerly numbered over one hundred paying members; at present there are only twenty-five. Let the good work have better encouragement. I have made reference to it, not in a carping spirit, but with a wholesome desire to revive its former efficiency and usefulness.

Already there are indications of a decided improvement in its affairs: the Home having been recently renovated, new furniture supplied, and a Superintendent elected, who begins his duty well, and it is to be hoped will continue faithful to his trust. Norwegian services are held in the Bethel every Sunday, conducted by the Superintendent, Capt. Christiansen, and it is the purpose of the newly elected Chaplain, Capt. W. J. Potter, to prosecute his work vigorously—in which it is to be hoped they will be sustained by all the friends of this good cause.

The officers of the Society are as follows:

GEORGE R. FRENCH, SR.,........ ..President.
GEORGE HARRISS,.............. ...Vice President.
GEORGE R. FRENCH, JR.,........ Secretary and Treasurer.
CAPT. W. J. POTTER,........ ....Chaplain.

Trustees—Messrs. George R. French, George Harriss, R. E. Heide, E. T. Hancock, H. B. Eilers, B. F. Mitchell, George R. French, Jr., E. S. Martin, Edouard Peschau, Roger Moore, Edward Kidder, Alexander Sprunt, F. W. Kerchner, W. I. Gore, C. H. Robinson.

Executive Committee—Messrs. E. T. Hancock, H. B. Eilers, R. E. Heide.

ST. JAMES' HOME.

"In the Spring of 1867 Dr. A. J. DeRosset, Senior Warden of St. James' Parish, Wilmington, N. C., conveyed to the vestry of the parish, an entire city square with a two story double wooden house thereon, as a free gift, for religious and benevolent use. The active exertion of the parishioners, aided by the liberality of friends in different portions of the United States, and supplemented by a very successful fair, enabled the vestry to restore the residence which had been seriously damaged during the war of secession.

In 1870, a Sunday and day school were opened in the building, for the gratuitous instruction of the poorer white children of the city. The object of the school, was the instruction of such children as might be reached by it in the more fundamental branches of an ordinary English education, in connection with the direct inculcation of moral and religious principles, with a view not merely to prepare its scholars for respectability and success in the world, but therewith also to make them good orderly citizens, both of the commonwealth, and of the church.

Since its commencement, the school has been maintained without interruption, except for the ordinary vacations. So far as the existing records of attendance supply material for the estimate, it is calculated that from 600 to 800 children of both sexes have, up to the present time, come under the influences, and enjoyed the training of the school. Though at no time having room for any very large attendance, the numbers of the school have steadily increased from the first, and there are now upon the roll more than 100 names. The growth of the school required very soon after its first opening, a separate school room, which was annexed to the main building. This has recently been enlarged to more than double its original size, and will, (thanks to the liberality of friends,) both in New York and Wilmington,) in a few weeks, be furnished with an entire set of new and handsome desks of the most approved pattern.

Teachers have been employed at fixed salaries during much of the time. But much or most of the work has been done—and well done—by the voluntary labor of educated women who have devoted themselves to good works, and who have had their home on the premises. Since the fall of 1878, the school has been in charge of members of the Sisterhood of the Good Shepherd, whose mother house is in New York, and whose work in this connection has been beyond all praise. The order and discipline maintained, have been such as would compare favorably with that of any other school in the country, and the advances in education have been creditable to both teachers and scholars.

In connection with the school, a general mission work among the poorer classes has been zealously maintained, and with the best and most evident results. It has been a part of the work of the ladies, resident at the Home, to visit the poor and the afflicted, and carry with them help and consolation—to be instructors in all good and useful things from house to house, especially among the parents of the school children. A large and varied work of this sort is incessantly done.

In addition to this, orphans, or half-orphans, have from time to time found a home in the house. The more helpless and homeless sick have, in several instances, been brought thither and cared for, and nursed till relieved of their sufferings by death, and then decently buried. Invalids from places at a distance, seeking the help of the skilled physicians of the city, have been received and nursed. Penitent women have found a refuge where the religious influences of the household, have aided them in their attempts at reformation. Beside all which, the Home has been a nucleus for the benevolence of the Parish, and has given wise form and direction to its alms. Nor should it be forgotten that to carry out more completely its influences for good among the children connected with its schools, instruction in needle work and in cooking have been added to its other departments of education. It is at this time, and in this way the only industrial school in the city known to the writer.

All this work has, of course, involved considerable expenditure, and at the same time required very rigid economy in the administration of the household.

The institution has so far been supported,

1. By a regular subscription kept up by a few gentlemen and ladies of the parish.

2. By the collections in its behalf of the Ladies' Association of the parish.

3. By public offerings on Ash Wednesday and Thanksgiving Day in each year.

4. By occasional contributions.

If to these resources a small endowment could be added —just enough to ensure the permanency of the work, independently of the fluctuations of individual fortunes, but not enough to relieve the parish of the duty and privilege and habit of giving to the maintenance of a good object— a great and good work would be made secure, and the minds of the faithful women who have surrendered all worldly prospects of support, in order to do their Master's work among the poor, would be comforted with the assurance, that after their work is done, and they have been worn out in doing it, they will not be turned adrift to die, but will find a shelter till death, in the institution to which they have given their lives.

At present there are three ladies resident at the Home, and constituting the Sisterhood family, all of them connected with the Sisterhood of the Good Shepherd, and all of them, together with another lady of the parish who comes daily, actively occupied in the work."

I am indebted for the foregoing particulars to the Rector of St James' Parish, who has given much of an unselfish and devoted life in his Master's cause to this most interesting and important work of benevolence.

NEWSPAPERS.

If we may believe the historian, Williamson, the Lords Proprietors and the Royal Governors were extremely hostile to the establishment of newspapers in the colony,

during their administration of affairs. We are told that
the Governor of Virginia would not suffer in the colony,
under any pretense whatever, the use of a printing press,
and Sir William Berkley, one of the Proprietors of North
Carolina, thanked God that there was not a printing office
in any of the Southern provinces. Doubtless they knew well
the power of an unfettered press, and dreaded its influence
upon the minds of the people; but notwithstanding their
opposition, printing was introduced into North Carolina,
and a paper published at Newbern, by James Davis, in
1749, one hundred and thirty-five years ago. It was called
the *North Carolina Gazette*, and printed on a small sheet,
and issued weekly.

The second press set up in North Carolina was at Wilmington, in 1763, by Andrew Stewart, called the *Cape
Fear Gazette and Wilmington Advertiser*. This paper
was discontinued in 1767, but was succeeded the same year
by the *Cape Fear Mercury*, published by Adam Boyd.
He was an Englishman, but a true friend to the Colonies,
was a member of the Committee of safety for the town of
Wilmington, in 1775, and greatly respected. He was a
prominent member of the Committee of Correspondence and
was endowed with versatile talents. In 1770 he entered the
ministry and was appointed Chaplain of the Continental
line.

We have no means of knowing how long the *Mercury*
existed, nor have we been able to find copies of any other
publications, prior to 1818. In that year, Mr. David Smith,
Jr., father of Col. Wm. L. Smith, the late Mayor of
the City, commenced the publication of the *Cape Fear
Recorder*, which continued under his management until
1835, when Mr. Archibald McLean Hooper assumed control of its management and for a number of years it was
the only paper published in this section of the State. Mr.
Hooper had large scholarly attainments and was fond of
the classics. He had the hand of a ready writer, and his

style was characterized by great ease and elegance, felic-
itous in expression, and clothing his ideas in language
beautiful and chaste. He was a near relative of Wm.
Hooper the signer of the Declaration of Independence, and
the father of Johnson Hooper, so well known to fame as the
author of "Simon Suggs," "Taking the Census," and other
humorous works.

About the year 1834, Mr. Henry S. Ellinwood came to
Wilmington, and assumed the editorial chair of the *Wilmington Advertiser*, a paper then published in the town.
He was an educated gentleman, and fitted for the duties of
a journalist. He courted the muses with considerable
success, and many of his pieces, which are still in
existence, give ample evidence of belles lettres culture, wit
and fancy. His connection with the paper was, however,
very brief, as he died suddenly a short time after taking
charge. After his death the paper was purchased by Mr.
Joshua Cochrane, of Fayetteville, and conducted by him
until the Summer of 1836, when he died, and Mr. F. C.
Hill became the Editor and Proprietor, and continued its
publication until about the year 1842, when it ceased to
exist.

Cotemporary with the *Advertiser*, was the *People's
Press*, a paper published by P. W. Fanning and Thomas
Loring, the latter being the editor in chief, which position
he held for some time, when he disposed of his interest and
purchased the *Standard*, the organ of the Democratic party
of the State, issued at Raleigh, and removed to that city,
assuming control of its management, he brought to the
discharge of his duties great energy, perseverance, marked
ability and a thorough familiarity with political history.
He was a man of sanguine temperament and a warm parti-
san, and in the excitement of controversy, often indulged
in expressions towards his political opponents, which, in
his calmer moments, his judgment condemned. He wielded
a political influence, at one time, second to but few men in

the State, and was an acknowledged leader of his party, but differing from them in 1842, in regard to their course towards the Banks of the State, he retired from the position he held, rather than continue to hold it at the sacrifice of his independence. Returning to Wilmington, he established the *Tri-Weekly Commercial*, which he conducted for a number of years, until failing health compelled its discontinuance.

The *Wilmington Chronicle* was established about the year 1838, by Asa A. Brown. It was an exponent of the principles of the Whig party, and advanced them with great zeal and ability. Mr. Brown was a capable editor, a good writer and a man of more than ordinary ability. In 1851, he disposed of the paper to Talcott Burr, Jr., who changed its name to the *Wilmington Herald.*

Under his management, the *Herald* became one of the leading papers in the State, and but for his untimely death in 1858, would have taken rank with any in the South.

Mr. Burr's peculiar characteristics as a writer, were his ready wit and sparkling humor, overlaying a deep vein of strong, impulsive feeling. Quick, vivid and flashing, never missing its point, yet never striking to wound, abounding in gay and pleasant fancies, and always warm and genial as the Summer air, it touched the commonest topic of every day life, and imbued it with new and charming attractiveness. He was struck down by the shaft of the great destroyer, in the prime of life, and in the midst of an active, useful and honorable career.

After his death, his brothers, C. E. and R. Burr, carried on the paper for a year or two, when it passed into the hands of A. M. Waddell, and ceased to exist on the breaking out of the war.

In the year 1844, Alfred L. Price and David Fulton, under the firm name of Fulton & Price, issued the first number of the *Wilmington Journal*, a paper destined to

exercise a controlling influence for many years upon the
political questions of the day. The editorial department
was under the control of Mr. Fulton, and very ably conducted until his death, which occurred a year or two after
the establishment of the paper, when his brother, James
Fulton, took charge of its management.

James Fulton was no ordinary man. He possessed a
vigorous intellect and a clear judgment, was quick at
repartee, and prompt to take advantage of any point
exposed by an adversary, in the controversies incident to
his position, but was always courteous, and rarely indulged
in personalities. He wrote with great ease, and his style
was chaste, graceful and vigorous. He had humor, too,
and it bubbled up continually, not that keen, pungent wit
that stings and irritates, but that which provokes merri-
ment by droll fancies and quaint illustrations. He had a
remarkable memory and read much, and remembered what
he read, and could utilize it effectively.

The *Journal* was a power in the State while he controlled
it. In this section, particularly, its influence was unbounded. Mr. Fulton died in the early part of the year
1866, and was succeeded by Major J. A. Engelhard, as
editor, who sustained the high reputation the paper had
acquired. Upon the retirement of Mr. Alfred L. Price,
Col. Wm. L. Saunders became connected with the paper,
the firm being Engelhard & Saunders, an intellectual com-
bination in journalism seldom surpassed. During the
troublous times, after the close of the war, its utterances
were manly, outspoken and fearless in condemnation of
measures regarded as oppressive to our people. It prac-
tised no temporizing policy, but boldly uttered what the
sincerity of its convictions might prompt it to declare. It
continued thus until 1878, when adverse circumstances
caused its suspension. It is now published as a weekly
paper, the name, *Wilmington Journal*, being retained by
Josh T. James, Editor and Proprietor.

But few copies of the earlier papers published in Wilmington, are now in existence, of some, not a copy can be found ; hence there may be, and doubtless are, omissions in the present list, but it is believed to be nearly accurate, at least approximately so. No mention is made of papers whose existence was but temporary.

There are now in Wilmington the following publications :

The *Morning Star*, daily, by W. H. Bernard, established September, 1867, and the *Weekly Star*, established in 1868.

The *Daily Review*, established by James & Price, in October, 1875, now conducted by Josh T. James.

The *Star* and the *Review* are the only daily papers published in the City, the former, a morning paper, and the latter issued in the evening.

The *Wilmington Post*, established in 1866, weekly.

The *North Carolina Presbyterian*, weekly, was first established in Fayetteville, January 1, 1858, the Rev. Geo. McNeill, and the late Bartholomew Fuller, being the editors. It was removed to Wilmington in November, 1874, John McLaurin being the editor and proprietor.

The *Africo-American Presbyterian*, published in the interest of the colored members of that denomination, by Rev. D. J. Saunders, a colored man of remarkable attainments.

The *North Carolina Medical Journal*, by Dr. Thomas F. Wood, was established January, 1878. It is a monthly publication, ably edited, and of great value to the profession.

A comparison between the papers of the day and of the past, will show the marvelous advance that has been made in science and in art. Then, months were required for the transmission of news, political or commercial; now, the lightnings flash has been made subservient to the wants or caprices of man, and he can know the same day what is

transpiring in countries thousands of miles distant. Do
we realize the advantages that we of this century enjoy,
and are we any better, as a people, than were our ances·
tors, who were content with a weekly newspaper, "no
bigger than a man's hand," while we have mammoth dailies
by the hundreds?

COMMISSIONERS OF NAVIGATION AND PILOTAGE.

The Commissioners of Navigation and Pilotage for the
Cape Fear River and Bars, were formerly elected by the
qualified voters of the city of Wilmington, but in 1870 the
Legislature of the State passed an act authorizing and requiring the Mayor and Aldermen of the city of Wilmington to appoint every year five persons, and the Mayor and
Commissioners of the town of Smithville two persons, to
serve as Commissioners of Navigation and Pilotage for the
Cape Fear River and Bars, and providing that the seven
persons so appointed should have power to do and perform
all acts theretofore authorized by law to be done by the
Board of Commissioners of Navigation and Pilotage. The
Commissioners have authority in all matters that may con-
cern the navigation of the waters from seven miles above
Negrohead Point downwards, and out of the bar ; and
with respect to throwing rubbish in the river at the
city of Wilmington, and in the construction of wharves
have concurrent jurisdiction with the Mayor and Aldermen
of the city.

The Commissioners are required to appoint a Harbor
Master, and prescribe the duties of his office, to make such
rules and regulations for the Port of Wilmington, and
respecting the duties of pilots, as they may deem most ad-
visable, and to impose reasonable fines, forfeitures and
penalties for the purpose of enforcing such rules and regulations. They are required to provide for the examination
by nautical men, of apprentices who have served three
years, and who desire to become pilots, and to issue com-

missions or branches to such as are found qualified to perform the duties of pilots, provided that there shall not be
at any one time more than sixty-five river and bar pilots
in commission. Three classes of licenses are required to
be issued—one to pilot vessels whose draught of water does
not exceed nine feet, one to pilot vessels whose draught
does not exceed twelve feet, and one unlimited, or full
license, to pilot vessels of any draught of water.

Every person, before he obtains a branch to become a
pilot, must give bond, with two sufficient sureties in the
sum of $500, payable to the State of North Carolina, for
the faithful discharge of his duties.

The number of pilots for the river and bars must not at
any one time be reduced below forty.

The Commissioners are authorized to fix the rates of
pilotage, provided they do not reduce them below the rates
established in 1869.

Pilotage is compulsory for all vessels of sixty tons burthen and over.

The present number of pilots (sixty-five) is about equally
divided between the bars and river.

The Commissioners are required to regulate the number
of apprentices, provided there shall not be less than twenty.
During and since the war, it has been impossible to comply
with this provision of the law, there having been at no time
since the war as many as twenty to serve, and now there
are not more than three or four.

A Harbor Master's fee, when no service is performed, is
not compulsory ; but, by an order of the Commissioners,
every vessel whose captain voluntarily pays the Harbor
Master three dollars, on her arrival, is entitled to his services
at all times, while the vessel is in port, without further
charge.

If this fee is refused, and the vessel so refusing requires
the Harbor Master's services, he is entitled to, and can col-
lect, $5 for the first visit, and $2.50 for every subsequent
visit.

The present Board is composed of James H. Chadbourn, Chairman ; Donald MacRae, David G. Worth, H. B. Eilers, and James Sprunt, of Wilmington, and G. F. Crapon and Edward Daniels, of Smithville.   Mr. Chadbourn has served upon the Board for fifteen years, for twelve of which, he has acted with great acceptability as Chairman.

During his administration, the character of the pilots has greatly improved, and the present body will compare most favorably with any of the profession in other ports.   Instances of drunkenness, neglect or incapacity, are very rare, and although the difficult navigation of our river has of late been more perplexing, in consequence of the changes being wrought by the engineers, there has been no serious damage sustained by any vessel for many years, while in charge of a Wilmington pilot.

Rules and Regulations of the Port of Wilmington, Revised and Adopted by the Board of Commissioners of Navigation and Pilotage, on September 18th, 1868, for the Government of the Port of Wilmington, River and Bars of the Cape Fear, to go into effect immediately.

Ordered, That hereafter all vessels arriving in this Port, the Master, Agent or Consignee of which shall voluntarily pay to the Harbor Master, the sum of Three Dollars, they may command, at all times, the services of said Harbor Master, as prescribed by the Port Regulations, without further charge, while the vessel shall remain in Port ; but where such Master, Agent, or Consignee, shall refuse to pay said amount of Three Dollars, the following fees are fixed, and shall be collected as provided in Revised Code, chapter 85, paragraph 3, page 461 :   When called upon to perform any duty required by law or Court Regulations— for the first visit or performance of duty, Five Dollars, and for each subsequent visit to the same vessel, Two Dollars and Fifty Cents.—*Adopted November 11th,* 1869.

1. All ballast, coal, or other substance calculated to injure the River, shall be safely placed not less than four feet from the cap of the wharf; and in delivering or landing, must be done under such precautions as to prevent the escape of any portion into the River, under the penalty of Fifty Dollars. No ballast or coal shall be discharged from any vessel, while in this Port, after dark or before sunrise, under a penalty of One Hundred Dollars for each and every offence, to be paid by the Captain. And no trash or substance calculated in any manner to injure the navigation, shall be thrown into the River, under a penalty of Ten Dollars, for each and every offence, to be paid by the party offending.

2. All vessels crossing the Bars, either in or out, or navigating the Rivers from or to the sea, shall be required to pay full pilotage to the Pilot offering his services, whether such craft be in tow or otherwise—and that any Pilot neglecting or detaining a vessel under his charge unnecessarily, shall suffer the severest penalty of the law. *Ordered further*, That any person without the authority of this Board, attempting to pilot a vessel, or charging for such service, shall pay a penalty of Forty Dollars.

3. Any vessel hoisting her colors for a Pilot, shall be compelled to pay the Pilot offering his services full pilotage, whether such Pilot be employed or not.

4. When no Pilot is in attendance, any person may conduct into port any vessel in danger from stress of weather or in a leaky condition; but if any person not duly qualified or licensed, shall presume to act as Pilot under any other circumstances, he shall forfeit and pay Forty Dollars.

5. No Master of a vessel having a Branch, or a Mate with a Branch, shall be compelled to take a Pilot, said Master or Mate first having a permit from this Board for leave of absence.

6. Every Master of a vessel who shall detain a Pilot after the time appointed, so that he cannot proceed to sea, though

wind and water should permit, shall pay such Pilot Three Dollars per day during the time of his actual detention ; and if any vessel, which shall be boarded by a Pilot, without or within any of the inlets, shall, by violence of the weather or otherwise, be driven to sea, the Master or owner of such vessel shall allow and pay the Pilot Three Dollars per day for every day he shall be on board, besides the fee of pilotage.

7. All vessels at anchor, or under way, within the bars of Cape Fear River, at night, shall exhibit a light in some conspicuous place, at least ten feet above the deck, so as to be seen by vessels or steamboats passing up or down the River, under a penalty of One Hundred Dollars for each and every neglect, and shall also be liable for all damage or the amount of injury sustained by any vessel or boat coming in contact, to be recovered for the benefit of the injured party. And it shall be the duty of the Pilots to notify the Master of each vessel coming over the bar of the existence of this order.

8. No vessel shall anchor in the River, or extend her fasts as to interrupt the navigation of said River, or the passage of the Ferry Boats to and from the usual place of landing on either side of the River, under the Penalty of Fifty Dollars for each and every offence, after notice from the Harbor Master.

9. No vessel shall extend her hull, bowsprit, yards, rigging or fasts, so as to interrupt the passage into or out of the public Docks, under the penalty of Five Dollars for each and every hour said offence shall continue, after notice from the Harbor Master.

10. No vessel that has discharged, or that is not engaged in discharging or taking on board a cargo, shall keep her place at any wharf, when, for the convenience of discharging or taking on board a cargo, said place may be required by any other vessel, under the penalty of Fifty Dollars for each and every day such offence shall continue.

11. No vessel shall careen for the purpose of burning, cleaning or repairing, at any wharf within the limits of Wilmington, except at regular ship-yards, under a penalty of One Hundred Dollars for each and every offence.

12. No Master or Commander of a vessel shall disobey or neglect such orders and directions as may be given by the Harbor Master, in times of gales of wind, relating to the safety of vessels in the harbor, under the penalty of One Hundred Dollars for each and every offence, to be paid by the Master or Commander of said vessel.

13. No vessel having on board grain, or articles evidently in a state of putrefaction, or offensive, shall haul to or lay at any wharf, but shall anchor in the middle of the River until the order of the Board shall be known, under the penalty of One Hundred Dollars for each and every hour said offence shall continue, after notice from the Harbor Master. Nor shall any vessel discharge offensive bilge water within the limits of the City of Wilmington, under a penalty of Fifty Dollars.

14. No vessel shall lay at any wharf with her yards and booms otherwise trimmed than as the Harbor Master shall direct, under the penalty of Fifty Dollars, for each and every day said offence shall continue, to be paid by the Master or Commander of said vessel.

15. No vessel, whether loaded or empty, shall lay at anchor in the River opposite the City, between Mulberry and Castle Streets, for more than twenty-four hours at one time, under a penalty of Fifty Dollars for each and every day said offence shall continue, after notice from the Harbor Master.

16. If a Branch Pilot shall go off to any vessel bound in, and offer to pilot her over the Bar, the Master or Commander of such vessel, if he refuses to take such Pilot (except lawfully exempt), shall pay such Pilot the lawful pilotage.

17. When any Pilot shall see any vessel on the coast, having a signal for a Pilot, or shall hear a gun of distress

fire off the coast, and shall neglect or refuse to go to the assistance of such vessel, such Pilot shall forfeit and pay One Hundred Dollars—one-half to the informer, the other half to the Master; unless such Pilot is actually in charge of another vessel.

18. The Board of Commissioners may designate the place whereat, within the waters under their control, may be cast and thrown ballast, trash, stones and such like matter : and if any person shall cast or throw from any vessel into said waters, any such substances, likely to be injurious to the navigation, he shall forfeit and pay Two Hundred Dollars. And if any Pilot shall knowingly suffer such unlawful act to be done, and shall not, within ten days thereafter, give information to some one of this Board, he shall be subject to the lawful punishment.

19. Authority is vested in the Commissioners to hear and determine all matters of dispute between Pilots and Masters of vessels, or between the Pilots themselves, respecting the pilotage of vessels—appeal in certain cases to be allowed.

20. On the arrival of any vessel at this port, it shall be the duty of the Harbor Master to go on board and deliver to the Captain or officer in charge of such vessel, the Port Regulations, under a penalty of Ten Dollars.

21. Any Pilot running a vessel ashore, by which means any injury or detention is sustained by such vessel, shall report the same without delay to the Chairman of this Board.

22. No vessel under sixty tons shall be compelled to take a Pilot or pay pilotage, unless a signal for a Pilot shall be made.

23. Any Pilot intending to absent himself from his station for over twenty-four hours, shall communicate his intention to the Chairman, who may grant a permit, and he shall likewise make known his return, under a penalty of Fifty Dollars for such neglect.

24. Should any hulk, raft, flat, or other obstructive substance become sunken, from any cause, in the River, the same shall be immediately removed, under a penalty of Five Dollars for each and every day such nuisance shall remain, after notice from the Harbor Master, to be paid by the parties interested or concerned; and in case exertions are not immediately made for the removal aforesaid, the Commissioners may exercise the discretion of using other means of abating the nuisance, even to the confiscation or condemnation of such obstructions.

25. The Harbor Master shall have power to regulate all fires which are burning or kindled on Rafts, Decks, or Flat Boats, or Lighters, and any owner or agent of the owner, refusing to obey the orders of the Harbor Master, shall be liable to a fine of Fifty Dollars for every violation.

26. It shall be the duty of the Harbor Master to see that all raft frames be taken out of the water by persons landing wood or lumber, and it shall be the duty of every Agent or Inspector of said rafts to have the same done, when so ordered, or at all times, under a penalty of Fifty Dollars.

27. Any person encumbering either of the public docks with logs, dilapidated hulks, or other trash or nuisance, shall forfeit and pay a fine of Five Dollars, if not removed immediately upon notice from the Harbor Master, and Five Dollars for every additional day the nuisance remains. And when the owner cannot conveniently be found, the Harbor Master shall take the most speedy method to clear the dock.

28. The Bar Pilots shall be divided into classes of not less than four each, whose duty it shall be by turns, to ascertain the depth of water at the several navigable points, and to report to this Board by the first regular meeting in each month, being Tuesday—penalty for neglect, Ten Dollars.

29. In all violations of these Ordinances, wherein no forfeiture is specified, a penalty not exceeding Fifty Dollars may be imposed, according to the aggravation of the case.

30. During the recess of the Board, the Chairman shall be empowered to try and determine all cases of delinquency occurring, and an appeal from his decision to this Board being allowed; and all matters connected with the navigation and regulations of the Port, during the recess of the Board, shall be under his immediate supervision and control.

31. No apprentice is allowed to pilot any vessel drawing over six feet of water, without permission from the Chairman of this Board.

32. Any Pilot, who, after having been notified for the purpose, shall fail to be on board any vessel at the time set for sailing, shall forfeit and pay the Captain Ten Dollars for each day's delay (unless at the time he shall have personal charge of some other vessel), and the further sum of one day's expense of such vessel. Pilots, however, may require advance pay for pilotage.

33. Pilots navigating vessels into Port, shall be entitled, exclusively, to navigate such vessels out of Port, provided a Pilot be in attendance when a vessel is ready to sail; otherwise the Captain may employ any other suitable Pilot. Any Pilot or other person navigating a vessel contrary to the meaning of this regulation, shall forfeit and pay the injured Pilot Forty Dollars.

34. Neglect to repair dilapidated wharves shall subject the owners or parties interested, after having been duly notified, to a fine of Five Dollars, for each and every day's neglect to make such repairs.

35. All flats, lighters, or other boats or vessels, employed within the limits of the City of Wilmington, propelled wholly or in part by gigs or poles, are hereby prohibited from using upon the ends of said gigs or poles, any iron or other metal points so sharpened as to make indentation into wood. And any vessel, steamer or package of goods, receiving damage from the use of said gigs or poles, the owners or agent of the owners of the flat or lighter, shall

be liable for the full amount of damage arising therefrom. And any person or persons employed as crew of said flat or lighter, who shall violate this Ordinance, shall be fined not less than Five Dollars for each and every offence.

36. Any person casting loose or adrift, any Flat, Raft or Raft of Turpentine, or any Boat or Vessel, without the consent of the Harbor Master, had and obtained, shall be punished by a fine of Ten Dollars for each and every offence. One-half of the said fine shall, when collected, be paid to the person or persons giving information to the Harbor Master.

37. From and after this date, any person piling wood, or any other material or merchandise, in such manner as to prevent or obstruct the fastening of vessels at any piling or ringbolt, placed upon any wharf for the purpose of securing any vessel, shall forfeit Five Dollars for each and every hour said obstruction shall remain, after notice from the Harbor Master; said fines to be collected in the same manner as other fines imposed by this Board.

All Ordinances, Rules or Regulations, conflicting with those above specified, are hereby repealed.

JAMES H. CHADBOURN, Chairman.

Jos. Price, Harbor Master.

Ordered by the Board of Commissioners of Navigation and Pilotage:

That hereafter no Pilot shall leave a vessel on the River without the consent of the Master, and when any detention shall occur, by fault of the Master of any vessel, the Pilot shall be entitled to Three Dollars per day for every day so detained.

When any vessel lying outside of the Rip, or at other exposed points, shall set her colors for a Pilot, the regular Pilot shall promptly answer her signal, or in his absence, some other Pilot, who has a branch entitling him to take charge of such a vessel, shall proceed to her with all possible dispatch, and for such service shall receive Five Dollars per day, until discharged by the Master.

Services rendered by any other than the regular Pilot, in answer to a signal, shall not deprive the regular Pilot of his right to carry the vessel to sea when she is ready.

Any Pilot failing to carry out this order, shall be liable to such fine as the Board of Commissioners, after investi gating the cause, may impose.

JAS. H. CHADBOURN, Chairman.

February 17th, 1874.

———

Rates of Pilotage for the Cape Fear Bars and Rivers, Established on the 2d day of August, 1870, in Accordance with the Existing Acts of the Legislature of North Carolina, to go into Operation on August 10th, 1870.

BARS:

									$	
Every vessel drawing 6 feet and under 6½ feet..........									$	9 00
"	"	"	6½	"	"	"	7	"	....	9 75
"	"	"	7	"	"	"	7½	"	....	10 75
"	"	"	7½	"	"	"	8	"	....	11 50
"	"	"	8	"	"	"	8½	"	....	12 00
"	"	"	8½	"	"	"	9	"	....	12 75
"	"	"	9	"	"	"	9½	"	.... —	13 50
"	"	"	9½	"	"	"	10	"	....	14 50
"	"	"	10	"	"	"	10½	"	....	15 25
"	"	"	10½	"	"	"	11	"	....	17 00
"	"	"	11	"	"	"	11½	"	....	18 50
"	"	"	11½	"	"	"	12	"	....	20 50
"	"	"	12	"	"	"	12½	"	....	22 50
"	"	"	12½	"	"	"	13	"	....	25 50
"	"	"	13	"	"	"	13½	"	....	28 50
"	"	"	13½	"	"	"	14	"	....	31 00
"	"	"	14	"	"	"	14½	"	....	34 00
"	"	"	14½	"	"	"	15	"	....	38 00
"	"	"	15	"	"	"	15½	"	....	42 00
"	"	"	15½	"	"	"	16	"	....	45 00
"	"	"	16	"	"	"	16½	"	....	50 00
"	"	"	16½	"	"	"	17	"	....	55 00
"	"	"	17	"	"	"	17½	"	....	60 00
"	"	"	17½	"	"	"	18	"	....	65 00

RIVER.	From Smithville to Wilmington, and vice versa.	From Five Fathom Hole to Wilmington and vice versa.
Every vessel drawing 6 feet and under 6½ feet	$ 9 50	$ 7 00
"　　"　　"　6½　"　"　"　7　"	10 50	8 00
"　　"　　"　7　"　"　"　7½　"	12 00	9 00
"　　"　　"　7½　"　"　"　8　"	12 50	9 75
"　　"　　"　8　"　"　"　8½　"	13 00	10 25
"　　"　　"　8½　"　"　"　9　"	13 50	10 75
"　　"　　"　9　"　"　"　9½　"	14 00	11 25
"　　"　　"　9½　"　"　"　10　"	15 00	12 25
"　　"　　"　10　"　"　"　10½　"	16 00	13 25
"　　"　　"　10½　"　"　"　11　"	18 00	14 50
"　　"　　"　11　"　"　"　11½　"	19 75	15 75
"　　"　　"　11½　"　"　"　12　"	22 00	16 75
"　　"　　"　12　"　"　"　12½　"	24 00	17 50
"　　"　　"　12½　"　"　"　13　"	26 50	20 00
"　　"　　"　13　"　"　"　13½　"	29 00	22 25
"　　"　　"　13½　"　"　"　14　"	32 00	24 25
"　　"　　"　14　"　"　"　14½　"	35 00	26 25
"　　"　　"　14½　"　"　"　15　"	40 00	28 25
"　　"　　"　15　"　"　"　15½　"	44 00	30 00

From Smithville to Brunswick, or from Brunswick to Wilmington, or *vice versa*, shall be one-half the Pilotage from Smithville to Wilmington. From Smithville to Five Fathom Hole, from Five Fathom Hole to Brunswick, from Brunswick to Campbell's Island, from Campbell's Island to Wilmington, or *vice versa* one-fourth of the Pilotage from Smithville to Wilmington: *Provided*, That vessels of 60 tons burthen, owned by the citizens of this State, shall not be required to take a Pilot.

　　　　　　　　By order,　　　　　　JOS. PRICE, Clerk.
August 10, 1870.

PORT WARDENS.

An Act of the General Assembly passed in 1802, authorized, empowered and directed the Commissioners of Navigation to appoint three fit persons to be Wardens of the Port, for the Port of Wilmington. And, in case of the death, refusal to act, or resignation of any Port Wardens so appointed, it is the duty of the Commissioners of Navigation, together with such Port Warden, or Wardens, as shall be then living and acting, to elect'some other person or persons in the place of the one so dying or refusing to act.

The act prescribes the duty of the Port Wardens substantially as follows:

On request made by the master or owner of any vessel arriving in port, or stranded within the bounds thereof, to survey and make report of the situation and condition of her, and the causes thereof, and whether she should be repaired or condemned. To inspect the condition of vessels which may arrive in distress, or may have suffered by gales of wind at sea. The condition and situation of goods, wares and merchandise, which may arrive in said vessels, or may have received damage at sea, and to report thereon and the probable causes thereof. To inspect the stowage of the cargoes of vessels arriving in port, having received damage at sea, before the same shall be discharged. To make surveys of goods, wares and merchandise, and the cargoes of damaged vessels, and to make and report estimates of the amount of damage sustained. To make and report (if required) surveys of vessels outward bound, and to report whether they are seaworthy or not, and fit for the voyage intended. All goods that are sold by reason of their having received damage, which shall have been surveyed or inspected by the Port Wardens, shall be sold under their inspection and direction.

The surveys and reports of the Port Wardens are considered as authentic documents, and as such, received as evidence in courts of law.

The present Wardens are George Harriss, B. G. Bates and R. G. Ross; and judging from the Act of General Assembly ratified in 1802, creating this office, it would appear that the appointments are for life.

PORT CHARGES AND FACILITIES.

Wilmington is proverbially a cheap port. Owing to its distance (about thirty miles) from the sea, the principal expenses to vessels are towing when required, and pilotage, which is compulsory. The service of towage is efficiently rendered by the steam tugs *Blanche, Italian, Passport, Alpha, Tioga* and *William Nyce*, at the following rates:

Towage from sea to sea, ...35 cents per ton.
   "   " Smithville and to sea, ...30 "   "   "
   "   " Wilmington   " " ....25 "   "   "

There are no Harbor dues, except the Harbor Master's fee of $3.00 on each vessel, which is not compulsory, but optional with the vessel, and which is recommended to be paid in all instances, as a retainer in case of need,—the Harbor Master being empowered to charge a vessel, other-wise, for services rendered, $5.00 for the first visit, and $2.50 for each subsequent one. There are over three miles of river front, about half of which affords wharf accommodation, free of charge to vessels, which are promptly moored on arrival, by the Harbor Master.

The present depth of water in the harbor is 10 to 45 feet, but below Wilmington, the river (now being dredged and deepened) on ordinary tides is only 14½ feet, so that vessels requiring more water, must lighter the remainder of the cargo to Smithville (near the bar) at a cost of, say, 8 to 12 cents per barrel rosin, 10 to 15 cents per cask spirits turpentine, 30 to 50 cents per bale cotton.

The charges for stowing cargoes are lower than in any other port; say,—rosin 3 cents, tar 4 cents, spirits turpentine 6 cents, cotton 40 to 50 cents, porting and stowing lumber 50 cents. Provisions and other ship stores are about the same as in other Atlantic ports.

Two years ago an attempt was made to establish a line of Steamers from Wilmington to Liverpool, and the Steamer *Barnesmore* was chartered as an experiment, but it was found that the depth of water was not sufficient to encourage further business.

The Captain of this Steamer, however, wrote, upon his departure for Liverpool, a very hopeful letter addressed to Mr. A. H. Van Bokkelen, President of the Chamber of Commerce, of Wilmington, which was as follows, and which may serve as a guide, should further efforts be made for direct steam communication:

"OFF SMITHVILLE, N. C., October 6th, 1881.
HON. A. H. VAN BOKKELEN,
   President Chamber of Commerce, Wilmington, N. C.
DEAR SIR :—

Agreeably to your request, I beg herewith to give you my opinion and experience of the approaches and port of Wilmington. The only danger to be apprehended in approaching Wilmington bar is the Frying Pan Shoal, which is well marked by buoys on each side, and the Light Ship at the extreme end ; but as ships bound to the southern ports endeavor to sight the Light Ship, the risk and danger is equally great to them as if they were bound to Wilmington. Any remarks therefore, on this head, would be superfluous, as it is abundantly shown they can have all the tonnage they require at any southern port ; and I am quite sure the approaches would not be considered by owners desirous of sending their steamers to this port, any more than to Charleston or Savannah.

The bar is straight, and well marked for crossing by day or night—and we passed in and out with perfect ease and safety.

Outward-bound, our draught was—forward, 13 feet, 4 inches ; aft, 14 feet, 9 inches.

We found not less than 18 feet of water on the bar—sufficient for a much larger steamer than the *Barnesmore* to pass safely.

I was prepared to find Cape Fear River shallow ; but I also expected to find the navigation intricate and troublesome, and in this I was agreeably disappointed, for excepting the Horse Shoe Bend, there is not a sharp turn in the river ; and I do not think any steamer that steered fairly well would have any difficulty in passing this. Indeed, navigating the Danube, compared with the Cape Fear River, is passing the Horse Shoe Bend all the time.

The shallowness of the water, however, is a great difficulty in the way of getting steamers to run regularly to this port. There are comparatively few steamers that can load a cargo large enough to pay them to cross the Atlantic on a draught of 14½ feet. If, however, the river was dredged to a minimum depth, at ordinary tides, of 16 feet, you could get as many steamers as you wanted to load a cargo of cotton at this draught ; and I have no doubt Wilmington would soon become one of the first cotton ports on the coast.

The dock and wharf accommodations are good, the cotton presses as powerful as any in the United States, and attached to them are warehouses capable of storing several thousand bales of cotton, where they are perfectly sheltered from the weather, and the risk of fire considerably lessened by the strict rules for the prevention of accidents of this nature being rigidly carried out.

The charges for compressing and stowing are about the same as in other U. S. cotton ports.

There is a fee of $3.00 to the Harbor Master ; but except this, ships are free of all charges whatever ; there are neither harbor nor wharf dues to pay. The pilotage is comparatively light, and referring to the men who piloted my steamer to and from Wilmington, I found them cautious and skillful. Provisions, although not as good as in most American ports, are moderate in price—and finally, comparing Wilmington with any other cotton-shipping port, it is a very cheap place.

The facilities for loading are good. We have been only nine days in taking in 3,458 bales of cotton, 673 barrels of spirits turpentine and 550 barrels of rosin ; and on days when cotton was coming forward briskly, we have received from the Champion Press alone, upwards of 600 bales.

Another important matter which will be taken into consideration when sending ships in this direction: The State has passed a law which provides for the arrest and imprisonment of persons enticing men away from their ships, and the authorities are willing and prompt in locking up deserters when properly certified by the British Consul; and I have no doubt this will have the effect of checking, and ultimately ending—at least in North Carolina—the endless expense and trouble, owners and shipmasters have hitherto been subject to, throughout America, in consequence of this evil. Personally, I owe the authorities here my best thanks for the manner in which they helped me in a matter of this kind.

I wish to acknowledge with gratefulness the kind reception that has been extended me by your most worthy fellow-merchants, whom I find really anxious to encourage any movement which tends to the welfare and progress of the place.

Of the zeal and energy of Messrs. Alex. Sprunt & Son, in despatching the *Barnesmore*, there is no question ; and I am satisfied that President Murchison and Manager Clark, of the Central Railway, are quite ready to aid, in the most substantial manner, toward establishing a regular steam service from this port.

I mention these gentlemen because there is no mistaking their cordiality with reference to this subject. But let the river dredging be pushed on vigorously, otherwise there is small scope for individual enterprise and energy. In conclusion, I wish to acknowledge the great attention and courtesy of Collector Canaday and Captain Gabrielson, and to say I shall not soon forget them or their kindly offices.   I remain, dear sir,

Your most obedient servant,

J. TRENERY,
Captain of S. S. Barnesmore."

CUSTOM HOUSE RETURNS.

The following report of the Collector of Customs for the Port of Wilmington, shows the returns for the fiscal year ending June, 1882.

"A" shows the transactions of the year, including the total receipts from all sources and the number of persons employed.

"B" the tonnage and the number of vessels documented in this district on June 30th, 1882, with the number of vessels built, lost at sea, etc.

"C" the exports to foreign countries classified.

The U. S. Revenue Steamer *Colfax* is attached to the Customs' Service at this port; her complement consists of seven officers, a pilot and thirty men, and her cruising extends from Body's Island, N. C., to Georgetown, S. C.

Connected, also, with the Customs' Service, is a Light Ship off Frying Pan Shoals, and a Light House on Bald Head, and another on Fort Caswell.

These lights, together with the Life Saving Station, make arrival and departure of vessels, to and from this port, comparatively safe.

During the winter season the *Colfax* is on the lookout for vessels in distress, along this course, and frequently renders timely assistance, without any expense to vessels, except for provisions furnished, or fuel expended.

The following persons are employed by the Department, at this office.

NUMBER OF PERSONS EMPLOYED.

1 Collector.	6 Other Employees.
1 Deputy Collector.	1 Weigher and Gauger.
2 Clerks.	6 Inspectors.
1 Messenger.	Aggregate 18.

A.

No. of Vessels entered from Foreign Ports 181
"   Vessels cleared for Foreign Ports........................ 267
"   Vessels entered from Domestic Ports.................... 170
"   Vessels cleared for Domestic Ports....................... 110
"   Entries of Merchandise for Duty......................... 60
"   Entries of Merchandise free of Duty.................... 26
"   Entries for Warehouse.......... 6
"   Entries from Warehouse for Consumption............ 5
"   Entries for Consumption Liquidated..................... 86
"   Entries for Warehouse Liquidated....................... 6
"   Certificates of Registry granted............................. 27
"   Certificates of Enrolment granted........................ 22
"   Licenses for Coasting Trade granted..................... 51
"   Licenses to Vessels under 20 tons granted... 23
Value of Exports—Domestic................. ....$5,793,188 00

RECEIPTS FROM ALL SOURCES.

Duties on imports.. $81,721 45
Tonnage.. .... 10,180 80
Marine Hospital Tax................................. .... 1,587 04
Fines, Penalties and Forfeitures............................... 15 00
Miscellaneous Customs Receipts..................................... 918 45
Inspection of Steam-Vessels... 567 70
Official Fees.. 2,244 79

     Total........ .... $97,235 23

B.

	No. of Vessels	Tonnage.	
		Tons.	100ths
Permanent Registers—Sail, Balance........................	1	312	23
Temporary " —Sail, "	15	3,235	14
Permanent Enrollments—Sail, "	21	1,059	98
" " —Wood Steam, Balance.......	11	1,018	85
" " Iron Vessels,Steam, "	6	800	93
Temporary " Sail, Balance......................	2	445	57
Licenses under 20 tons, Sail,Coasting Trade,Balance	25	366	89
Total number of vessels and total tonnage of District	81	7,245	59
Licenses of Enrolled Vessels in the Coasting Trade—Balance...	47	5267	30
Statement of Vessels Built.....................................	2	158	45
" Vessels Lost at Sea and Wrecked........	2	213	07
" Vessels Abandoned as unfit for service	1	7	00

C.

Statement of Domestic Commodities Exported to Foreign Ports During Fiscal Year Ended June 30th, 1882.

Cotton.			Rosin and Turpentine.		Tar & Pitch.		Spts.Turpentine		Lumber.	
Bales	Lbs.	Dollars.	Bbls.	Dolls.	Bbls.	Dolls.	Galls.	Dolls.	Feet.	Dolls.
63,833	20,922,175	3,370,000	347,504	813,346	1,4880	33,253	2,850,552	1,326,244	12,721,000	225,614

Shingles.		Miscel-laneous.	Portion Carried in American Vessels.	Portion Carried in Foreign Vessels.	Total Value of Exports of Domestic Merchandise.
M.	Dolls.	Dolls.	Dollars.	Dollars.	Dollars.
3,031	20,880	3,851	155,772	5,637,416	5,793,188.

FOREIGN CARRYING TRADE.

The foreign carrying trade of Wilmington is done principally by Norwegian, German and British vessels, in the order named, although there are a number of Swedish, Danish and Italian ships entered, with a few of other nationalities during the year.

The class of vessels most suitable for cargoes of naval stores, are from 250 tons to 350 tons register, and these are generally of Scandinavian nationality. The German and British vessels in our trade, average about 350 tons ; several British ships trading here being 550, 700 and 950 tons register respectively. It is well known that small sailing vessels are fast disappearing from the sea, experience having proved that large vessels, at even considerably lower rates of freight, are more profitable, the ratio of running expenses being largely in favor of increased tonnage. This fact shows the necessity of our River and Harbor improvement, if we would keep pace with the changes already referred to. River and Bar lighterage has always been an objectionable clause in our Charter Parties, both on account of the delay and expense to the vessel, and the increased hazard to marine underwriters.

During the year 1882 the total number of Scandinavian vessels entered in Wilmington was 99, aggregating 39,926

tons register, and 1,053 men ; of German vessels there were
50, aggregating 18,481 tons, and 525 men ; of British vessels there were 40 arrivals, with a total registered tonnage
of 10,769 tons, and 334 men.

The other foreign vessels entered during the year were as
follows :

```
3 Russian  vessels.  Tonnage...................... 1,052
3 Italian      "         "     ...................... 1,132
2 Austrian     "         "     ......................   744
1 Greek        "         "     ......................   307
1 Costa Rican  "         "     ......................   268
1 Haytien      "         "     ......................   109
2 Dutch        "         "     ......................   407
                                                      -----
13                                                    4,019
```

Appended herewith is a carefully prepared statement of
vessels of all nationalities and their registered tonnage,
entered and cleared in Wilmington during the years 1881
and 1882.   The apparent discrepancy between the Consular
returns and this table for 1882, may be accounted for by
the fact that some of the entries of the year 1882 extend
into the clearances of 1883 :

Classification of Clearances of Shipping for the Years 1931 and 1882.

STEAMERS.

FLAG.	1881.		1882.	
	No.	Tons.	No.	Tons.
American	73	63,707	78	73,501
British	1	1,518	....	....

BARKS.

FLAG	1881.		1882.	
	No.	Tons.	No.	Tons.
German	50	18,300	37	13,575
Norwegian	105	37,408	77	31,801
Swedish	18	6,795	8	2,922
British	19	7,340	15	6,358
Danish	5	1,783	8	2,832
Russian	1	260	2	708
Dutch	....	....	1	250
Italian	....	....	2	854
Austrian	....	....	2	744
Haytien	1	298	....	....
American	4	1,324	10	3,309

BRIGS.

FLAG.	1881.		1882.	
	No.	Tons.	No.	Tons.
German	13	3,343	11	3,028
Norwegian	19	5,262	12	3,369
Swedish	5	1,439	2	497
British	15	4,243	10	2,505
Danish	2	494	1	247
Russian	1	367	1	311
Portuguese	1	172		
Costa Rica			1	268
Haytien	2	258	1	109
Greek			1	307
Italian			1	274
Dutch			1	157
American	20	5,962	12	3,244

SCHOONERS.

FLAG.	1881.		1882.	
	No.	Tons.	No.	Tons.
American	210	50,580	197	51,220
British	12	1,214	9	1,159

TOTAL.

STEAM AND SAIL.	1881.		1882.	
	No.	Tons.	No.	Tons.
Steamers	74	65,225	78	73,501
Sailing Vessels	503	146,822	422	130,085

FOREIGN CONSULS

In Wilmington, are as follows :

NAME.	RANK.	NATION.	WHEN APPOINTED.
Frederick J. Lord	Vice Consul	Spain	May, 1843.
O. G. Parsley, Jr	"	Brazil	1859.
Alexander Sprunt	"	Great Britain	March 31, 1866
Jacob Loeb	"	France	May 29, 1867.
Wm. L. DeRosset	"	Portugal	March 30, 1868
R. E. Heide	"	{ Norway { Sweden { Denmark	Dec. 10, 1870.
George Harriss	"	Argentine Republic	October, 1871.
Edouard Peschau	{ Vice Consul { Consul	Germany	Nov. 8, 1871. Dec. 7, 1874.
W. A. Cumming	Vice Consul	Hayti	March, 1874.

NOTARIES PUBLIC

Appointed in the City of Wilmington since the passage of the Act of 1881, whose terms expire, under the provisions of this act, two years from the date of their qualification, are as follows .

NAME.	DATE OF APPOINTMENT.
Alex. S. Heide...	April 11th, 1881.
Wm. L. Smith, Jr...	May 18th, 1881.
Thos. D. Meares..	June 1st, 1881.
Jno. W. Atkinson..	"
Wm. A. Willson..	"
Thomas Evans..	"
Andrew J. Howell...	June 6th, 1881.
Elbridge G. Barker..	June 8th, 1881.
Michael Cronly, Jr..	June 15th, 1881.
C. P. Mebane..	June 17th, 1881.
Asa K. Walker..	June 24th, 1881.
Hanson M. Bowden..	
Matthew P. Taylor...	July 1st, 1881.
B. G. Empie...	January 11th, 1882.
H. H. Heide...	February 6th, 1882.
Louis Poisson Davis........	July 29th, 1882.
John K. Brown..	September 20th, 1882.
John R Latta...	December 26th, 1882.

UNITED STATES COURTS.

The Circuit Court for the Eastern District of North Carolina meets at Raleigh, on the first Monday in June and the last Monday in November. Hon. Hugh L. Bond, of Baltimore, is Circuit Judge, with a salary of $6,000 a year. William S. O'B. Robinson is United States Attorney for this District, N. J. Riddick, Clerk, and Joshua B. Hill, Marshal.

The District Court meets at Elizabeth City on the third Monday in April and October; at New Berne on the fourth Monday in April and October, and at Wilmington on the first Monday after the fourth Monday in April and October. Hon. Augustus S. Seymour is District Judge; salary $3,500 a year, with residence in New Berne. W. S. O'B. Robinson is also Attorney of this Court, and J. B.

Hill, Marshal; W. H. Shaw, is Clerk, and Joseph H. Neff, Deputy Marshal.

Jurors in this Court are paid $2.00 per day and mileage, and witnesses $1.50 per day and mileage.

E. H. McQuigg and E. H. King are United States Commissioners in Wilmington.

THE IMPROVEMENT OF CAPE FEAR RIVER BELOW WILMINGTON.

Upon the ultimate success of the present operations by the General Government for the deepening of Cape Fear River and Bar, depends, in a great measure, the future prosperity of Wilmington. All classes of our citizens are therefore directly interested in the accomplishment of this great undertaking, which means cheap through railway rates on grain and provisions from the Western States, to be handled and trans-shipped at less cost in Wilmington than in any other Southern port; the development of our almost inexhaustible Coal and Iron region in the Deep River Valley, now waiting a cheap outlet; the enhance-ment by one hundred per cent. in the value of real estate, and especially of our three miles of water front, which is now of so little value; the substantial encouragement of all our manufacturing industries; the establishment of regular steam lines of first-class ships at cheaper and more reliable rates of freight to the principal seaports of the world, enabling us to compete more successfully with our Southern neighbors in those products which now depend for movement, in a great measure, upon slow sailing ships, extra insurance premiums and fluctuating rates of freight. A few of our citizens, appreciating the importance of this work, have, under many discouragements, kept their shoulders to the wheel, and by steady perseverance and the invaluable aid of our Representatives in Congress, accomplished nearly all that has been done to promote the desired end.

The late Mr. Henry Nutt, as Chairman of the Committee appointed by the Chamber of Commerce, was, during the last years of his life, indefatigable in his unselfish efforts, and had the satisfaction of seeing the most difficult part of the scheme—the closing of New Inlet—successfully accomplished.

The Hon. A. H. VanBokkelen, President of the Chamber of Commerce, has for three years past given a great part of his time and energy to the uninterrupted progress of the Engineers, by encouraging reports to our Senator, and by personal attendance at Washington.

To Col. Craighill, United States Engineer, we are greatly indebted, not only for his skillful direction of the work, but also for his steady support of the scheme in his reports to the War Department. Assistant Engineer Bacon, in charge of the operations on the river, has kindly furnished me with the technical information on this subject.

The Cape Fear River, from its mouth nearly to Wilmington, is properly a tidal estuary of about thirty-eight square miles. The river and its branches drain an area of about eight thousand square miles. The amount of fresh water passing out at the mouth, though large, is insignificant when compared with the tidal flow which alternately fills and empties this great reservoir. The mean fresh water discharge of the river does not exceed 9,000 cubic feet per second, while the tidal flow at the entrance averages about 175,000 cubic feet per second. This is the real force which creates and preserves the channel across the shifting sands of the coast at the mouth of the river. No demonstration is needed to prove the importance of concentrating this force. It is also apparent that such a force would be most efficient in preserving a passage across a bar and shoals which are in a position sheltered from the prevailing winds and heaviest storms of the coast. This we have at the natural mouth of the river, which is wholly sheltered from northerly, north-easterly, and in a great measure from easterly winds, by its position in the bay, protected by Cape Fear and the Frying Pan shoals. From the old maps of the river and harbor it appears that there was at the entrance a least depth of about 14 feet at low water. When, therefore, in 1761, the sea made a breach across the narrow sand-beach, which divided the sea from the river, some seven miles above the mouth, which from that time became known as the New Inlet, the deterioration which afterwards occurred was anticipated, as appears, negatively, by the letter of Governor Tryon, in February 1769, in which he says: "H. M. ship Foly came in at the entrance at half-tide, drawing 14 feet of water. The New Inlet, which was broken through a few years since, is used only by vessels drawing 7 or 8 feet of water. The New Inlet seems to have had no bad effect at the entrance." But the bad effect came gradually, as appears by subsequent maps and surveys, which show continual deterioration. The accurate and elaborate survey of Lieutenant Glynn, in 1839, shows 9 feet depth at low water at the Bald Head channel, and the same at the other, or Western Bar of the entrance, and 10 feet at the New Inlet. The coast survey of 1851 shows 8 and 7 feet depth at the Rip, and 8 feet at the New Inlet. The coast survey chart of 1869 does not show much change, the available depths appearing to be about the same. The careful survey of Mr. Vinal, of the coast survey of 1872, shows 9 feet at low water at the Bald Head, and the same depth on the Rip of the western channel of the entrance, and 10 feet at the New Inlet Bar. No changes appear to have occurred in the upper river until improvements were made. [These soundings do not agree with the record of the Commissioners of Navigation.]

The improvement of the river below Wilmington was begun by the State of North Carolina, and continued from 1823 to 1828. In 1829 it was taken in hand by the United States, and from 1829 to 1838 inclusive, Congress made annual appropriations amounting to $202,539, which were

expended in improving the river from Wilmington to
Campbell's (Big) Island, about 9 miles below. The operations consisted mostly of pile and plank jetties, made to
concentrate the currents; some dredging was also done.
The plans initiated by the State were continued by the
United States. An available increase of about 2 feet was
obtained, so that 9 to 9½ feet could be carried at low water.
Projects for improvement were revived in 1852, when Congress appropriated $20,000, and $140,000 was appropriated
in 1854. These appropriations were expended for the
improvement at the entrance by jetties at Bald Head
Point, and by closing the breaches between Smith's and
Zeke's Islands. When the latter works were nearly completed and the appropriation exhausted, a great storm in
September 1857, destroyed, to a considerable extent, the
works at Zeke's Island, leaving the stone foundations.
Nothing further was done toward improvement until 1870,
when the work was begun again. The following appropriations have been made by Congress:

By act approved July 11, 1870 .... $100,000
By act approved March 3, 1871 75,000
By act approved June 10, 1872 100,000
By act approved March 3, 1873 100,000
By act approved June 23, 1874 150,000
By act approved March 3, 1875 150,000
By act approved August 14, 1876 132,500
By act approved June 18, 1878, ... 160,000
By act approved March 3, 1879 100,000
By act approved June 14, 1880 70,000
By act approved March 3, 1881 140,000
By act approved August —, 1882 225,000

        Total.................................. $1,502,500

The project adopted in 1870 was the closure of the breach
between Smith's and Zeke's Islands, with the ultimate
closure of the New Inlet in view. In 1873 and 1874 the

additional work projected was the dredging of the new channel behind the Horse Shoe Shoals, near Snow's Marsh, and dredging the Bald Head Channel (which had already begun to improve), and also dredging and removing obstacles from the river between Campbell's Island and Wilmington, so as to obtain 12 feet depth at mean low water. In 1875 the work of closing the New Inlet was begun in earnest. A continuous line of mattresses, composed of logs and brush, sunk and loaded with stone, was laid entirely across the New Inlet, from October, 1875, to June, 1876. This was the first foundation of the dam.

As fast as appropriations were available, the work was continued from year to year, by piling small stone rip-rap on and over this foundation, and finally bringing it up to high water, and then covering it with heavy granite stones on the top and slopes to low water. There were many *real* discouragements during the progress of the work, not to speak of the almost universal prediction of ultimate failure by the pilots and others, who were well acquainted with the forces to be contended with. The great rush of the tidal currents in and out can hardly be realized, even now, when it is shown that the alternate difference in level on the sea and river sides of the dam at the different stages is usually from 1 to 2 feet, and a difference of 3½ feet has been observed.

This rush and over-fall caused a scour on both sides of the foundation to a depth of from 6 to 16 feet below the bottom of the mattresses, and the water found its way under the mattresses, and the scouring caused their irregular subsidence. In some instances the settlement was 10 or 12 feet within twenty-four hours. The only, or at least the best remedy, was to continue to pile on the stone and let them go to their limit, thus making the foundation from 90 to 120 feet in width at the base, where the original mattresses were from 45 to 60 feet. The whole work, from shore to shore, Federal Point to Zeke's Island, is nearly a

mile in length. For about three-fourth's of a mile of this
length the stone go to an average depth of about 30 feet
below the top of the dam ; in many places the depth is
more than 30 feet. The limit of subsidence was reached
during the year 1878, since which it has only been necessary to widen the foundation and cover the dam with heavy
rock. This was carefully done by the use of three floating
derricks—one of which was operated by steam—between
December 1879 and July 1881. The stone used in its construction amounts to 181,600 cubic yards, including the
16,756 gross tons of heavy granite. During the progress
of the work the small stones below half-tide were being
cemented into a solid mass by oysters and barnacles ; and
now the whole structure, with its granite surface, is like
one solid rock. Its crest is above the level of ordinary
Spring tides, and there can be no question of its permanence.   .

When the magnitude and apparent and real difficulty of
the work are considered, the cost has been small. The
whole cost, from its inception, in 1875, to its thorough completion, in 1881, has not exceeded $480,000.

During the first three years of the construction of the
dam, it did not much affect the quantity of the in-and-out
flow of tides at the New Inlet, but as it approached completion, the stoppage was more and more, and the effect on
the Bald Head channel increased ; this was also assisted
by the operation of the suction dredge Woodbury, which
was thoroughly rebuilt and put in operation on the Bald
Head channel early in April 1879, and continued work until
October 1881, during which time 169,491 cubic yards of
sand were dredged and dumped in deep water. In good
weather the amount of compact sand dredged and carried
to deep water for dumping, would often amount to 500 cubic
yards per day, and occasionally to more than 600 cubic
yards. The large amount of materials removed by the
dredge, bore a small proportion to the amount carried out

by the natural force of the tidal currents, as frequent surveys have proved. The following were the shortest soundings in the Bald Head channel at the end of the fiscal
years :— 1878, 9 feet ; 1879, 11 feet ; 1880, 13 feet ; 1881, 14
feet ; 1882, 14 feet. It is probable that there would have
been farther increase of depth in 1882 if the operations of
the suction dredge had been continued. As it is, the
results are gratifying, being greater than our predictions or
expectations, bringing the channel into as good or better
condition that before the breach of the New Inlet in 1761. It
is a practical demonstration of the advantage of closing
the New Inlet by the completed dam. The mean range of
the tides being 4½ feet, 17½ feet draft can be carried over
the bar and shoals at ordinary high water and 18½ feet at
Spring tides.

The available depth of water between Smithville and
Wilmington only allows about 14½ feet draft at high water.
The importance of obtaining a greater depth was apparent.
An estimate for it was placed before Congress at the
instance of the Hon. Senator M. W. Ransom, in January,
1881, and an appropriation of $140,000 designed in part for
it was made by Congress by act approved March 3, 1881.
The project adopted was for a channel to be dredged,
where dredging was needed to obtain it, of 270 feet width
and 16 feet depth at mean low water, from the deep water
at Smithville harbor to Wilmington.

The first contract for dredging was made in May, 1881,
and it is not yet completed. Another appropriation of
$225,000 was made in August, 1882. A portion of this is
already applied to the dredging referred to, and the work
under the second contract is to be completed according to
its terms, by June 30, 1883. This will finish the channel
to 16 feet depth about half the distance from the harbor to
Wilmington. About half of the last appropriation is reserved
for the probable requirement to defend the long narrow
beach at Smith's Island against the encroachments of the

sea. The breaches through this, though at present remote from the river, with long shoal water intervening, might in the course of years become connected by deep water with the river, and thus repeat the history of the New Inlet in a new location. To guard against this, a defence must ultimately be made, and it can now be made at a comparatively small cost. It is under advisement by a Board of Engineers, who will probably decide to make it, by a continuation of the work of the New Inlet dam, or the Zeke's Island works across the shoal water to the Big Marsh, thus cutting off the connection of the Swashes across Smith's Island and the river. Such a work would probably cause the reformation of the beach, or at least of a wide inner beach at a considerable distance from the defensive work.

If the needed appropriations are made by Congress the projected channel of 16 feet depth will be completed to Wilmington during the year 1885.

There is no doubt that by a proper jetty system 20 feet depth at low water can be obtained at the mouth of the river and on the bar. The question of obtaining it from the harbor to Wilmington is only one of dollars and cents.

It is greatly regretted that Congress has adjourned without the usual appropriations for this important and necessary undertaking, as it is of vital moment that the operations in the Cape Fear are not retarded at this important stage of the work; although the present available means will suffice for a few months to come, the defeat of the River and Harbor Bill threatens a serious blow to probably the most important public work ever projected in North Carolina.

OCEAN AND RIVER STEAM NAVIGATION COMPANIES.

The following list comprises the Steam Lines engaged in the Wilmington carrying trade. The "New York and Wilmington Steamship Company" is a corporation chartered by the State of New York, and owns the following iron propellers:

"Gulf Stream," 998 tons,

"Benefactor," 844 "

"Regulator," 847 "

Mr. Thos. E. Bond is the Superintendent at Wilmington, and Messrs. W. P. Clyde & Co. General Agents at New York.

The imports and exports by this line of first class steamers for the year 1882 were as follows:

EXPORTS.

Cotton, bales,	58,655.	Rice, meal, sacks,	4,306.
Lumber, feet,	5,640,707.	" rough, "	4,131.
Shooks,	2,935.	Molasses, hhds,	130.
Shingles,	1,292,000.	Peanuts, sacks,	1,197.
Naval Stores, bbls,	95,607.	Pig Iron, tons,	174.
Spirits Turpentine "	27,400.	Yarn, bales,	306.
Rice, cleaned, tcs,	3,950.	Merchandise, pkgs,	7,676.

IMPORTS.

Syrup, bbls,	1,379.	Ties, bundles,	3,162.
Sugar, "	6,195.	Bagging, rolls,	15,875.
Bacon, boxes,	10,318.	Cement, bbls,	600.
Lard, pkgs,	1,570.	Water Pipe, pieces,	916.
Corn, sacks,	114,503.	Brick,	10,200.
Oats, "	7,251.	Sulphur, tons,	437.
Hay, bales,	25,328.	Railroad Iron, rails,	2,785.
Liquor, pkgs,	686.	Merchandize, pkgs,	143,601
Oil(lubricating only)		Shoes, cases,	3,776.
bbls,	144.	Barrels, empty,	21,346.
Coffee, sacks,	5,913.	Guano, sacks,	40,510.

EXPRESS STEAMBOAT COMPANY.—CAPITAL $50,000.

WILMINGTON AND FAYETTEVILLE.

	CAPACITY.	COST.	
"D. Murchison,"	1,000 barrels.	$22,000.	Iron Hull.
"Wave,"	800 "	13,000.	" "

CAPE FEAR AND PEOPLE'S STEAMBOAT COMPANY.—
CAPITAL $75,000.

WILMINGTON AND FAYETTEVILLE.

	CAPACITY.	COST.	
"Gov. Worth,"	1,200 barrels.	$45,000.	Iron hull.
"A. P. Hurt,"	400 "	17,000.	" "
"North State,"	700 "	·17,000.	Wooden "

By these two lines we have a daily (except Sunday) boat,
and on Tuesdays and Fridays, two boats.

WILMINGTON AND FAYETTEVILLE.

	CAPACITY.	COST.	
"Bladen,"	500 barrels.	$6,000.	Wooden Hull.

WILMINGTON AND POINT CASWELL.

	CAPACITY.	COST.	
"John Dawson,"	350 barrels.	$6,500.	Wooden Hull.

WILMINGTON AND SMITHVILLE.

	CAPACITY.	COST.	
"Passport,"	250 passengers.	$8,000.	Wooden Hull.
"Minnehaha,"	200 "	7,000.	" " .

IMPROVEMENTS OF CAPE FEAR RIVER BETWEEN
WILMINGTON AND FAYETTEVILLE.

From a report of Capt. James Mercur, in charge of the
work, I learn that an examination or survey of this part of
the Cape Fear was directed by the River and Harbor Act of
Congress, June 14, 1882.

The improvements proposed consisted in the removal of
snags and logs, the clearing away of overhanging trees on
the banks, a small amount of dredging, and the construction of jetties or dykes. The total estimated cost of the

work proposed was about $56,000, which, however, was only for a part of the work that will be required for the entire portion of the river in need of improvement. The Act of March 3, 1881, appropriated $30,000 with a proviso that $10,000 of this sum was to be expended in extinguishing before December 1, 1881, the interest or franchise of the Deep River Navigation Company, which claimed the right to collect tolls, &c , under its State charter ; which after a careful investigation by Capt. Mercur, of the Engineer Department, was expended in full accordingly.

In June, 1882, work upon the river was begun under the direction of Capt. W. H. James, Civil Engineer of Wilmington, and is still in progress,—clearing the channel of such obstructions as sunken logs, snags, stumps and fallen trees, and in cutting and hauling back from the banks over-hanging trees on the channel side, which were liable to fall, or damage the upper works of steamers, thrown by the set of the current near the banks.

The further work contemplated by the Engineer is to reduce the width of the river channel at 22 Shoals, (lying between Fayetteville and Cypress Shoals, a distance of 52 miles) by the use of jetties of timber, plank and scantling, which are intended to scour the narrowest channel to a depth of about 4 feet at ordinary low water.

There is also some blasting of sandstone rock, dangerous to navigation at points between the limits referred to.

Every freshet brings down trees, logs, snags, and other debris, which will necessitate a moderate amount of work in removing obstructions from year to year ; and even if the river was satisfactorily scoured and jettied, new shoals are likely to form at other points, requiring attention in future. Probably, with this in view, a further appropriation was made by Congress, in August, 1882, of $35,000, the use of which, it is thought, will greatly facilitate the navigation of this important and historic stream.

As a matter of interest in this connection I have appended

the following report of Mr. George H. Elliot, U. S. Engineer, which is so complete in detail as to require no further reference to the subject.

NORFOLK, VA., January 24th, 1881.

CAPTAIN:—

I have the honor to submit herewith report of the examination of the Cape Fear River, North Carolina, between Wilmington and Fayetteville, made in compliance with your instructions in the early part of the present month. This examination was for the purpose of ascertaining the cost and practicability of clearing away logs and overhanging trees, and of dredging out such shoals as interfere with commerce.

A survey of this river was made in 1871, when that portion of it now under consideration was carefully sounded. It was thought that no material change had taken place in the general character since that time, and that a resurvey would be unnecessary ; and the testimony of pilots and others conversant with the river, is to this effect. The examination was therefore limited to ascertaining, so far as practicable, the number of snags, sunken logs, and overhanging trees to be removed.

A freshet which had commenced to raise the water in the river, prevented the observations being as thorough as was desirable, but it is believed that the information obtained from pilots and captains is as satisfactory with regard to the objects at present in view, as could be had except from an expensive survey, which would have to include the dragging of the river, to ascertain with any exactness the number of sunken logs and snags. Under these circumstances, trips were made up and down the river between Wilmington and Fayetteville, when notes were taken as to the locality of such snags, &c., as they (the pilots) had knowledge of ; these are indicated on the charts herewith (11 in number), which are tracings of the maps of the survey of 1871, with such slight changes as have been found necessary.   A tabulated list of the snags is also given at the end of this report.

In addition to the snags, &c., which are individually mentioned, there are several stretches of the river where such obstructions exist ; these are also stated in the list. The overhanging trees are very frequent from Fayetteville for some sixty miles down the river ; below that they are less so.   Few of the trees are large, and at present they do not much obstruct navigation, but their tendency is to fall into the river when the banks are weakened by the action of the freshet water; for this reason a large number of them ought to be removed.

The bed of the river for some 66 miles below Fayetteville is composed almost entirely of sand, which is constantly changing in position from the action of freshets.   During the Summer months the volume of water is insufficient to give a continuous channel, the river then presenting a succession of sand bars and shoals, with occasional deep water, principally in the bends.

Any improvement, to be permanent, will necessitate the contraction of the channel way in many of the straight reaches over a large portion of the distance named.

With the exception of one place (Thames' Shoal), dredging would be useless, as the first freshet would fill up any channel excavated through the shifting sand.   Thames' Shoal is a bed of pipe-clay, through which it is proposed to dredge a channel of 60 feet in width to a depth of 5 feet at low summer water.

The bed of the river contains, also, many sunken logs, under the sand in some cases, as is stated by the pilots who have been engaged in removing snags, &c., overlying each other; to what extent cannot well be ascertained except by actual operations in removing them.

The improvements needed in the river are confined principally to the 75 miles from Fayetteville down ; over this entire portion the banks need trimming of the overhanging trees, and snags and logs should be removed from the river-bed. To accomplish this work will require the employment of a hoister with the necessary appliances for dragging the bottom to find and raise snags, &c. This work can only be done satisfactorily at a low stage of water, and will cost about $500 per mile; an estimate for this sum is submitted.

As previously stated, there is no continuous channel for some 60 miles, and to provide one will require the contraction of the water-way. I am not prepared to submit an estimate for this entire work, but respectfully suggest that an amount of $5,000 be appropriated for the construction of experimental jetties or dikes of cheap character, to be placed at right angles to the axis of the stream, at intervals, from either side, to be built a little above the ordinary low summer water, and to be placed first in the shoalest of the straight reaches. Dikes of piles wattled between have proved quite successful in other rivers of similar character, and can be constructed for about $1 per running foot. An estimate is also submitted for the excavation of a channel through Thames' Shoal (previously mentioned).

I would mention, incidentally, that while on the river, the Steamer *Governor Worth* struck a log which had lodged in a tree near Council's Bluff, and, after running about 1½ miles, sunk ; the locality of the wreck is indicated on chart. She will doubtless be raised by her owners as soon the freshet subsides.

ESTIMATE.

For clearing 75 miles of river, at $500 per mile, ... $37,500
For dredging at Thames' Shoal channel, 1,900 feet
    by 60 feet, 15,000 cubic yards, at 40 cents, ...   6,000
For construction of experimental dike, say 5,000
    linear feet, at $1 per foot, ...   5,000

                                        $48,500
And for contingencies and engineering, 15 per cent,   7,275

      Total, ... $55,775

*   *   *   *   *   *   *

Fayetteville, the head of steamboat navigation proper, is situated about a mile from the river, 113 miles above Wilmington. It is a flourishing town, with a popluation of some 7,000 and is, next to Wilmington, the principal depot for naval stores in the State. Within a few miles, are several cotton and woolen mills, and others are now projected. For miles, in either direction, turpentine distilleries are found. Cotton is raised to a considerable extent in the vicinity ; it is estimated that 10,000 bales will be brought in for shipment this season, and the production is continually increasing. There is also quite an extensive industry in flouring mills, the product of which is shipped in considerable quantities. Five steamers are regularly engaged plying between Wilmington and Fayetteville ; these, with one exception (the *Governor Worth*, a side-wheel steamer), are stern-wheel boats, with a load-draught of something less than 4 feet. There is also railroad communication with the seaboard via Raleigh and Weldon, at Norfolk. Full statistics of the commerce of Fayetteville and the river generally were expected to be furnished by parties engaged in the shipping interests, but have not yet been received. This is to be regretted, as from what the writer learned in conversation, they would show a very marked increase over those obtained in 1871.

The only town between Wilmington and Fayetteville is Elizabeth, the county seat of Bladen ; a small population is scattered in the vicinity, engaged in the manufacture of naval stores, which are brought here for shipment. River landings are very numerous, there being about one hundred on the river, most of which are places for shipment of the staple of this section.

*   *   *   *   *   *   *   *

Very respectfully, your obedient servant,

GEO. H. ELLIOT, Assistant Engineer.

Capt. CHAS. B. PHILLIPS,

Corps of Engineers U. S. A."

LILLINGTON RIVER IMPROVEMENTS.

Captain W. H. James, Engineer, is entrusted with this work, for which the General Government has appropriated $6,000.

Until a petition was sent to Congress for improvements, this stream was known as Long Creek. The improvements consist in clearing out snags and logs, cutting down over-hanging trees, and the dredging off of a few abrupt points, with the intention of securing five feet of navigable water from the mouth of the river, where it empties into the Cape Fear, to the village of Lillington, about eleven miles above.

This stream is very tortuous, and the natural course is similar to a double inverted S. The engineers propose to cut through the loops of the S, and dredge the channel, thus saving both distance and expense.

Instead of a gradual slope downwards, towards the bottom of the channel, the banks overhang the stream, and the slope above the river surface being soft clay, retards the progress of flats and rafts, and renders the river other-wise difficult of navigation, which these *cut-offs* are intended to obviate.

The estimate for the work is $6,003.75, and the following letter from Captain Phillips, to the Chief of Engineers, will convey a correct idea of its importance to our city :

"UNITED STATES ENGINEER'S OFFICE, }
NORFOLK, VA., January 29, 1881. {

"GENERAL:—Your letter of the 17th of June, 1880, placed me in charge of the examination or survey of Lillington River, North Carolina, provided for in the last river and harbor appropriation act of Congress. I entrusted the examination to a party in charge of Assistant J. P. Darling, who took up and completed the field work during the month of August last.   *   *   *   *   *

" His report, as well as tracings, two in number, from his original map, exhibiting the present condition of the river, and the localities of the proposed improvements, are respectfully transmitted herewith.

" Lillington River is a tributary to the northeast branch of the Cape Fear River, emptying into the latter from the west, at a point about twelve miles above the city of Wilmington, North Carolina.

"Transportation upon the river is at present limited to rafts of timber and flat-boats, loaded chiefly with naval stores and cord-wood.

" Above the village of Lillington, a little over eleven miles from the mouth of the river, it appears to be impracticable to attempt any improvement of the river ; or at least the amount of trade, both present and prospective, does not seem to warrant any expenditure upon the portion of the river in question.

" Below the village of Lillington, and from thence to the mouth of the river, the trade is of more importance, and it would no doubt be greatly stimulated if the produce of the vicinity could be reached by light-draught steamboats.

" The obstructions to a 5-foot navigation, outside of a few snags and leaning trees, consist solely in a few abrupt bends, which can be rectified at a slight expense by dredging at six points, which are indicated upon the accompanying tracings.

" Mr. Darling's estimate for the whole work, including dredging and the removal of snags and other obstructions, amounts to but $6,000. The estimate seems to be low, but as he has allowed a large margin for contingencies, I think the amount sufficient to cover the cost of the desired improvements ; and it appears to me that the amount might well be devoted to developing the section of country adjacent to the river.

" Lillington River is in the collection district of Wilmington, North Carolina.   *   *   *   *   *

" I am, General, very respectf'y, your ob't serv't,
                    "CHAS. B. PHILLIPS.
                              Captain of Engineers.
" *The Chief of Engineers U. S. A.*"

DRY DOCKS.

The Empire Sectional Dock was built in this place several years ago by the present proprietors, Messrs. J. R. Blossom & Evans, at a cost of about $34,000.

The dock, which is considered one of the best in the South, comprises three sections, thirty feet wide and seventy feet long, equal to about 1,200 tons. The keel room is at present only 150 long, but other sections will be added in case of need. Until our bar and river improvement work will admit a much larger class of vessels than are now trading to Wilmington, the Empire Dock affords ample facilities.

The rates for sailing vessels are 25 cents per ton for taking up, with no further charge until the expiration of twenty-four hours, when the rate for each subsequent day is 12½ cents per ton.

Steamers and vessels with cargo on board are charged higher rates, in proportion to their weight. There is also a

MARINE RAILWAY,

long established, in the lower part of the harbor, and now leased by Capt. S. W. Skinner, whose facilities are ample, and the charges about the same as those of the Empire Dock.

WILMINGTON & WELDON RAILROAD.

This railroad was projected solely by the Wilmington people, and completed in 1836. Its length is from Wilmington to Weldon, 163 miles, through New Hanover, Pender, Duplin, Wayne, Wilson, Edgecombe, Nash and Halifax counties, with branch roads from Rocky Mount to Tarboro, a distance of 17 miles, and from Halifax to Scotland Neck, 20 miles. It is beyond question the best equipped, and most successfully managed road in the South, and will compare favorably with any Northern

railroad for travelling comfort and speed, as well as in its
facilities for the dispatch of freight business, and in the
efficiency of its employes. In response to my request for
information upon matters of interest discussed by the
Exchange at a previous meeting, President Bridgers has
made the following reply, from which it would appear that
the complaints of discrimination against Wilmington upon
the local tariff are hardly justified by the facts :

"In consequence of the enquiries made of me by you a
few days ago, I instructed our Auditor to make a minute
analysis of the rates we now have, as compared with those
in existence before the war. I enclose his letter, showing
the reductions between Wilmington and local stations.
We could have gone much more into detail on the various
items, but it would have made too long a document for
your consideration.

We have no hesitation in saying that the average diminu-
tion of these rates is about 40 per cent. The reduction in
rates has been much more rapid than the increase of
tonnage.

So much has been said about the difference between
"through" and "local" shipments, that I will refer briefly
to the causes therefor.

From the closest comparison we can make, we find the
cost of transporting local freights, with the extra handling
and other incidental expenses added, is about 2½ times the
cost of transporting through freight. To illustrate, a
through train, having to make no stops, goes from Wilmington to Weldon in one day. A local train requires two
days. A local train burns more fuel in a day than a
through train, and requires about three times as many
laborers.

Thus, you see, one through train does as much work as
two locals, the latter being run at a much greater expense
by increase of fuel and labor.

If you wish to look into the details of our operations

for the last year, you will find them published in our annual reports, copies of which are herewith enclosed."

WILMINGTON, N. C., February 13th, 1883.

"HON. R. R. BRIDGERS, *President:*

SIR :—As requested by you, I have examined the freight rates on the Wilmington & Weldon Railroad, and find that reductions have been made on all classes of goods from the rates in effect before the war. I cannot find any rates on cotton and lumber earlier than 1869, at which time the rates on other freights were similar to those in effect before the war—the high rates having been cut down to those of 1860.

The following will show the reductions between Wilmington and local stations :

						REDUCED.	
First class freight in 1882, compared with				1860,		53 per cent.	
Freight on Bacon,	"	"	"	"	"	60 "	"
"	" Salt,	"	"	"	"	53 "	"
"	" Flour,	"	"	"	"	24 "	"
"	" Cotton,	"	"	"	" 1869,	24 "	"
"	" Lumber	"	"	"	"	26 "	"

Average reduction on all classes, from rates of 1860, 40 per cent.

Yours Respectfully,

W. A. RIACH,
General Auditor."

The reduction in rates (40 per cent.), claimed by President Bridgers should not be taken as exceptional. I have ascertained that the same ratio of reduction obtains upon other roads in the South, and that the proportion is very much greater in favor of Northern railways.

Comparing the rates on New York railroads in 1860, upon such articles as bacon, salt, flour and cotton, with those now current, I find an average reduction of nearly 70 per cent., or 30 per cent more than on the Wilmington

& Weldon Railroad. Such a comparison would be manifestly unfair, however, when the volume of traffic and number of competing lines are so much greater in the North.

President Bridgers' last annual report, November 21st, 1882, shows :

Gross earnings,	$ 783,790.27
Total expenses,	574,318.30
Leaving a net of	$ 209,471.98

The receipts show an increase of $32,873.43 which is made up as follows :

Through Freight,	$ 1,033.88	
" Passengers,	16,877.07	
Local Passengers,	24,042.30	
Mail and Express,	11,930.97	$53,884.22
Decrease in Local Freight,		21,010.79
Net Increase,		$32,873.43

"Large expenditures have been made during the year in betterments—bridges, warehouses, new cars and engines— amounting to $121,749.16.

Also a large quantity of material for the erection of machine shops at Wilmington, which has been paid for.

It is very necessary that improvements should be made at Tarboro, during this year, and that the warehouse at Wilmington be built, and machine shops completed. So much of the old iron rail has been replaced with steel that in future the expenses of this important item will be materially diminished.

New sleeping cars have been contracted for and will be delivered on or before the first of January. They will be furnished with all the modern improvements, and will add very much to the attractiveness of this route and to the comfort of its passengers.

The track of the main line has been very much improved in every respect during the year and is in fine condition.

The road from Scotland Neck to Halifax has been completed at a cost of $79,950.58, and was regularly opened for the transaction of business on the 1st day of October, 1882. Its track is laid with forty pound steel rail and is now in good running condition, and the road is doing a very fair business.

There has been an exemption from accidents, due to the good condition of the track and machinery, and the faithful discharge of the duties of the employes in the various departments."

ADMINISTRATIVE DEPARTMENT.

R. R. BRIDGERS,.... ....President.
B. F. NEWCOMER,...... ....Vice-President.
J. W. THOMPSON,........... ...Secretary and Treasurer.

BOARD OF DIRECTORS.

W. T. WALTERS,	A. J. DEROSSET,
B. F. NEWCOMER,	DONALD MACRAE,
S. M. SHOEMAKER,	E. B. BORDEN,
H. B. PLANT,	W. H. WILLARD,
H. WALTERS,	GEORGE HOWARD.

EXECUTIVE DEPARTMENT.

JOHN F. DIVINE,...............General Superintendent.
SOL. HAAS,............................Traffic Manager.
T. M. EMERSON,........Gen'l Freight and Passenger Ag't.
W. A. RIACH,........................General Auditor.
JOHN R. LATTA,.....................Assistant Auditor.
JAMES KNIGHT,................Master of Transportation.
JOHN BISSET,.............. ....Master of Machinery.
JOHN BARRY,.............................Road Master.
E. F. CASON,............................Store-Keeper.

THE WILMINGTON, COLUMBIA & AUGUSTA RAILROAD.

This road is 189 miles in length, and passes from Wilmington into South Carolina, through Brunswick and Columbus counties, North Carolina, and continues its route through Marion, Darlington, Sumter and Richland counties, South Carolina.

The President's annual report, dated November 21, 1882, gives the following:

"The gross receipts for the year are $692,628.52, being an increase of $51,672.22 over those of the preceding year, which is made up as follows:

Through Freight	$ 6.59
Local Freight	20,578.41
Through Passengers	9,704.64
Local Passengers	8,272.02
Mail and Express	13,110.56
Total increase	$51,672.22

The expenses are $553,036.57, in addition to which the following amounts have been paid for improvements:

Two New Engines		$ 25,898.10
One Hundred and Fifty Box Cars	$88,471.50	
Two Baggage Cars	4,986.00	
Two Postal Cars	7,412.56	100,870.06
Warehouse at Timmonsville	4,865.09	
" Whiteville	4,536.85	
" Wilmington	12,773.45	22,175.39
Total		$148,943.55

Also 2,200 tons of steel rail and necessary fastenings have been put in the track.

For the present year we will not require more than 1,000 tons of rail, less than one-half of the quantity used last year. It is a subject of congratulation that we have replaced iron with steel rail to such an extent that the expenditures for rail will be considerably less than for several years past.

With the increased equipment, which was completed about the close of the fiscal year, increased receipts may be expected another year. The receipts would have been larger with more motive power and a larger number of freight and passenger cars. It is submitted whether it would not be policy to buy two locomotive engines and four passenger cars during the current year.

The warehouse at Wilmington, so long needed, will be completed in a few weeks, and will fully meet the requirements of the business.

Contracts have been made for the thorough equipment of the Roads constituting the Atlantic Coast Line with new Pullman Sleeping Cars, and this Company's proportion of the cost of the same will be about $48,000.00, to meet which, and to furnish two additional locomotive engines and new passenger cars, it will become necessary to increase the floating debt or to suspend dividends for a limited time.

The tonnage in freights has largely increased, and but for a general reduction in rates, would have given much larger net receipts.

The Central Railroad of South Carolina, which has been leased jointly by this Company and the North Eastern Rail Road Company, was delivered to the Lessees on April 1st, 1882. Considerable expenditures were necessary to perfect its new road-bed, quite equalling what would have been required for an old road-bed. The receipts will appear from the Superintendent's Report. The net above rental and operating expenses has been $3,009.02.

The Central Road has diverted considerable business at Sumter and other near stations from this Road, the profits on which diverted traffic have been about made up by the additional business received at Columbia. No regular through passenger trains have been run between Charleston and Columbia because of the deficiency of motive power and cars.

This Road has been remarkably free from accidents, due to its good condition and the efficient discharge of the duties of the various officers and employes of the several departments.

Abstract from the Superintendent's Report.

WILMINGTON, COLUMBIA & AUGUSTA R. R. Co., }
GENERAL SUPERINTENDENT'S OFFICE, }
WILMINGTON, N. C., November 21, 1882. }

HON. R. R. BRIDGERS, *President Wilmington, Colum bia & Augusta Rail Road Company:*

SIR:—The following report of the operations of this Company, for the fiscal year ending 30th September, 1882, is respectfully submitted:

RECEIPTS AND EXPENDITURES.

RECEIPTS.

From Through Passengers	$ 89,177 45		
" Local "	80,789 69	—$169,967 14	
" Through Freight	$120,431 36		
" Local "	304,305 77	— 424,737 13	
" Express		10,426 10	
" U. S. Mail		58,269 35	
" Telegraph		1,098 18	
" Rent of Old Rail		3,009 51	
" Minor Sources		25,121 11	
Total			$692,628 52

EXPENSES.

Conducting Transportation	$100,892 23	
Motive Power	124,795 57	
Maintenance of Cars	70,049 95	
Maintenance of Roadway	218,841 55	
General Expenses	38,457 27	—$553,036 57
Net Receipts		$139,591 95

JOHN F. DIVINE,
General Superintendent.

ADMINISTRATIVE DEPARTMENT.

R. R. BRIDGERS,......................President.
W. T. WALTERS,......................Vice-President.
J. W. THOMPSON ....Secretary and Treasurer.

BOARD OF DIRECTORS.

W. T. WALTERS,   J. D. CAMERON,
S. M. SHOEMAKER,   GEORGE S. BROWN,
B. F. NEWCOMER,   H. B. PLANT,
GEORGE C. JENKINS,   R. R. BRIDGERS.
ENOCH PRATT,   H. B. SHORT.

EXECUTIVE DEPARTMENT.

JOHN F. DIVINE................General Superintendent.
SOL. HAAS............................Traffic Manager.
T. M. EMERSON,......Gen'l Freight and Passenger Agent.
W. A. RIACH...........................General Auditor.
JOHN R. LATTA........................Assistant Auditor.
JAMES KNIGHT,................Master of Transportation.
JOHN BISSET.....................Master of Machinery.
PETER LAUGHLIN.... .....Road Master Eastern Division.
A. N. FREELAND. ......Road Master Western Division.
E. F. CASON...........................Store-Keeper.

THE CAROLINA CENTRAL RAILROAD.

The Wilmington, Charlotte & Rutherford Railroad was chartered February 13, 1855, and built 103 miles on the Eastern Division, and to Lincolnton, on the Western Division, before the war. It was sold April 10, 1873, and reorganized as the Carolina Central Railway Company, and completed to Charlotte and Shelby in the latter part of 1874, comprising a total distance of 242 miles.

The Carolina Central *Railway* was sold May 31, 1880, and reorganized as the Carolina Central Rail *Road* Company July 14, 1880.

It traverses the counties of New Hanover, Brunswick,

Columbus, Bladen, Robeson, Richmond, Anson, Union, Mecklenburg, Gaston, Lincoln and Cleaveland—a section highly productive of Turpentine, Cotton, and other articles of export; the class and style of Cotton grown in Anson and Union counties being superior to that of any other section of the State.

The Directors and Officers are as follows :

DIRECTORS.

J. S. WHEDBEE...........................Baltimore.
C. M. STEDMAN..........................Wilmington.
W. W. CHAMBERLAINE....................Portsmouth.
R. S. TUCKER.......................... ....Raleigh.
J. M. ROBINSON................. ....Baltimore.
D. W. OATES...............................Charlotte.
J. C. WINDER...............................Raleigh.
M. P. LEAK................................Wadesboro.
R. C. HOFFMAN...........................Baltimore.
J. L. MINIS..............................Baltimore.
SEVERN EYRE.......... ....Baltimore.

OFFICERS.

J. M. ROBINSON.. ....President.
J. C. WINDER.......................General Manager.
L. C. JONES.... ....Superintendent.
F. W. CLARK.......General Freight and Passenger Agent.
A. J. HOWELL......... ....Auditor.
JAMES ANDERSON....................... ....Treasurer.
W. H. ALLEN.................Master of Transportation.

CLINTON AND POINT CASWELL RAILROAD.

This is a railway projected from Point Caswell to Clinton, the county seat of Sampson, via Kerr's Landing and Harrell's Store, connecting with the daily steamers from Point Caswell, on Black River, with Wilmington, 28 miles distant, for the purpose of bringing the produce of Pender and Sampson counties to this market.

The Railroad was chartered by our last Legislature, February 1883, capital stock $150,000, of which $32,500 has been subscribed. The charter requires that the Road shall be completed within two years, and proposals are advertised for the work, which will begin at once. The officers are as follows :

F. W. KERCHNER,............................President.
E. W. KERR,.............................Vice-President.
J. H. BOATWRIGHT,..............Secretary and Treasurer.
J. D. O'HANLAN,.......................Chief Engineer.

THE DUPLIN CANAL COMPANY

was chartered by the Legislature in 1874. In 1873 a project to direct the North East River (Cape Fear Branch) into a straight channel by a canal through Angola Pocosin, by way of Bannerman's, to the mouth of Goshen Swamp, and thereby draining 121,000 acres of overflowed and valuable land in Pender and Duplin counties, was undertaken by Major Young, Engineer, resulting in the appointment by a number of Wilmington gentlemen of Mr. A. R. Black and Mr. W. L. Young as a Committee to make a careful survey of the route proposed and report upon its feasibility.

THE DUPLIN CANAL.

[Report of A. R. Black, Esq., in regard to the feasibility of the Enterprise.]

Messrs. Edward Kidder and others :

GENTLEMEN :—About the 10th of November, in company with Major Wilton L. Young, I set about to make reconnoissance of the Valley of the North East River, preparatory, as I understand, to locating a canal for shortening distances, improving the navigation and draining the swamp lands along and contiguous to the river; also for the further purpose of collecting all the information I could as to the character of the country and its resources.

In order to its being better understood, I found it necessary to prepare

A MAP

in connection with this report.

The map has been carefully drawn, and is founded on
the best information that could be obtained without an
actual survey.

The location of the river has been determined, generally,
by certain known directions and distances between places
on the river and railroad. The meanderings of the river
were given by persons in the neighborhoods, who professed
to be familiar with its curves, which are not fancy sketches,
but are believed to approximate the truth. The contour of
the country, and general quality of the lands, together with
the growth of timber, when seen, are represented as they
appeared, and when not seen, they are represented according to descriptions given by persons well acquainted with
the country.

The entire feasibility of constructing

THE CANAL

will readily suggest itself as soon as a glimpse is taken of
the parallel red lines on the map, running from the mouth
of Goshen, in a southerly direction, along the margin of
the flat lands on the western side of the river to Fed's
Landing, a distance of about sixteen miles; thence across
the river and down the swamp in a westerly direction one-
half mile, to "Burton's old field;" thence in a southerly
direction across the main divide at "Burton's old field,"
to the mouth of Fishing Branch, about one mile; thence
in the same direction across the upper end of Gum Swamp
and along the eastern margin of Angola Pocosin; thence
in the same direction across Holly Shelter Creek and North
East River to Peggy's Island—an entire distance from the
mouth of Goshen to Peggy's Island of about thirty-one
miles.*

*Reported distance by the course of the river: Mouth of Goshen to Sarecta 20
miles, thence to Hallsville 16 miles, thence to Chinquepin 25 miles, thence to Bowses'
16 miles, thence to Rafting Oak 15 miles, thence to Abe's Point 20 miles, thence to
Bannerman's 9 miles, thence to Peggy's Island 6 miles—in all 111 miles.

No serious obstacles appear to be presented to the construction of the canal. Nearly all the ground on which it
is located, from the "mouth of Goshen" to "Burton's
old field," is overflowed in high freshets ; the portions not
overflowed being low islands, scarcely rising above the water.
At "Burton's old field" there is a low divide, which, I am
informed, during the recent September freshet, only lacked
six or seven feet of being covered. From thence to Peggy's
Island the cutting will appear plain and simple.

This route is taken only as a sample; others may be
selected equally practicable, and perhaps more so, when
the test of instruments is applied. It appears that, in
reality, there is not much room for a display of great skill
in engineering. Almost any old woman can do the
engineering.

THE SWAMP LANDS

to be affected by the drainage are extensive, and most of
them very rich. This will also appear by an inspection of
the map. I heard the remark repeated several times, by
intelligent men in Duplin county, that the drainage of all
the swamps in the county would be benefited by the canal,
except two small streams west of the railroad, Stewart's
Creek and Turkey Creek. I found the swamps more
extensive and much richer than I expected. I have never
seen better lands than those of Gum Swamp and Goshen
Swamp, not to mention other bodies equally good. An
abundance of marl is generally found underlying or contiguous to the swamps. The growth is principally black
gum, sweet gum, cypress and ash, much of the cypress
being very fine. I estimate that if the rich swamp lands of
Duplin county were laid down in one body, they would
constitute a belt of swamp one mile wide by seventy miles
long. If the growth of timber could be separated and laid
down in different bodies, I think it would average nearly
as follows: cypress would occupy about fifteen miles of
the belt, black gum about the same, sweet gum about five

miles, ash about five miles, poplar about two miles, maple two miles, spruce pine two miles, hickory two miles, birch one mile, and holly one mile. The map will show where bodies of timber may be found.

THE UPLANDS

have generally a clay subsoil. I think it would be safe to say that two-thirds of the land in Duplin county has a clay subsoil. Most of this land produces good crops, and is admirably adapted to improvement, and with the vast amount of muck and marl interspersed throughout the country, almost every foot of this land may be made rich. What a tidal wave of prosperity awaits Duplin county when her swamps can be reclaimed and her people become fully awakened to the wonderful agricultural advantages that surround them.

When the Duplin Canal is constructed—and it can only be a question of time when this shall be done, for sooner or later this Canal surely will be constructed—Wilmington will be greatly benefited by it. This is no doubtful enterprise for Wilmington. It will not turn the products of the country away from her, as some others have done, but as sure as water runs down stream, it will pour them into her lap. Cast your eye over the map and note the green chain marked "Trade Line." See what a scope of country it embraces. It sweeps along within fifteen miles of Goldsboro, within twelve miles of Kinston, and within twenty-five miles of New Berne. What a splendid country this is. This line marks out the section of country that is likely to trade with Wilmington when the Duplin Canal is completed. All along the route of the Canal will be found, in Pender county, also, large bodies of excellent land.

We now come to speak of

"THE PINES ! THE STATELY, TOWERING PINES !"

How shall we speak of them in terms sufficiently lauda-tory ? They have been the mainstay of the people of all this region for over a hundred years, and are still profitable.

I am told that turpentine lands worked before the Revolutionary War, still continue to yield profitable crops. By the time one growth of pines is worked off another springs up. So that, for the production of turpentine, the forests are not likely to be exhausted. But it is not so for

MILL TIMBER.

Between the railroad and North East River most of the large timber has been cut off, but still, in some places, large bodies of excellent timber may be found, and a good deal of scattering timber throughout this region. Dr. Calhoun Hill informed me that there was a very fine body of heavy pines in the fork of Goshen and North East River, supposed to be ten or twelve thousand acres in extent. He also spoke of other fine bodies between these two streams. He informed me that there was a splendid body of white oak and ash, reaching for ten miles along Goshen Swamp, on the north side. Good timber was reported on the south side of Goshen, on Nahungar Creek, as also on Persimmon, on Maxwell, near the confluence of Elder and Stocking Head, and on both these streams, on the head waters of Grove, and on the back of Lochlin Pocosin.

On the East side of North East River, between Cypress Creek and Moore's Creek, on the east and south sides, and Marl Swamp and Gum Swamp and the North East River, on the west and north, large bodies of excellent timber are reported, some of which I saw.

On the east side of Cypress Creek, and along the east side of the North East River, after leaving the streams two to four miles, excellent forests of large timber are reported. I saw the borders of some of these forests, which were very fine. Vast quantities of lightwood, suitable for the manufacture of tar, may be found throughout all the region east of the North East River, also between Goshen and the North East River.

We found the people everywhere on our journey very

anxious for the Canal. They fully comprehend its importance to them. Its accomplishment is looked forward to as the dawn of the good time to come; and verily it will be so if it enables them to reclaim their swamp lands. The people were everywhere hospitable and obliging—anxious and willing to furnish any information in their power. We are greatly indebted to them for many favors, and shall always retain very pleasant recollections of our Canal explorations.

In conclusion, and not to repeat what has already been said, by way of summary, we recommend to the very favorable consideration of Messrs. Kidder and others, the construction of the "Duplin Canal."

I am, gentlemen,

Your obedient servant,

A. R. BLACK."

ESTIMATE OF ACREAGE OF SWAMPS IN DUPLIN COUNTY.

Island Creek	1,200
Lochlin Pocosin	5,000
Cypress Creek and tributaries	1,500
Muddy Creek	1,000
Maxwell Swamp and tributaries	5,000
Big and Little Limestone and tributaries	3,000
Grove Swamp	1,500
Persimmon	500
Dark Branch	300
Hell Swamp	600
Goshen Swamp and tributaries	12,000
Burnt Coat Creek	500
Wild Cat Creek	500
Great Branch	400
Green Swamp and part of Gum Swamp, in Duplin county	5,000
Back Swamp	3,000
North East River, in Duplin	10,000
Total acreage in Duplin	51,000

Dr. Blount, of Kenansville, aided me in this estimate.

I estimate the swamps of Pender county at about 20,000 acres.   A. R. B."

I am indebted to that patient and indefatigable Engineer, Major W. L. Young, for the following statement with reference to this work up to the present time, 25th March :

"Mr. Black's report only refers to overflowed lands belonging to individuals, viz : 51,000 acres in Duplin, and · 20,000 acres in Pender county—making in all 71,000 acres.

There would also be reclaimed 50,000 acres of State land lying in the counties of Pender and Duplin—making in all, both private and public lands, 121,000 acres that would be reclaimed from overflow by the canal.

It is more than probable that in all the Southern States there is not another locality where there is such an enormous amount of overflowed land which could be reclaimed by the cutting of a canal of only 30 miles in length.

The practicability of the result is made plain when the fact is taken into consideration, that the Northeast river has not only a very tortuous channel, but also makes enormous bends which environ great bodies of land, and which are overflowed during freshets, and which, also, submerge all the tributary swamps.

Owing to this peculiar formation of the river, rafts and freshets are actually seven days in passing down the river from the mouth of Goshen to Bannerman's, which by the route of the canal, is only 30 miles, while by the river it is 140 miles ; whereas, if the canal was constructed, and the river diverted to this new channel, the water flow would be reduced from seven days to ten hours ; and freshets would be a thing of the past.

As a means of navigation, this canal would be of much importance to the great triangle or section of country lying betwen the coast and the Wilmington & Weldon Railway, south of the Neuse and Pamlico Sound, and also to the isolated portions of Pender, Onslow, Duplin, Wayne, Lenoir and Jones.

The sluice way has been cut and the timber removed

more or less for the distance of six miles, and a dam—perhaps the largest structure of the kind in eastern North Carolina—442 feet long, has been constructed across Shelter Creek. This dam, when repaired at one point, will be capable of holding 14 feet head of water, which can be thrown at will into the sluiceway of the canal at various points, thus forcing the water of Shelter Creek to seek the new and direct channel of the canal.

The northern terminus of the canal is within two miles of a natural fall of 17 feet. When this fall is reached, an outlet will be given for a great basin of over-flowed land that is ten miles long and from three to four miles wide, that would be reclaimed as the work progressed. And further, as soon as this fall is gained, and the upper section of five miles of the canal is sluiced out so as to be navigable for barges, the Company would receive, without further extension of the work, annually, the "tolls" on 30,000 or 40,000 barrels of naval stores, and upon timber and lumber. It should be remembered that all this is before the river is reached at the first crossing by the canal."

The officers of the company are as follows :

Wm. Larkins,............ ....President.
W. T. Bannerman,.....................Vice-President.
J. H. Boatwright,............ ....Treasurer.
David Farrior,.........................Pay Master.
W. L. Young,.............Superintendent and Engineer.

INLAND WATER-WAY.

I am also informed by Major Young, that in the year 1874 a charter was granted by our State Legislature, for an inland canal from the South Carolina line to Virginia. The scheme proposed is to avoid the dangers of Hatteras, by connecting the North East Cape Fear River and Chesapeake Bay.

A survey of this route was made by the United States

Government in 1875, and it was ascertained to be practicable, and that by utilizing the 47 miles of the navigable river of the North East and other intermediate streams, it would only require about 40 miles of canal to connect Wilmington with Pamlico Sound and all the other inland water system of North Carolina—Croatan and Albemarle Sounds, the Neuse, Tar, Roanoke and Chowan rivers, and also with Norfolk and Baltimore, by the way of the Dismal Swamp and Albemarle canals.

It has further been ascertained, in connection with this scheme, that it only requires four miles of canal at Oak Island, and five miles between Little River and Waccamaw River, to connect the Cape Fear, Waccamaw, Pee Dee and Santee rivers by an inland water route—thus connecting Wilmington with Georgetown.

THE FIRST NATIONAL BANK OF WILMINGTON,

Was organized July 6, 1866—the capital stock is $250,000.

DIRECTORS.

DAVID G. WORTH,   GEORGE CHADBOURN,
JAMES SPRUNT,   EDWIN E. BURRUSS,
                ALFRED MARTIN.

OFFICERS.

E. E. BURRUSS, ...President.
A. K. WALKER, ...Cashier.

The following statement of Resources and Liabilities, on December 23rd, 1882, shows the condition of its affairs at that date :

Statement of the Condition of the First National Bank of Wilmington,
N. C., December 23rd, 1882.

RESOURCES:

Loans and Discounts	$ 613,642 31
U. S. Bonds to secure Circulation	50,000 00
Other Stocks, Bonds and Mortgages	75,111 60
Due from Banks and Bankers	103,246 70
Current Expenses	8,446 71
Cash on Hand	85,610 99
Real Estate and Furniture and Fixtures	76,327 22
	$1,012,385 53

LIABILITIES:

Capital Stock	$ 250,000 00
Circulation	44,990 00
Surplus Fund	37,160 19
Undivided Profits	59,351 29
Due Individual Depositors	591,037 05
Due Banks and Bankers	29,847 00
	$1,012,385 53

BANK OF NEW HANOVER.

This organization was effected January 12th, 1872—the capital stock is $300,000.

The following statement of its condition was published February 1st, 1883:

Statement of Condition of Bank of New Hanover, including Branches,
February 1st, 1883.

RESOURCES:

Loans and Discounts		$ 795,591 51
Cash in New York, Philadelphia, Boston and Baltimore Banks.	$ 98,624 53	
Currency and Specie	210,903 36	
Checks on other Banks	6,527 78	316,055 67
Due from other Banks not included above		88,648 51
Sterling Exchange (value in Currency)		5,148 14
Real Estate		89,099 24
Office Furniture and Safes		7,082 37
Bonds and Stocks		21,252 41
Checks and Drafts in Transit		14,445 97
		$1,340,326 85

LIABILITIES:

Capital Stock	$ 300,000 00
Due Depositors	915,296 32
Due other Banks	52,052 17
Surplus Fund	72,978 36
	$1,340,326 85

Statement of Condition of Bank at Wilmington, February 1st, 1883.

RESOURCES:

Loans and Discounts..		$633,062 62
Cash in New York, Philadelphia, Boston and Baltimore Banks.$	85,639 10	
Currency and Specie..	127,256 76	
Checks on other Banks..	6,527 78—	217,423 64
Due from other Banks not included above...................		53,908 58
Sterling Exchange (value in Currency).............		5,148 14
Real Estate................................		83,604 18
Office Furniture and Safes..		3,843 66
Bonds and Stocks..		7,723 94
		$1,004,714 76

LIABILITIES :

Capital Stock..................................... ....$		225,000 00
Due Depositors...		616,926 07
Due other Banks..		49,025 64
Due other Branches of this Bank...		78,043 73
Surplus Fund.....		35,719 32
		$1,004,714 76

Statement of Condition of Bank at Goldsboro, February 1st, 1883.

RESOURCES :

Loans and Discounts...		$119,118 10
Cash in New York and Baltimore Banks....................................... $	8,936 46	
Currency and Specie..	52,835 47—	61,771 93
Due from other Banks not included above.......................................		32,959 58
Due from other Branches of this Bank...		23,764 05
Real Estate...		5,495 06
Office Furniture and Safes...		1,877 21
Wilmington & Weldon R. R., Mortgage Bonds.............................		16,528 50
		$261,514 47

LIABILITIES :

Capital Stock..................................... ....$		50,000 00
Due Depositors...		178,389 72
Due other Banks		2,610 82
Surplus Fund...		30,513 93
		$261,514 47

Statement of Condition of Bank at Wadesboro, February 1st, 1883.

RESOURCES :

Loans and Discounts........ .... $		43,413 70
Cash in New York Banks... .... $	6,048 97	
Currency and Specie..	30,811 13—	36,860 10
Due from other Banks not included above.....................................		1,780 40
Due from other Branches of this Bank...		68,725 65
Office Furniture and Safes...............................		1,361 50
		$152,141 35

LIABILITIES :

Capital Stock ....$		25,000 00
Due Depositors...		119,980 53
Due other Banks....		415 71
Surplus Fund...		6,745 11
		$152,141 35

Its officers are as follows :

ISAAC BATES, ... President.
G. W. WILLIAMS, ... Vice President.
S. D. WALLACE, ... Cashier.

DIRECTORS.

R. R. BRIDGERS,	W. I. GORE,
I. BATES,	E. B. BORDEN,
C. M. STEDMAN,	JAS. A. LEAK,
G. W. WILLIAMS,	J. W. ATKINSON,
H. VOLLERS,	D. MCRAE,

F. RHEINSTEIN.

COTTON COMPRESSES.

The first Cotton Compress operated in this city was established by the Confederate Government during the war, in 1864. It was located on the west side of the river, just south of the Brunswick Ferry, and was under the entire control and supervision of the Government, and used for compressing cotton for running the blockade.

Its capacity was from 450 to 500 bales a day. It was set fire to and totally destroyed, together with a large amount of other property, by order of Gen. Bragg, on the evening of February 21st, 1865, the eve of the evacuation of the town by the Confederate forces. It was brought to this place from Charleston, the port of Wilmington being the only one at that time where the business of blockade-running was carried on.

Wilmington has now three first class Cotton Compresses in successful operation, viz: The Wilmington Compress Company, (2 presses), of which George W. Williams is President, and George Sloan Secretary and Treasurer ; and the Champion Compress Company, (1 press), E. J. Penny-packer, President, and T. B. Harriss, Secretary and Treasurer. They are stock companies, the former with a capital of $85,000, and the latter $70,000. The first was organized during the summer of 1875. Valuable wharf property was purchased near what was known in the early history of the town as "Paradise," in the northern portion of the city, and adjoining the terminus of the Carolina Central Railroad,—on which were erected the latest improved cotton presses, a Taylor Steam and Hydraulic Press and a Tyler Steam press, and extensive warehouses for the storage of cotton. The increase of business within two years after its erection, warranted the establishment of an additional press, and during the summer of 1879, the Champion Compress and Warehouse Company was organized. The wharf property at the foot of Red Cross street, and adjoining the depot of the Wilmington, Columbia & Augusta, and the Wilmington & Weldon Railroads, was purchased, on which was erected the "Morse" Cotton Compress, with brick warehouses and sheds, together with the largest guano warehouse in the State—located on the west side of the river.

The estimated pressure is about 1,500 tons, and the capacity of each press is about 50 bales an hour. Both companies are kept actively engaged during the cotton season, in compressing cotton for foreign shipment, and business has steadily increased from 15,000 bales the first year to about 100,000 bales during the last cotton season. It is a business that has increased each succeeding year since its commencement, and when the advantages offered to shippers at this port become generally known, it must assume larger proportions.

The facilities for handling cotton cheaply here, are not surpassed, if equaled, by any other Southern port. The railroads centering at this point, deliver cotton at the different presses ; there is ample room at the wharves of the companies, and sufficient depth of water for the largest sized vessels that visit this port, to load without the least difficulty, thereby saving the expense, which is very heavy at other ports, of drayage and lighterage, which of course have to be borne by the shipper, and which aggregates a very large amount.

The port charges are less than at other points, and the expenses generally are more moderate.

Quick dispatch is given, for the presses are run day and night when necessary, and delays seldom occur, unless from some unavoidable accident. When we take into consideration the improved character of these presses, their capacity for doing well the work which is required, the fact that cotton is handled cheaper here than at other places, and the expenses in every way much lighter to the shipper, we certainly have reason to anticipate a largely increased business to our city from the success of this important industry.

WILMINGTON COTTON MILLS.

These mills were built in 1874, at an original cost of $150,000, and reorganized in 1878, with a reduced capital of $60,000.

The list of officers is as follows:

DONALD MACRAE,.........................President.
WM. A. FRENCH,............... ....Vice President.
W. G. MACRAE, ...Treasurer and Superintendent.

DIRECTORS.

EDWARD KIDDER,   F. W. KERCHNER,
JAS. H. CHADBOURN,   B. G. WORTH.
JOHN WILDER ATKINSON.

The Machinery is 100 horse power (steam); and the fuel —wood and sawdust.

There are in operation 156 looms, 5,712 spindles, 34 cards, 7 fine spuders, 4 slubbers, and 1 picker and opener.

The goods manufactured are Print Cloths and Batting; and during the past year, the mill has turned out 168,000 yards per month, or say, 2,016,000 yards per year,—part of which is sold for home consumption, but the product is principally sold to calico printers in Philadelphia and New York.

The mill employs 3 superintendents of departments, 12 men, 15 boys, 80 women and 20 girls,—total, 130. The cost of production of goods and pay of operatives is about the same as at Fall River and other manufacturing places North.

The number of bales of cotton used is 780 per annum, costing $40,000, and value of goods manufactured per year, $80,000 to $100,000.

THE NAVASSA GUANO COMPANY, OF WILMINGTON

was established in 1869, with a capital stock of $200,000. The following named comprise the officers:

R. R. BRIDGERS,..............................President.
DONALD MacRAE,........... . .Secretary and Treasurer.
C. L. GRAFFLIN,...................... Superintendent.

The works are situated at Meares' Bluff, Brunswick county, N. C., about 4 miles from Wilmington, and manufacture annually 18,000 tons of "Navassa Guano" and Acid Phosphate.

There are in operation two Sulphuric Acid, and one Muriatic Acid chambers, of a capacity of 240,000 cubic feet.

About 100 workmen are employed.

The power (steam) used is 150 horse, and fuel,—wood.

The value of product is $450,000 annually.

The company owns and works a valuable rice plantation of about 300 acres, situated about a mile below the factory, and which produces about 12,000 bushels of rice yearly.

THE SOUTHERN ORE COMPANY.

This is a new industry, recently established in Wilmington, and the only one of the kind in North Carolina. It is located on South Water street, at the foot of Ann street.

It is an incorporated Company, and was organized on February 1st, 1883, with a capital of $50,000, with power to increase to $500,000.

A local Board of three resident Directors manage the affairs of the corporation.

Its business is the purchase and reduction of all minerals that contain the precious metals, such as gold and silver, and also ores containing copper, zinc, lead, etc.

The ores are purchased at different points within the State, and shipped to this place by rail, and by a peculiar process, the details of which are not made public, the precious metals are extracted. The prices offered by the Company for ores have already resulted in engagements for, it is thought, a sufficient supply to keep the works employed, and the enterprise is of course materially helping to develop the mineral resources of the State.

Mr. J. Beno, of New York, is the projector of this scheme.

TOBACCO FACTORY.

Wilmington is the only point east of Raleigh where a Tobacco Factory is in successful operation. The Cape Fear Tobacco Works were established here in the spring of 1879, and are now located on Bladen street, near the Wilmington & Weldon Railroad, on the site formerly known as Camp Lamb. The proprietors are Messrs. Meadows and Kidder. The capacity of the works is about 500,000 pounds annually, making plug, twist and smoking tobacco, and the quality of the goods turned out will compare favorably with other factories in the State. The leaf used, is obtained principally from Granville county, and the counties adjoining, long celebrated for their fine quality of tobacco ; and the standard of goods manufactured at the Factory is never allowed to deteriorate. About sixty hands are employed, and the demand for their goods here and in the surrounding country is increasing. The engine is about ten-horse power, with a fifteen-horse power boiler, and the machinery, of the most approved kind.

THE CAROLINA RICE MILLS.

In 1881 the increasing rice crop along the Cape Fear and in the up country induced Messrs. Norwood Giles and Pembroke Jones, of Wilmington, to venture upon the establishment, at great expense and considerable risk, of a first-class Rice Mill, which was completed the year following, and which will compare favorably with any mill in the country. These enterprising young men have not only brought energy and capital to this important undertaking, but a degree of intelligence and sound business judgment which is bound to make them successful. Already the product of the Carolina Mills has attracted attention in New York and in Liverpool, and pronounced by competent and recognized authority, the best milled rice in the South. They have a capacity of double the present crop, and they are increasing their facilities constantly to meet every requirement of the trade.

The Mills are of brick, 106 feet long, 42 feet wide, and four stories in height. Pitch of floors 14 feet. An engine room connected with the Mill is 18 feet wide and one story high. The engine is 45-horse power, and the capacity of the Mill is 1,800 to 2,000 bushels per twenty-four hours. There are 18 patent Brotherhood pestles on the first floor, and the spouting necessary for turning out the clean rice. On the second floor are all the receiving bins for ground and beat rice, and also the stones. On the third floor stands two large brushes for polishing and the necessary fans and screens. The fourth floor is entirely devoted to machinery for cleaning the rice before going to mill.

The elevators are many in number and wonderfully assist in handling the grain. The number of people employed is 13. The storage capacity of the warehouse is 75,000 bushels.

GRAIN MILLS.

There are four grain mills in successful operation in Wilmington at this time, two of which are also flouring mills, viz: Messrs. B. F. Mitchell & Son, on North Water street, between Market and Princess streets, and the Cape Fear Flouring Mills, now carried on by Mr. C. B. Wright. The former was originally established by Ellis & Mitchell in the year 1849, and continued under that firm name until 1866, when Mr. Ellis retired. He was succeeded in the firm by Mr. Huggins, and the business was conducted under the name of Mitchell & Huggins, until 1871, when Mr. Huggins died. Since that time it has been B. F. Mitchell & Son.

The power used is 76 horse, with four run of stones capable of turning out 450 bushels of meal, and 20 barrels of flour per day. It is the only mill in the State in which there is a purifier for purifying the middlings; and it has besides, all the modern improvements and conveniences.

THE CAPE FEAR FLOUR MILLS, C. B. WRIGHT, PROPRIETOR.

This mill is located at the foot of Walnut, corner of North Water street. It was first built in 1855, on the lot directly opposite its present location, but was destroyed by fire in 1866, and then built upon its present site. It has a power of 85 horse, capable of turning out from 500 to 600 bushels of meal, and 20 barrels of flour a day, runs three stones on wheat and corn, and three on hominy. In 1868, the proprietor, Mr Alex. Oldham, bought the patent for the State for making pearl hominy, and it is the only mill in North Carolina that has the right and is engaged in manufacturing that article.

/ Our flour mills cannot compete successfully with the Western mills, on account of the tariff of freights. Flour is handled at a much cheaper rate than wheat, which operates greatly to the disadvantage of our mills. The quality is as good as that made anywhere, and compares favorably with the best brought to this market from other points.

Messrs. Preston Cumming & Co.'s mill, located at the foot of Dock street, and Mr. W. P. Oldham's, on the south side of Dock street, are grain mills alone. The first was established in 1869, has two sets of runners, uses 40 horse power, and is capable of turning out about 400 bushels of meal a day.

Mr. W. P. Oldham's mill was erected in 1875, has two sets of runners, 35 horse power, and a capacity of 350 bushels of meal a day.

These grain mills are complete in every way ; advantage is immediately taken of any improvements in machinery or otherwise to add to their efficiency, and they are managed with the skill and energy which generally commands success.

THE ACME MANUFACTURING COMPANY.

In a communication from Messrs. Cronly & Morris, Agents of the above-named Company, with reference to its origin and endeavor, and in response to my request for information, I learn that "Cronly," on the Carolina Central Railroad, is the site of its operations, and that some months ago the proprietors in Wilmington, Messrs. Latimer and others, entered into negotiations for the establishment of a fertilizer manufactory on the tract of land owned by Cronly & Morris at Livingston Creek, on the Carolina Central Railroad. Pending these negotiations last spring, their attention was called to a patent device for curling vegetable fibres for upholstering purposes in imitation of horse-hair, and a rubbing machine for the treatment of fibrous plants and material. As in the treatment of the fibres, chemicals were used which were valuable fertilizing agents, they attempted to obtain control of these processes, with a view either to consolidation with the fertilizer factory, or to operate both to mutual advantage.

After a thorough examination of the two schemes, they became convinced of their value, and finally completed negotiations for the establishment of the enterprise.

For more than a year, attention had been directed to the manufacture of cotton-seed oil, and enquiries instituted with reference to the process ; and although convinced of its practicability, the excessively high prices demanded by manufacturers of the necessary machinery, and the necessity of convincing the planters of the advantage to them by selling their cotton-seed, and receiving in return cotton-seed meal, possessing greater fertilizing properties than the seed itself, deterred them from the undertaking. Subsequently attention was called to an article of Mr. Edward Atkinson, of Boston, the cotton statistician, on the production of cotton-seed oil, in which he characterized as extremely wasteful and thriftless, the present method of obtaining the oil, and strongly advised the adoption of a process recommended by him whereby the oil was obtained by certain chemical reaction. Full enquiries were made into his process, and being satisfied that the oil could be so obtained, and at a much smaller cost for the plant and for working than by the present method, they entered into an arrangement for the establishment of a factory, with Dr. L. H. Friedburg of New York, an expert-chemist, who had been most highly recommended by Dr. C. F. Chandler, President of the Board of Health of New York City, and Dean of the Faculty of the School of Mines of Columbia College.

A short time ago, they effected a consolidation of the three enterprises, which under this arrangement can be conducted in a much more economical manner, and with greater assurance of success. The Legislature has incorporated the joint enterprises under the name of the Acme Manufacturing Company.

The capital of the Company will be $152,000, all of which is subscribed. The location of the Factories is particu-

larly desirable, having water communication with the river
by Livingston Creek, and being situated on the Carolina
Central Railroad, at a distance of about a mile and a
quarter from the Wilmington, Columbia & Augusta Railroad with which they expect to connect the Factories by
private or public railway, and thus obtain greater facilities for shipment of the manufactured product.

The beds of marl and phosphate rock are adjacent to the
Factory sites. Dr. Ledoux, who analyzed the marl, showed
it to be valuable, which is verified by subsequent analyses
made by him, and published in his report for 1880, giving
to one of the marls over 51 per cent. of phosphate lime,
and to another 27 per cent. of phosphoric acid. The results
of analyses of several other marls from the same locality,
though much lower than the above, showed them to be
valuable as fertilizers.

A fibre factory 100x150x48 has already been built at
"Cronly," and all the machinery for it has been received,
and is now being put up. This factory will manufacture
fibre from the long-leaved pine-straw for upholstering purposes (turning out about ten tons per week), oil from the
pine leaf, and fibres from palmetto, bear, and other grasses,
and material from West Indies and Bahama Islands.

The Fertilizer Factory will produce a first-class fertilizer,
and also place within reach of our farmers prepared marl.
Its capacity at first will be about 5,000 tons per annum.

The Cotton-Seed Oil Factory will, during the cotton season, manufacture cotton-seed oil and cake, and, during the
summer months, oil and cake from peanuts, palm kernels,
linseed, flax-seed, or any other oil-yielding substance which
they can obtain, either in this country or abroad.

In connection with the fibre factory, they expect to make
bagging for the fertilizer and for sale, and eventually from
the coarser fibres which abound in our section, to make
barrels from paper pulp for the oils.

Mr. John G. Stephens of New York, the patentee of fibre

processes will have charge of the fibre factory as Superintendent, and Dr. L. H. Friedburg, assisted by Mr. Thos.
Radcliffe, will have charge as Superintendent and Chemist
of the fertilizer and oil mills.

About 70 tons of machinery have been received, and
about 30 tons more are expected.

The fertilizer and oil mills of the same size as the fibre
factory are now in course of erection, also houses and a
store for the use of operatives. The fibre factory will be
ready for operation about April 1st, and the oil and fertilizer mills about May 1st.

The principal stockholders of the new Company are the
Messrs. Latimer, Messrs. Cronly & Morris, Messrs. Chas.
V. Ware and G. W. Warren, of New York, Mr. J. G.
Stephens and Dr. L. H. Friedburg.

TURPENTINE DISTILLERIES.

The following comprises the Turpentine Distilleries
operated in Wilmington :

NAME.	NO. OF STILLS.	CAPACITY PER DAY.
"Empire,"	7,	400 barrels crude turpentine.
Morton & Hall,	4,	250 " " "
"Ætna,"	2,	100 " " "
"Point Peter,"	3,	150 " " "
"Clay,"	3,	160 " " "
Mahn's,	1,	75 " " "
"Union,"	4,	250 " " "
Bowdens,	3,	160 " " "
Total,	27,	1,545 " " "

There are in addition 2 rosin oil stills, operated as a part
of Clay Distillery, the product of which also comprises:

Rosin Oil, 4 grades ; Rosin Oil Naptha, crude and rectified ; Tar Oil ; Spirits of Tar, crude and rectified ; Metalic
Paint Oils ; Deck and Spar Oils, for the preservation of the
decks and spars of vessels, and all wood not covered with

paint, against the action of the weather, and of dry rot ; Bright and Black Varnishes ; Venice Turpentine, for printer's ink ; Navy, or Shipbuilder's Pitch ; Shoemaker's Wax Pitch ; Brush Maker's Pitch ; Brewer's Pitch.

The Carolina Oil Company also operates 3 stills, the product of which is 20 barrels of oil per week. They also manufacture Tar Oil and Pine Wood Creosote Oil.

WILMINGTON GAS LIGHT COMPANY.

This company was chartered January 27th, 1851, and organized February, 1855.

Its capital stock is $100,000.

The Works are located on the corner of Surry and Castle streets.

Capacity of holders, 40,000 cubic feet of gas ; process of manufacture, wood and rosin ; price of gas per 1,000 cubic feet, $2.50 ; public lamps, $24.00 per year for each lamp ; length of mains, about 9½ miles.

BOARD OF DIRECTORS.

EDWARD KIDDER,	DONALD McRAE,
GEORGE R. FRENCH,	DR. A. J. DeROSSET,
WM. H. McRARY,	E. S. MARTIN,
	R. J. JONES.

OFFICERS.

EDWARD KIDDER,............................President.
RICHARD J. JONES,.............Secretary and Treasurer.
JNO. W. REILLY,... ....Superintendent.

CLARENDON WATER WORKS COMPANY.

This Company was organized April 16, 1881 ; the Works were completed the following autumn, and began supplying water in December, 1881. The hydrant service was accepted by the city in January, 1882.

It has about 12½ miles of main pipes from 4 to 12 inches in diameter, and about 1½ miles of service pipes and small mains ¾ of an inch to 2 inches in diameter.

There are 105 public fire hydrants and 260 consumers. The present daily consumption is upwards of 100,000 gallons.

The Company uses what is known as the combined stand-pipe and direct pressure system. The water is pumped into the stand-pipe for ordinary use, but in case of fire, it is pumped directly into the mains, the pressure being increased as the exigencies of the case demand.

The stand-pipe is 20 feet in diameter and 90 feet high, which gives a domestic pressure of from 25 to 50 pounds per square inch. The fire pressure is usually 100 pounds per square inch. The capacity of the stand-pipe is 210,000 gallons.

These Works have two Worthington Duplex Pumping Engines—one high pressure of 500,000 gallons daily capacity, and the other a compound non-condensing engine, of 1,000,000 gallons daily capacity. This can be increased about 25 per cent. if necessary.

The capital stock is $50,000.

The Works cost about $150,000, the balance being represented by bonds.

DIRECTORS :

E. E. BURRUSS,	H. A. BURR,
F. W. KERCHNER,	J. F. DIVINE,
EDWARD KIDDER,	D. G. WORTH.

OFFICERS :

J. F. DIVINE...............................President.
EDWARD KIDDER..............Secretary and Treasurer.
J. C. CHASE...........................Superintendent.

RATES :

" The following rates will be charged annually for the use of water, to be collected quarterly in advance :

Dwelling houses occupied by one family of not exceeding five
   persons, for the first faucet................................ ....$6 00

For each additional faucet.......... ....$2 00
For the first bath-tub.. 4 00
For each additional bath-tub.. 2 00
For the first water-closet... 4 00
For each additional closet...:........ 2 00
For the first urinal... 2 00
For each additional urinal.. 1 00

For each additional person in the family, exceeding five, ten per cent. of the above rates.

Water-closets and urinals without self-closing valves, double the above rates.

Where hot and cold water faucets discharge into one vessel, but one charge will be made for both.

For each additional family using the same fixtures, 75 per cent. of the above rates.

Stores, warehouses, offices, shops, etc., requiring no more than the ordinary supply of water, the same price for fixtures as dwelling houses.

Stables.—For the first horse...$3 00
For each additional horse... 2 00
For each cow.. 2 00

The above rate includes the use of water for washing carriages, etc., *without* hose. Where hose is used in any stable an extra charge will be made for each horse of $2 00.

Use of hose for sprinkling streets, gardens, etc., per thousand
      square feet...$1 00

Provided that the amount charged for the use of hose shall be in no case less than five dollars per annum, and that one-half of the annual rate will be collected April 1st, and the balance July 1st.

Meter rates, per 100 cubic feet..15 cents.
                         (20 cents per 1,000 gallons.)

Provided, however, that in no case where a meter is used by request of the consumer, shall the annual charge be less than ten dollars.

When the quantity used exceeds 15,000 cubic feet per month, special rates will be made."

OAKDALE CEMETERY COMPANY.

The charter for this Corporation was granted on the 27th day of December, 1852, the company was organized on the 16th of November, 1853, and the grounds were opened, and the first interment made on the 6th of February, 1855. The necessity for the formation of this corporation grew

out of the fact that the old time-honored custom of interments within the city church-yards was fast giving way, in
other places, to the Cemetery system of burials, and a few
public-spirited gentlemen of Wilmington suggested the
location of a central Cemetery, "to be universally adopted
as a substitute for the old grave-yards then in use." Acting
upon this suggestion, the grounds just east of the "Old
Burnt Mill Creek," containing 60 acres, were purchased
and named "Oakdale," and dedicated to the preservation
and continued protection of our dead.

Of the fifteen gentlemen named in the charter of this
corporation, one now resides in California, one in Con-
necticut, two in other counties of this State ; six are still
actively engaged in their business vocations in this city,
and the other five have passed over the river, while their
remains "rest under the shade of the trees" in "Oakdale."

All revenue, from whatever source it may be derived, is
devoted to the maintenance of the grounds.

Up to the present time, about one third, or probably
one-half, of the grounds have been improved and formed
into sections, and sections into lots,—each lot containing
four hundred square feet.   The sections vary in size to suit
the conformation of the grounds, as follows :

Section A has 4 lots ; section B has 151 lots ; section C
has 23 lots ; section D has 110 lots ; section E has 42 lots ;
section F has 70 lots ; section G has 25 lots ; section H has
124 lots ; section J has 87 lots ; while the last section, K,
which has been opened, contains 150 lots, without including
the plot donated to the Ladies' Memorial Association, for
the Confederate dead, to which 453 bodies were removed
and buried in two semi-circular graves, and upon which
stands the most beautiful monument erected to the Confederate dead in the South.

Owing to the loss of some of the records during the war,
as well as to the confusion growing out of that terrible
epidemic of 1862, the yellow fever, which carried hundreds

to their graves, including both the Secretary and Superintendent of this company, the present Secretary, Mr. R. J. Jones, says:

"I cannot give a correct list of the interments since the opening of the grounds. My records, commencing February 4th, 1867, show 1,825 for the past sixteen years, or up to the first of January, 1883; and it is but fair to presume that with the casualties of the war and yellow fever combined, there were at least 2,000 buried before my record commences."

The present managers are:

DONALD MACRAE, ...President.
TIMOTHY DONLAN, ...Superintendent.
RICHARD J. JONES, ... Secretary and Treasurer.

DIRECTORS.

EDWARD KIDDER,	W. H. NORTHROP,
WM. J. YOPP,	GEORGE R. FRENCH,
JAMES H. CHADBOURN,	DR. A. J. DEROSSET,

I have thought that it would be appropriate, and perhaps a matter of interest to some, to recall the names of a few of our prominent citizens who now sleep in Oakdale Cemetery, and many of whom were distinguished in our annals, for wealth, intelligence and virtue. The old graveyard adjoining St. James' Church was for many, many years the common receptacle of the dead of the town, and within its walls, the ashes of more than one of our distinguished citizens still repose. It is now almost deserted, but one can learn a lesson of the vanity of life from the still remaining records of those, who, "after life's fitful fever, sleep well," within its hallowed precincts.

In August, 1763, Thomas Godfrey, son of the inventor of

the Quadrant, and the author of the first dramatic work
written in America, died and was buried in that old church-
yard.   He was but twenty-seven years old.   His grave is
undistinguishable from those of the numerous congregation
of the dead who sleep around him, for time has long since
levelled the incumbent sod, and no stone was erected to
mark the spot where his ashes repose.   The memorials of
him are few.   He was born in Philadelphia, and when
grown to manhood removed to this place and entered into
business as a merchant and factor.   While living here he
wrote his tragedy, "The Prince of Parthia," and many
fugitive pieces of local interest, which survived for years
in the recollection of the people of this section.   His tragedy,
as already stated, was the first dramatic work written in
America.   Extracts from it may be found in Duycinck's
Cyclopedia of Literature.

The spot where Cornelius Harnett sleeps is in the north-
east corner of the old grave-yard, and is marked by a red
sandstone, about two feet high, on which is inscribed, now
nearly illegible, the following :

CORNELIUS HARNETT,

Died April 20th, 1781.

"Slave to no sect, he took no private road,
But looked through nature, up to nature's God."

Such is the brief and artless biography written by the
men of 1781, of the first President of the Provincial Council,
the first member of the Provincial Assembly from the
Borough of Wilmington, and one of the three delegates
from North Carolina, who signed the original articles of
Confederation of the United States.   He was the representative man of the Cape Fear, bold, eloquent and incor-
ruptible, with a genius equal to the greatest occasions and
loftiest efforts.   He did not live to witness the success of
that cause which was so near his heart.   While lying sick
at the house of Mr. Spicer, on the Sound road, he was

captured by a party sent out by Major Craig, the British commandant of the town, and brought into Wilmington. The effect of severe and almost barbarous exposure, inflicted while a prisoner, upon a system enfeebled by disease, could have but one result. He died while a captive in their hands, and the old graveyard of St. James' contains all that was mortal of the first scholar, statesman and patriot, of the age in which he lived.

The State has honored his memory by assigning his name to the county of Harnett; but what has New Hanover county ever done to honor him whose name so much honors her. Should not a monument have been erected to his memory long ago? Is it too late to do it now, either upon the spot where he lies, within the town he so faithfully served, or upon one of those lovely mounds in Oakdale Cemetery, whither the ashes of some of his compeers have been carried to slumber midst their children's children, apart from the bustle of the town, amidst the beauty and grandeur of the country? Are there not some who will undertake this pious task, this labor of love, for one whose only descendant is his memory and his name?

Major George Blaney, who died in 1835, aged 40 years, belonged to the corps of Engineers of the United States Army. He was a prominent officer of the service, superintended the building of Fort Caswell, at the mouth of the river, and the works at the jetties, which were undertaken by the government to deepen the channel, but did not have the effect anticipated.

Dr. William J. Harriss, a skillful physician and a man of parts, died in 1839, leaving numerous descendants.

Christopher Dudley, for many years Postmaster at Wilmington, died in 1840, in the 65th year of his age.

Alexander Anderson, distinguished for his integrity and sound judgment, and who was a very successful dry-goods merchant, died in 1844, aged 59 years.

Robert McLaughlin, the first principal of the school established by the society of Odd Fellows, died suddenly in 1845. He was a man of great force of character.

Lieut. William Henry Wright, of the United States Corps of Engineers, died in 1845, at the early age of 31 years. He graduated at West Point with the highest distinction, General Beauregard being in the same class, and ranking second on the list. Lieutenant Wright was engaged upon the defences of Boston Harbor, and while thus engaged, published a treatise on mortars which is still recognized by the Engineer Corps as standard authority. He was one of the foremost men in his profession of his age, and was faultless in the discharge of the duties of life. Vices, he had none, and the elevated tone of his morality exerted a wholesome influence over all who came within the sphere of its action.

Capt. J. H. K. Burgwyn, of the United States Army, was killed in battle, during the Mexican war, in 1847, aged 37 years.

William C. Lord, formerly Collector of the port, remarkable for sound judgment and business qualifications, departed this life also in the year 1847, in the 54th year of his age.

Dr. John Hill, connected for many years with the Bank of Cape Fear—first as Cashier and afterwards as President —died, also, in 1847. He wielded a pen at once graceful and vigorous, and would, without doubt, have attained a high rank in the republic of letters had he devoted himself to literary pursuits.

Gov. Edward B. Dudley died in 1855. He rose to distinction by his native force of character, and intrinsic worth. He served in the Legislature for several terms, and was the last representative from Wilmington under the old Constitution, which allowed borough representation. He was a member of Congress in 1829, served one term and declined a re-election, giving as a reason, that Congress was not a place for any one who desired to be honest. He identified himself with the cause of internal improvements, was the active and ardent friend of that great work, the Wilmington & Weldon Railroad, was its first President, and did more, perhaps, than any other one man, to secure its completion. He was the first Governor elected by the direct vote of the people in 1836, and so satisfactory was his administration that there was no organized opposition to his re-election. He was a man of liberal and enlarged views, of generous impressions and spotless integrity.

Robert W. Brown, a successful merchant and a man of great probity, whose word was as good as his bond, died in 1856, aged 70 years.

Talcott Burr, Jr., a journalist of distinction, died in 1858, at the early age of 38 years.

In the year 1859, at the ripe age of 92 years, died Dr. Armand John DeRosset, identified with our city by ancestral descent, for more than a century. There are few brighter pages in the history of North Carolina than those which record the actions of such men as Harnett, Ashe, Waddell, Lillington, Moore, Howe and others, all of this section of the colony. It was among such a people that the youthful days of Dr. DeRosset were passed. He had advantages in early life for the attainment of knowledge, and in 1788 went to Philadelphia to attend the lectures at the Medical College, rendered famous by the genius of Dr. Benjamin Rush, and became the pupil of that celebrated man. He received his medical diploma in 1790, and immediately entered upon the practice of his profession in this city, which soon became large and remunerative, and so continued until age compelled him to retire. For more than half a century he was affectionately called the "old doctor"; outliving all of his contemporaries, and dying at the patriarchal age of four score and twelve years, leaving behind him not an enemy in the world.

Mr. Geo. W. Davis, merchant, died in 1860, aged 52 years.

Rev. Adam Empie, a distinguished divine in the Episcopal church, died also in 1860, in the 75th year of his age.

In 1861, Dr. Frederick J. Hill, Dr. Thomas H. Wright, aged 61, President of the Bank of Cape Fear, and Mr. Henry R. Savage, Cashier of the same Bank, and of the same age, passed to their rest.

The year 1862 will ever be remembered by our people as a period of terror and dismay. That dread pestilence, the yellow fever, raged with terrible malignity, sweeping off many of our most prominent and valuable citizens, among them Rev. R. B. Drane, Rector of the parish of St. James, aged 62 years.

James S. Green, Treasurer of the Wilmington & Weldon Railroad Company from its organization, aged 63 years.

Dr. James H. Dickson, an accomplished physician, a man of letters and large scientific attainments, aged 59 years.

J. W. K. Dix, a prominent merchant, age 35.

Isaac Northrop, a large mill owner, age 67.

James T. Miller, an intelligent and useful member of society, a genial, amiable, kind-hearted man, who served in the Legislature for two terms, was Mayor of the town for many years, Chairman of the County Court, and Collector of the Customs at the time of his death, aged 47 years.

Rev. J. L. Pritchard, Baptist minister, fell at the post of duty, aged 51 years.

Thomas Clarkson Worth, merchant, of the firm of T. C. & B. G. Worth, aged 45 years, who was born to be a merchant of the first class and of the highest principle, could endure nothing vile or mean. He had a benevolent, feeling heart, in sympathy with the suffering poor. He possessed a delightful temper, and carried a stock of good nature which never failed him. During the dark days of the yellow fever, September and October, 1862, he resolved not to fly from the pestilence, but to abide here and assist in tending the sick and dying. In fact, it was an offering up of himself, on the altar of duty, in behalf of the poor and suffering. Dr. Worth took the fever and died on the 1st of November, 1862.

Cyrus Stowe VanAmringe, one of the most gifted and promising of our young business men, remarkably pleasing and attractive in his person, ardent and faithful in his devotion to his friends, and of great purity in his life and character, fell at his post, with many other devoted people, during the pestilence, aged 26 years.

During the epidemic, none of our devoted citizens who , stood in the breach, were more unceasing in their work of humanity, or more constant in their attendance upon the sick of all classes, than Rev. Father Murphy, the Roman Catholic Priest, of St. Thomas' church, and Rev. A. Paul Repiton, of the Baptist church. The former succumbed to the disease towards the close of the epidemic, universally regretted by all denominations of christians. The latter outlived the disease, and closed a long and useful life, some years after, in Norfolk, Va., and now sleeps in Oakdale.

Mr. Edward P. Hall, President of the Branch of the Bank of the State, died in 1863, aged 77 years, as did also Joshua G Wright, a prominent member of the bar, at the age of 54 years.

Timothy Savage, Cashier of the Commercial Bank, died in 1864, in the 72nd year of his age.

James Cassidey died in 1866, aged 74 years ; and James Fulton, journalist, in the same year.

P. K. Dickinson, one of our most public-spirited citizens, died in 1867, aged 73 years.

Daniel B. Baker, of the legal profession, died in 1868, aged 62 years.

General Alexander McRae, Civil Engineer, died also in

1868, aged 72 years; and Nicholas N. Nixon, aged 68 years.

In 1869, Nathaniel Greene Daniel, of Worth & Daniel, departed this life at the early age of 36 years, mourned by many devoted friends, in his untimely death, and regretted by the entire business community. At the time of his death he was among the most successful and enterprising of our business men. Quick in perception, vigorous in action, and steadfast in routine duty, he gave promise of a long and useful career, to be cut off in the prime of life, after months of painful suffering. Also Mr. John Wooster, an experienced man of business, and Hon. Samuel J. Person, formerly a Judge of the Superior Court, the former aged 78 and the latter 46 years.

Daniel L. Russell, an extensive planter, and a very successful one, died in 1871, aged 68 years.

Alfred L. Price, one of the founders of the *Wilmington Journal*, died in 1873, aged 56 years; and during the same year, Robert H. Cowan, the accomplished scholar, polished declaimer, and graceful elocutionist, passed from earth at the age of 48 years. "Whom the gods love, die early."

In 1873, John A. Taylor, who was intimately associated with every work of public utility that would advance the interest and increase the prosperity of Wilmington, departed this life at the age of 74, followed in the same year by Miles Costin, a retired merchant and prominent in every good work, 73 years of age, and Junius D. Gardner, formerly an officer in the Bank of Cape Fear, at the age of 77 years.

Dr. William A. Berry, for many years a successful practitioner of medicine, died in 1875, aged 71 years.

Dr. F. J. Cutlar, a most estimable gentleman, aged 75 years, died, also, in 1875.

In 1877, Robert Strange, the chivalrous gentleman, the accomplished scholar, the able jurist, while arguing a case in court, passed from an earthly to a higher tribunal, in the 53rd year of his age. The same year witnessed the death of Silas N. Martin, who had been Mayor of the city, and President of the Carolina Central Railroad, aged 49 years, also of Capt William B. Whitehead, an old and highly esteemed naval officer of the United States and Confederate States service, and Adam Empie, an advocate of rare powers, in the 56th year of his age.

In the year 1878, William A. Wright, died, aged 71 years, also Isaac B. Grainger, aged 37 years, and Hon. Hugh Waddell, aged 79 years. Mr. Wright and Mr. Waddell were both distinguished members of the bar. The latter won fame on the hustings, as an advocate in Legislative halls, and was prominent in the politics of the State. Mr. Wright preferred office practice, made no pretentions to oratory, but his mind was thoroughly disciplined and stored with legal lore. As a corporation counsel he had no superior in the State, and his ability in in that branch of the profession was recognized abroad. In private life he was distinguished for his playful humor, his fund of anecdote, his amiability and joyous vivacity. He was a close observer and diligent student, and his advice was sought by the old and grave, who valued his wisdom and learning as much as the more volatile his pleasantry and fun. Capt. Grainger was the architect of his own fortunes, and by his industry and energy attained a position which gave him great influence in financial circles. He was President of the Bank of New Hanover, whose affairs he managed with skill and success.

Dr. J. Francis King died in 1879, aged 48 years, and the following year, P. W. Fanning died, aged 81 years.

In 1881, Dr. Moses John DeRosset, aged 42 years, F. D. Poisson, attorney at law, aged 45 years, John Dawson, merchant, aged 80 years, Zebulon Latimer, retired merchant, aged 70 years, T. C. James, journalist, aged 43 years, and Henry Nutt, whose name will for all time be connected with our river and harbor improvements, passed away.

In 1882, they were followed to the grave, by Hon. R. S. French, formerly Judge of the Superior Court, and an ornament of the bar, aged 66, by General William McRae, one of the most gallant and distinguished officers in the Confederate army, and for many years prior to his death a successful railroad Engineer, Superintendent and President, aged 47 years, then by his attached friend and companion in arms, Captain David R. Murchison, one of our most successful merchants, who united boldness with sound judgment in business transactions, aged 44—a man of most extraordinary endowments, and unbounded industry—and possessing an indomitable spirit, which grappled with all opposing forces, overcame all obstacles, and which placed him, in spite of disease and constant physical suffering that would have prostrated an ordinary man, at the head of his profession; recognized by his fellow merchants as a leader, and esteemed by many who knew that under his uncompromising business exterior, shone a nature warm in sympathy with all distress and suffering, to which he responded quietly and liberally, and full of love and tenderness to those who knew him best, and to whose welfare and happiness he devoted his life. He was the first President of the Produce Exchange, having been the means of its organization, and for a few years prior to his death was largely interested in the Carolina Central Railway, of which he was its President. Levi A. Hart, a prominent citizen and proprietor of the Foundry Works, aged 73; Dr. J. C. Walker, a skillful physician and an amiable gentleman, aged 49, and James Dawson, a successful Banker, long identified with our city, and esteemed most by those with whom he was intimately related as a kind-hearted and devoted friend—aged 67.

Very many others could be mentioned, but the limits of this publication would not admit of its being done ; enough have been given, however, to show that there has been no degeneracy in our people since the old Colonial times. It is to be hoped that, in the not distant future, some one competent to the task may sketch the characters of those who once trod our streets and acted so well their parts in the busy scenes of life. It would not only be of great interest to those who are still upon the stage, but would excite future generations to imitate their example and to practice their virtues.

I wish to acknowledge most gratefully the courtesy of Mr. Richard J. Jones, through whom I have obtained much of the above interesting data, and the kindly offices of Col. James G. Burr, in matters of detail upon this subject, without whose invaluable assistance I could not have accomplished a satisfactory record.

In addition to "Oakdale," there are Bellevue, Pine Forest, (colored), and the National Cemeteries, all of which are well situated and carefully attended.

THE CHAMBER OF COMMERCE

was organized in Wilmington, September 11, 1866, for the mutual interests of those engaged in mercantile pursuits, and for the purpose of instituting a uniform system for the government of trade and commerce ; of adjusting amicably by arbitration, causes of dispute, and of exercising a general supervision of all matters pertaining to the commercial interest of the port.

In 1873 the organization of the Produce Exchange assumed control of certain branches of our trade not fully provided for by the Chamber of Commerce ; and on the 12th of June, 1873, the Constitution of the latter body was amended in all points at conflict with the new organization. The following named members have served as President of the Chamber : William L. DeRosset, five years ; Alfred

Martin, two years; Dr. W. W. Harriss, two years; A. H. VanBokkelen, seven years.

The present officers and members are as follows:

A. H. VANBOKKELEN..... ....President.
E. PESCHAU......................First Vice-President.
DONALD MACRAE...............Second Vice-President.
JOHN L. CANTWELL............Secretary and Treasurer.

EXECUTIVE COUNCIL.

WILLIAM CALDER,   GEORGE HARRISS,
JAS. H. CHADBOURN,   WM. L. DEROSSET,
R. E. HEIDE,   (and JAMES SPRUNT,
        ex-officio President Produce Exchange.)

MEMBERS.

Adrian & Vollers,	Kerchner & Calder Bros.,
Blossom, J. R., & Evans,	Kidder, Edward, & Son,
Burruss, E. E.,	McRary, W. H., & Co.,
Bank of New Hanover,	Martin, Alfred,
Cantwell, John L.,	Mitchell, B. F., & Son,
Chadbourn, J. H., & Co.,	Navassa Guano Company,
DeRosset & Co.,	Peschau, E. & Westermann,
DeRosset, Wm. L.,	Robinson, C. H.,
Eilers, H. B.,	Sprunt, Alex., & Son,
Harriss, Geo., & Co.,	VanBokkelen, A. H.,
Hall & Pearsall,	Worth & Worth,
Heide, R. E.,	Williams, Geo. W., & Co.

HONORARY.

George Davis.

The following is a record of the proceedings of the last annual meeting of the Chamber, held 7th March, 1883:

The annual meeting of the Chamber of Commerce not having been held in October, was ordered to be held yesterday at 12 o'clock.

The meeting was called to order by the President, who read his annual report, as follows:

CHAMBER OF COMMERCE, }
WILMINGTON, N. C., 7th March, 1883. }

The annual meeting of this Chamber has been delayed beyond the regular time by causes which were in a measure unavoidable.

The duties which remained to the Chamber of Commerce upon the formation of the Produce Exchange, in 1873, were "all questions arising bearing upon transportations, harbor and improvements, and other public interests of our city or State," including the general commerce of the country and its advancement, which duties since the last annual meeting have been confined to the improvement being made by the United States Government on the Cape Fear River from Wilmington to the ocean, and such other matters as were calculated to be of benefit to the commerce of our own port, as well as the general commercial interests of the United States.

The work now being carried out by the United States Government will be delayed in its completion because of the failure of Congress at its session just closed to pass a River and Harbor Bill. The present contracts, for which funds remain in hand, will soon be completed, giving a depth of sixteen feet at low water, twenty feet at high water from good anchorage, well protected at a point twelve miles below the city to Smithville, which will reduce the expense of, and detention by, lighterage greatly. Vessels can now load to fifteen feet at wharves in the city. Bald Head Channel, out to the ocean, shows on its bar a depth of fourteen feet at low water, with eighteen to twenty feet at high water.

A report kindly furnished by Mr. Henry Bacon, the efficient United States Assistant Engineer in charge of the improvements, under Lieutenant Colonel William P. Craighill, of the United States Engineer Corps, will be presented by Colonel William L. DeRosset, Chairman of the River and Harbor Committee of this Chamber, showing fully the present condition of the work.

The foreign and domestic commerce of this port shows a steady and healthy increase in amount of tonnage employed and value of exports and imports. Railroad connections now existing, and others contemplated, which will be completed when the depth of sixteen feet low water is obtained to the city, will bring, in addition to what will come by rivers to this port, three to ten-fold the present receipts. Larger coastwise steamers, with additional lines, are contemplated. Steamers to Europe will be employed for the next cotton crop, this port showing advantages as a shipping port over most others.

Our people who have desponded over seeing Wilmington a great commercial centre, now have good reason to hope and soon will have facts to assure them of a great future for our city by the sea.

Respectfully submitted,
A. H. VanBOKKELEN,
President.

The report of the Committee on River and Harbor Improvements was read by Colonel W. L. DeRosset, Chairman of that Committee, together with the accompanying letter of Mr. Henry Bacon, Engineer in charge, as follows:

A. H. VanBokkelen, Esq., President Chamber of Commerce:

SIR:—Your Committee have lately visited the Government works at New Inlet and Snow's Marsh, and having been favored with the accompanying report of Mr. Henry Bacon, United States Engineer in charge, which covers all the ground, and being prepared to fully endorse the statements of Mr. Bacon, beg leave to present the same in connection with this as their annual report.

Respectfully submitted,
WM. L. DeROSSET, Chairman,
GEO. HARRISS,
Committee on Bar and River Improvement.

A. H. VanBokkelen, Esq., President of the Chamber of Commerce, Wilmington, N. C.:

SIR :—At your request, I take pleasure in making a concise statement of the condition of the improvements of the Cape Fear River.

At the end of the fiscal year in 1878 the shortest soundings (or available depths) on the Bald Head Channel were 9 feet at mean low water, 11 feet in 1879, 13 feet in 1880, and 14 feet in 1881 and 1882.

The suction dredge *Woodbury* was in operation on the Bald Head Channel from April, 1879, to October, 1881. During the time 169,491 cubic yards of sand were dredged by it, and dumped in deep water, and a much larger amount was moved by the natural forces of the tidal currents from the channel and large area in the vicinity.

The work of closing the New Inlet by the dam was begun in October, 1875, but the practical stoppage of the water was not perceptible until the years of 1878 and 1879. The dam was thoroughly completed in June, 1881.

There can be no doubt of the beneficial effect of the operations of the suction dredge in concentrating the tidal currents, especially at the outer crest of the bar ; and it is probable that the available depth of the channel would have been further increased if the work had been continued. As it is, the results are more gratifying, as proving the power of the *natural forces* in the preservation of the Bald Head Channel.

It is obvious that the value of all improvements depends on the preservation of the entrance channel.

Much has been said about the "swashes" across the narrow beach of Smith's Island. During past years, and before the present improvements were initiated, breaches were made by the sea across this beach, and were closed by natural causes. Those of 1857 were especially remarkable. The great storm of April 13th, 1877, caused the present breaches or swashes. They were subsequently partially closed by natural causes, but the completion of the New Inlet dam created a greater difference in the relative times of the tides in the bay and sea, and thus increased the velocity of the tidal currents, out and in the swashes, which has prevented the natural closures.

The nearest swash is about two miles from the main river channel, and there are wide intervening shoals, and there is, therefore, no immediate danger from the swashes; and they have no perceptible effect on the main currents of the river. But, inasmuch as the sea is gradually encroaching on the beach and shoals, and producing an indenture at the swashes, it is only a question of time when a defence must be made.

The matter is now under consideration by a board of engineers. It is probable that they will decide that it is best to begin the work soon on an inner line, from Zeke's Island to the big marsh across the shoal waters, and nearly on the neutral line of the tidal currents, thus completely separating the river from the bay and swashes, in which case there can be but little doubt of the natural closure of the swashes and the re-formation of the beach.

A large portion of the available appropriation—from $110,000 to $130,000—is now in reserve and can be used for this purpose, if so decided.

The work of dredging now in progress is under two contracts. Those of G. H. Ferris, of May, 1881, for about 750,000 cubic yards, and the National Dredging Company, of October, 1882, for 450,000 cubic yards. Both contracts terminate June 30, 1883. They will complete the channel along Snow's Marsh, and to the deep water above, to 270 feet in width and 16 feet deep at mean low water; and also the channel across the next shoal above to the same depth, and probably to the same width, thus securing 16 feet depth at low water to a point about twelve miles below Wilmington, where there is good anchorage in 16 feet depth at low water. The prospect of finishing the contracts at the appointed time is, perhaps, a little doubtful, but it is certain the channel by Snow's Marsh and above to deep water will be finished so far that it can be used within the next two months. This will completely avoid the Horse Shoe Channel and practically save at least one day in getting deep draft vessels from Wilmington to the sea. At the present time the new channel is finished to 200 feet width along Snow's Marsh, and to 235 feet for the first half mile above. Then it is 130 feet wide for the next quarter of a mile, and on the remaining or upper portion it is 75 feet in width—and the cut making it 100 is in progress. The reach of the new channel above Snow's Marsh is approximately in the line with the ebb and flood tidal currents, and there is every reason to expect its permanence in depth and width. The New Inlet dam remains as finished in 1881. There has been no settlement or other signs of deterioration; on the contrary, it is constantly becoming more and more solidified by oysters and barnacles. The passage of water through the small stones is becoming less and less. The sand beach is forming fast over the site of the Carolina Shoals, and is above high water for nearly half the distance from shore near Fort Fisher to the head of Smith's Island, and the shoals are bare at low tide over most of the remaining distance. There is a prospect at no distant time that the New Inlet basin will be converted into a *Sound*, with perhaps one or two small inlets across the newly formed outer beach.

It is unfortunate that Congress has failed to make any appropriations for the coming fiscal year. It is hoped that one will be made early after the meeting of Congress in December next, in which case the delay will be less serious.

My estimate of the amount required for the two years ending June 30, 1884, was $674,308, of which $225,000 was appropriated in 1882, leaving a balance needed—say of

$450,000—to complete the dredging for 16 feet depth at low water to Wilmington and the thorough defence against the swashes.

Very respectfully, &c.,

HENRY BACON,
United States Assistant Engineer.

QUARANTINE.

Prior to 1868 all quarantine power was invested in the Commissioners of Navigation, who were required to appoint a Port Physician, and to make and enforce such rules and regulations for the protection of the inhabitants from infectious diseases, as they deemed necessary. But in that year (1868) the Legislature passed an Act which divested the Commissioners of all quarantine power and authority, and relieved them of all responsibility.

The Act provided that a quarantine station should be established opposite Deep Water Point, and that the Governor should designate some physician who should act as medical quarantine officer for that station, where all vessels subject to quarantine should be brought to anchor, and be subject to such rules and regulations as the medical quarantine officer might prescribe.

In 1879 this law was amended so as to provide for the appointment, by the President of the State Board of Health, of two physicians residing in Wilmington, who, with the medical quarantine officer, should make and enforce all necessary quarantine regulations for the port of Wilmington. This law is still in force.

This amendment was a wise provision against the introduction of infectious diseases by the error or oversight of a single individual empowered to act with unlimited discretion ; and the present arrangement has been found to satisfy all classes of our people. The present Board is composed of Dr. W. G. Curtis, medical quarantine officer appointed by the Governor, resident at Smithville, and

Drs. Thomas F. Wood and George G. Thomas, residing at Wilmington, who issue quarantine rules and regulations every spring.

The Regulations for 1882 are given below ; at this date (20th March) the Regulations for 1883 have not been issued, but it is thought by the Board that no material change will be made :

QUARANTINE REGULATIONS, }
PORT OF WILMINGTON, N. C., March 23, 1882. }

The quarantine will go into effect on the first day of May.

The following Quarantine Regulations will be enforced for the port of Wilmington, and the penalty of $200 for every violation thereof strictly enforced. Pilots violating the same are liable to a loss of their branch :

To entitle a vessel to free pratique' in the port of Wilmington, from whatever port she may come, she must show—

1st. A clean bill of health, in accordance with the recommendations of the National Board of Health.

2d. She must show, to the satisfaction of the Quarantine Board, that no case of infectious disease has occurred on board at the port of departure or during the passage.

3d. She must be thoroughly cleansed and disinfected and ballast discharged at the Quarantine Station, and perform any other requirements that may be designated by the Quarantine Physician.

4th. After performing all these requirements, she may receive a permit in writing from the Quarantine Physician, which permit must be endorsed by the Quarantine Board before she will be allowed to come to the city.

5th. Vessels subject to the above regulations will be designated by notice from time to time to their pilots and others interested in commerce, and all such vessels must come to anchor at the Quarantine Station, opposite Deep Water Point, as far to the eastward of the channel as is practicable, so as to allow them swinging room, and not depart thence without written permission from the Quarantine Physician.

6th. Universal cleanliness must be preserved on board all vessels detained in quarantine—the forecastle, steerage and cabin must be scrubbed, all foul wearing apparel and bed clothing of officers, passengers and seamen must be washed and aired, and all infected articles destroyed, and disinfection practiced as directed by the Quarantine Physician.

The bilge water must be pumped out twice a day, and water from alongside put in until the water pumped out shall be clear and free from any offensive smell; and wind sails must be kept up in each hatchway, and trimmed to the wind whenever the weather permits.

Commanders of vessels are accountable for all irregularities committed on board their respective vessels, and for the conduct of such of their people as they may send on shore by permission of the Quarantine Officer; and if any person shall leave a vessel in quarantine, or go on board of such vessels without the written permission of the Quarantine Officer, he shall, on conviction, suffer punishment as by law provided; and all persons belonging to a vessel in quarantine are strictly forbidden to take on board any person who did not arrive in such vessel, without a regular permit from the Quarantine Officer.

All communication between vessels in quarantine is expressly prohibited, and no boat or craft is permitted to go alongside a vessel in quarantine except the master thereof have a written permission from the Quarantine Officer.

Provisions and other necessaries intended to be sent on board vessels at quarantine must follow the same rules and regulations which apply to other communications with the vessels, and all arrangements for discharging and taking a cargo must be made with the sanction of the Quarantine Officer.

Colors must be worn, and a light must be hoisted at night so long as the vessel is detained at quarantine.

7th. Whenever for any reason the Quarantine Board resident in Wilmington shall not consider it safe for a vessel to go to the city she may be allowed to discharge and take in cargo at the Quarantine Station, under the following conditions: After receiving a permit in writing from the Quarantine Physician, allowing her to load, the captain may permit all necessary lighters, stevedores and laborers to go on board or alongside; but such lighters, stevedores and laborers shall be considered in quarantine, and subject to all the rules and regulations which apply to the vessel itself, according to the tenor of these regulations, and shall be subject to detention for observation, fumigation and such other measures as the public safety may require, and the expenses of fumigation, inspection and permits shall be paid by the vessel for which the lighters, stevedores or laborers are employed; and any vessel, stevedore, lighterman or laborer violating these regulations, shall, in addition to the penalty of $200 provided by law, be liable to be sent out of the limits of the city of Wilmington until November 1st, next ensuing.

Vessels engaged in discharging ballast, or any other service performed previous to fumigation, must remain in quarantine during the entire season unless permitted in writing by the Quarantine Physician to engage in other business.

8th. All persons residing in the city of Wilmington who desire to visit vessels in quarantine, must first get a written permit from the Quarantine Board resident in Wilmington enabling them to return to the city, and must present this permit to the Quarantine Physician for his indorsement before they can go on board of any vessel in quarantine.

9th. Pilots are notified that they must make inquiry as to the existence of contagious disease on board of vessels before boarding, and if by any means they become exposed to infection, they must remain on board such vessel until permitted to go ashore by the Quarantine Physician.

10th. Tow Boats and Steamboats are notified that they must not go alongside of any vessel subject to quarantine for any purpose until such vessel is regularly discharged from quarantine by written permit from the Quarantine Physician.   W. G. CURTIS, M. D.,
                                  Quarantine Physician.

J. C. WALKER, M. D.,   } Consultants.
THOMAS F. WOOD, M. D. }

THE WILMINGTON PRODUCE EXCHANGE

was organized April, 1873, and incorporated September 16, 1873. The object of this organization was to provide and regulate a suitable room for a Produce Exchange in the city of Wilmington, to inculcate just and equitable principles of trade, to maintain uniformity in commercial usages, to acquire, preserve and disseminate valuable business information, and to adjust controversies and misunderstandings between its members.

The following named members have served as President since its organization: D. R. Murchison, D. G. Worth, C. H. Robinson, R. E. Calder and James Sprunt.

The present officers and members are as follows:

JAMES SPRUNT........ ....President.
H. C. McQUEEN........................Vice President.

BOARD OF MANAGERS.

R. E. CALDER,   R. MOORE,
B. F. HALL,   ALFRED MARTIN,   .
W. R. KENAN.

MEMBERS.

Adrian & Vollers,   Bond, T. E.,
Atkinson & Manning,   Burruss, E. E.,
Barker, E. G., & Co.,   Bank of New Hanover,
Boney, G., & Sons,   Cantwell, John L.,

Chess-Carley Co.,
Carolina Central Railroad,
Crow, John E.,
Covington, E. P. & Son,
Cazaux, A. D.,
DeRosset & Co.,
Daniel, John H.,
Gore, D. L.,
Gore, Albert,
Greene, A. H.,
Gordon, John W. & Bro.,
Hall & Pearsall,
Heide & Co.,
Hicks, R. W.,
Harriss, W. W.,
Wilmington & Weldon R.R.
Johnson, Harding,
Kerchner & Calder Bros.,
Kenan & Forshee,
Lilly, E.,
Love, C. S. & Co.,
Metts, James I.,
Mitchell, B. F. & Son,

Martin, Alfred,
Mebane, C. P.,
McNair, S. P.,
Northrop, Samuel,
Northrop & Cumming,
Newbury, F. A.,
Oldham, W. P., & Co.,
Peschau, E. & Westermann,
· Paterson, Downing & Co.,
Pennypacker, E. J.,
Rankin & Birdsey,
Robinson & King,
Sprunt, Alex. & Son,
Shotter, S. P., & Co.,
Smith, C. E., & Co.,
Turrentine, J. R.,
VanBokkelen, A. H.,
VanAmringe, Geo.O.,
Whitehead, W. A.,
Worth & Worth,
Williams, Geo. W., & Co.,
Woody & Currie,
Willard, A. A.

SUBSCRIBERS.

The Daily Review.   *The Morning Star.*

The rooms of the Exchange are quite inadequate, not more than half the members being comfortably provided for. It is hoped that the next Board of Managers will furnish more suitable accommodations, and that the rooms may not only be attractive to the members, but serve as a place of resort for our business people at any hour of the day. The stock reports and other statistics required by the organization are most creditably prepared by the Secretary, Col. J. L. Cantwell, whose long experience and remarkable accuracy especially fit him for this important duty. The Board of Managers have much pleasure in testifying to his skill and faithfulness.

In an old pamphlet "On the Trade of Wilmington, "North Carolina, and of the produce exportable from the "River Cape Fear, the season and prospects taken into "view May 1st, 1815," by Joshua Potts, the following interesting information is given under the head of "*Remarks*" : "It is unadvisable, and often disadvanta. geous, for a merchant in a distant State or foreign port, to dispatch a ship to Wilmington under orders for a cargo of our produce, without first having written to his correspon. dent of particulars required. *Four to six weeks previous notice* to the agent is always requisite, that he may have time and opportunity to procure the produce described, at the best advantage, and have it in readiness by the time of the arrival of such ship. Great detention and disap. pointment often happens in consequence of voyages being abruptly commenced, as, but seldom, peculiar kinds of produce can be had on sudden notice."

The above contrasts strangely with the method of the present day. Several cargoes at a time are now frequently sold within as many hours by cable to foreign markets. A remarkable instance of improved facilities occurred here a few weeks ago, when a member of this Exchange offered by cable to Liverpool, at 9.30 A. M., a cargo of cotton, which was not only immediately accepted, but confirmed by a cable received in the Wilmington office 63 minutes after the dispatch of the first message to Liverpool. Thus an entire transaction was made and confirmed with a foreign market within an hour and a quarter—*annihilating time* to the extent of about three hours and three-quarters.

WESTERN UNION TELEGRAPH.

There is no record of the date of the first appearance of the telegraph in Wilmington, but an office was probably established here by the old Washington and New Orleans

Magnetic Telegraph Company, about the year 1850. The system then generally in use was the old Morse register system—everything being recorded on paper in Morse characters, and transcribed by the operator—a slow and tedious process.

About 1858, the use of paper began to be laid aside by a great many operators, who discovered that *sound* reading was quite as safe ; and while lessening the labor, it expedited the business by saving a great deal of time that had before been consumed in translating from the paper. Now, and for fifteen years past, the use of the old Morse paper register has been discontinued almost entirely. Hence the system in use here at present is that in general use in this country—the "Morse"—by which the message is taken from the instrument by sound, at the very moment it is sent by the transmitting office, and is ready for delivery at the end of the line as soon as the last word is finished by the sending office.

There are other systems such as the "Automatic," the "Harmonic," and some of which very little is known, but they all work by complicated means, and require a small army of clerks to translate and transcribe that which has been received. None have yet stood a *practical* test that would make them desirable as a substitute for the old, first invention, of Morse.

During the past three years there have been built here two new wires, in which Wilmington has some interest— as they have given us better facilities for handling an important class of business. One of them is the New York Cotton Exchange wire, giving us direct communication with the Cotton Exchange, and Wall Street, in New York.

The other is the Carolina Central wire, which, in the cotton season is an important one to cotton merchants.

The present facilities of the office are as follows : 1 New York Commercial News Department wire—direct with the New York Main office ; 1 New York Cotton Exchange wire, direct ; 2 Charleston wires ; 2 Augusta wires, (one of these used to Savannah at times) ; 1 Washington and Raleigh wire ; 1 New Berne and Raleigh wire ; 2 Richmond wires ; 2 Charlotte wires, (one extending to Shelby).

Some of these wires of course take in a number of intermediate stations between Wilmington and Augusta, and between Wilmington and Weldon.

During the past two years rates have been reduced very materially, the reduction averaging at least twenty per cent. The volume of business here has increased in the last three years about one-fourth, and the receipts about ten per cent.

Good progress has been made with us in the manner of handling business during this period. There has been a gradual lessening in the time of dispatching business, and in the transmission of the replies thereto, notably on northern and western lines. Of course there is still room for improvement, especially in the further reduction of rates in view of the yearly increase in the dividends declared by this immense monopoly.

The cable business, up to last month, has been larger this season than ever before—showing that our foreign business is growing, or that people are becoming habituated to the use of the cable.

The staff of this office is as follows :

W. H. STERLING,.......................... ...Manager.

OPERATORS.

N. B. TOPPING,   R. J. McILHENNY,
C. W. PETERSON,   J. T. HAMBRICK.

CLERKS.

E. B. BURKHEIMER,   JOHN SHOLAR.

Besides six messengers and two battery and line men.

Our general business community will bear cheerful testimony, not only to the unvarying courtesy and obliging

disposition of Manager Sterling, but to the remarkable
industry and wonderful accuracy and patience of those
quiet, solemn people, upon whom so much depends in our
daily business transactions.

WILMINGTON TELEPHONE EXCHANGE

is licensed under patents of Alexander Graham Bell, and
was opened in 1879. The present number of subscribers is
81, and the system is generally adopted by our business
people. The city of Wilmington was one of the first
in the South to show its enterprise in the adoption of the
Telephone Exchange system. In 1880 the method of working was much improved by the introduction of the "Law
System" of Central Office "switching," which is claimed
to be the best in the world.

Wilmington was the second city in the United States to
adopt the Telephonic Fire Alarm System, the wisdom of
the action being frequently demonstrated.

Private lines are in operation with the main office to the
Navassa Guano Works, at Meares' Bluff, and to Mason-
boro' Sound.

There is probably no more obliging and intelligent
Manager in the service than Mr. J. C. White, in charge
here, who affords every facility for prompt and satisfactory
communication with the members of the Exchange.

It is a matter of interest with reference to this subject
that experience has proved the impossibility of using the
telephone satisfactorily for greater distances than a hundred miles.

Laboratory telephonic tests have worked through a
"resistance" of wire equal to 150,000 miles of telegraph
line, but on actual lines the leakage of electricity from the
wire to the ground, dampness in the atmosphere, and other
magnetic disturbances render the transmission of speech
far less easy than was at first expected by electricians. By
submarine wire the circuit is confined to lesser distances--

that is to say, a land wire will work satisfactorily five times longer than a cable wire, so that, although telephonic messages have been sent by cable sixty to eighty miles, they are practically of no use at a greater distance than twenty or thirty miles.

A recent publication asserts that experiments made with the Gray-Harmonic system and Dorrance telephone between Cleveland, Ohio, and New York, over the heavy, copper wire of the Postal Telegraph Company have demonstrated the feasibility of connecting the larger cities of the Middle and Eastern States by telephone, and a record is made of alleged thoroughly successful tests over a wire of 650 miles in proof of this. The statement is also made that a test of speaking over 1,000 miles of wire has been successful; but it is believed by many electricians to be either a mistake or altogether untrue.

WILMINGTON POST-OFFICE STATISTICS.

For the year ending January 31, 1883.

Number of pieces of mail matter originating and received at this office for transmission :

First class matter, number of pieces, . . 1,568,580	
Second " " " " " ..1,227,920	
Third " " " " " .. 191,568	
Fourth " " " " " .. 20,448	
Total number of pieces mailed. . . .	3,008,516
Number of pieces received at this office for delivery,. . . . . .4,036,240—4,036,240	
Total No. of pieces handled	7,044,756

MONEY ORDER BUSINESS.

Receipts.

Deposits received from other offices. . . . $124,800	
Received from Money Orders issued, . . 78,330— $203,130	

Disbursements.

Money Orders paid,................ $108,140
Deposited order of Department........ 94,990— $203,130

Total Money Order business,...... $400,260

REGISTERED LETTER BUSINESS.

Number letters registered at this office, 8,325
Number of registered letters delivered
  at this office,...................... 7,440
Number of registered letters in transit, 37,420

Total number of registered letters
  handled,...................... 53,185

RECEIPTS FOR SALE OF STAMPS,

Stamped envelopes, Postal cards, &c., $32,342

International Money Orders are issued in

The Dominion of Canada,	France,
New Foundland,	Algiers,
England,	Switzerland,
Scotland, ·	Austria,
Wales,	Hungary,
Ireland,	Italy,
British India,	Jamaica,
Germany,	New Zealand,
Denmark,	New South Wales,
Sweden,	Victoria,
Norway,	Belgium,
Luxemberg,	Tasmania.
The Netherlands,	

The general business of the office has increased fully forty per cent. in the last four years, and the administration of its affairs by the present Post-Master, E. R. Brink, who has been repeatedly renominated, is most efficient, and, I believe, entirely satisfactory to all classes of our citizens.

Arrangements are being made for a free delivery of the mails throughout our city, which has been proposed through Post-Master Brink, and our city government is preparing for this improvement by a proper designation of the streets and numbering of the houses.

LUMBER.

In the beginning of this century Michaux, with reference to the long-leaf pine (*Pinus Australis*), wrote as follows : "This invaluable tree is known both in the countries which produce it and in those to which it is exported, by different names: in the first it is called long-leaved pine, yellow pine, pitch pine, and brown pine; in the Northern States, Southern pine and red pine ; and in England and the West Indies, Georgia pitch pine. I have preferred the first denomination, because this species has longer leaves than any other eastward of the Mississippi, and because the names of yellow pine and pitch pine, which are more commonly employed, serve, even in the Middle States, to designate two species entirely distinct and extensively diffused. The specific epithet *Australis* is more appropriate than that of *Palustris*, which has hitherto been applied to it by botanists, but which suggests an erroneous idea of the situations in which it grows.

Towards the north the long-leaved pine first makes its appearance near Norfolk, in Virginia, where the *pine-barrens* begin. It seems to be especially assigned to dry, sandy soils, and it is found, almost without interruption, in the lower part of the Carolinas, Georgia and the Floridas, over a tract more than 600 miles long from northeast to southwest, and more than 100 miles broad from the sea towards the mountains of the Carolinas and Georgia. I have ascertained three points, about 100 miles apart, where it does not grow : the first, 8 miles from the river Neuse, in

North Carolina, on the road from Louisburgh to Raleigh; the second, between Chester and Winnsboro, in South Carolina; the third, 12 miles north of Augusta, in Georgia. Where it begins to show itself towards the river Neuse, it is united with the loblolly pine, the yellow pine, the pond pine, the black jack oak and the scrub oak; but immediately beyond Raleigh it holds almost exclusive possession of the soil, and is seen in company with the pines just mentioned only on the edges of the swamps enclosed in the *barrens;* even there not more than one stock in a hundred is of another species. With this exception the long-leaved pine forms the unbroken mass of woods which covers this extensive country. But between Fayetteville and Wilmington, in North Carolina, the scrub oak is found in some districts disseminated in the *barrens*, and, except this species of pine, it is the only tree capable of subsisting in so dry and sterile a soil.

The mean stature of the long-leaved pine is 60 or 70 feet, with an uniform diameter of 15 or 18 inches for two-thirds of this height. Some stocks, favored by local circumstances, attain much larger dimensions, particularly in East Florida. The bark is somewhat furrowed, and the epidermis detaches itself in thin transparent sheets. The leaves are about a foot long, of a beautiful, brilliant green, united to the number of three in the same sheath, and collected in bunches at the extremity of the branches; they are longer and more numerous on the young stocks, which are sometimes cut by the negroes for brooms. The buds are very large, white, fringed, and not resinous.

The bloom takes place in April; the male flowers form masses of divergent, violet-coloured aments about 2 inches long; in drying they shed great quantities of yellowish pollen, which is diffused by the wind and forms a momentary covering on the surface of the land and water. The cones are very large, being 7 or 8 inches long, and 4 inches thick when open, and are armed with small retorted spines.

In the fruitful year they are ripe about the 15th of October, and shed their seeds the same month. The kernel is of an agreeable taste, and is contained in a thin white shell, surmounted by a membrane ; in every other species of American pine the shell is black. Sometimes the seeds are very abundant and are voraciously eaten by wild turkeys, squirrels, and the swine that live almost wholly in the woods. But in the unfruitful year, a forest of a hundred miles in extent may be ransacked without finding a single cone ; this probably occasioned the mistake of the French, who, in 1567 attempted a settlement in Florida, that the woods were filled with superb pines that never yielded seed.

The long-leaved pine contains but little sap ; several trunks 15 inches in diameter at the height of 3 feet, which I have myself measured, had 10 inches of perfect wood. Many stocks of this size are felled for commerce, and none are received for exportation of which the heart is not 10 inches in diameter when squared.

The concentric circles, in a trunk fully developed, are close and at equal distances, and the resinous matter, which is abundant, is more uniformly distributed than in the other species ; hence the wood is stronger, more compact, and more durable ; it is, besides, fine-grained and susceptible of a bright polish. These advantages give it a preference over every other pine ; but its quality is modified by the nature of the soil in which it grows ; in the neighborhood of the sea, where only a thin layer of mold reposes on the sand, it is more resinous than where the mold is 5 or 6 inches thick ; the stocks that grow upon the first mentioned soil are called pitch pine, and the others yellow pine, as if they were distinct species.

This wood subserves a great variety of uses in the Carolinas, Georgia and the Floridas ; four-fifths of the houses are built of it, except the roof, which is covered with shingles of cypress ; but in the country the roof is also of pine, and is renewed after 15 or 18 years, a considerable interval in a climate so warm and humid.

A vast consumption takes place for the enclosure of cultivated fields. In naval architecture this is the most esteemed of the pines : in the Southern States, the keel, the beams the side-planks, and the pins by which they are attached to the ribs, are of this tree. For the deck, it is preferred to the true yellow pine, and is exported for that purpose, to Philadelphia, New York, etc., where it is in request, also, for the flooring of houses.

In certain soils its wood contracts a reddish hue, and it is for that reason known in the dock-yards of the Northern States by the name of red pine. Wood of this tint is considered the best, and in the opinion of some ship-wrights, it is more durable on the sides of vessels, and less liable to injury from worms, than the oak.

The long-leaved pine is the only species exported from the Southern States to the West Indies. A numerous fleet of small vessels is employed in this traffic, particularly from Wilmington, in North Carolina, and Savannah, in Georgia.

The stuff destined for the Colonial market is cut into every form required in the construction of houses and of vessels ; what is sent to England is in planks from 15 to 30 feet long and 10 or 12 inches broad ; they are called *ranging timbers*, and are sold at 8 or 10 dollars a hundred cubic feet. The vessels freighted with this timber repair chiefly to Liverpool, where it is said to be employed in the building of ships and of wet-docks : it is called Georgia pitch pine, and is sold 25 or 30 per cent. higher than any other pine imported from the United States.

From the diversified uses of this wood an idea may be formed of the consumption ; to which must be added a waste of a more disastrous kind, which it seems impossible to arrest. Since the year 1804 extensive tracts of the finest pines are seen covered only with dead trees. In 1802 I remarked a similar phenomenon among the yellow pines in East Tennessee. This catastrophe is felt among the Scotch firs which people the forests of the north of Europe, and is wrought by swarms of small insects, which lodge themselves in different parts of the stock, insinuate themselves under the bark, penetrate into the body of the tree, and cause it to perish in the course of the year.

The value of the long-leaved pine does not reside exclusively in its wood : it supplies nearly all the resinous matter used in the United States in ship-building, and a large residue for exportation to the West Indies and Great Britain. In this view its place can be supplied by no other species : those which afford the same product being dispersed through the woods or collected in inaccessible places. In the Northern States the lands which, at the commencement of their settlement, were covered with the pitch pine, were exhausted in 25 or 30 years, and for more than half a century have ceased to furnish tar. The *pine-barrens* are of vast extent, and are covered with trees of the finest growth ; but they cannot all be rendered profitable from the difficulty of communication with the sea. Formerly tar was made in all the lower parts of the Carolinas and Georgia, and throughout the Floridas vestiges are everywhere seen of kilns that have served in the combustion of resinous wood. At present this branch of industry is confined to the lower districts of North Carolina, which furnish almost all the tar and turpentine exported from Wilmington and other ports."

Professor Kerr, in his Physiographical Description of North Carolina, refers to the trees of this State as follows :

"It will be seen from the United States Census tables for 1870, that of its 50,000 square miles of territory, 40,000 are still covered with forests. The range and variety of prevalent and characteristic species of growth, being of course proportioned to those of the climate and soil, are very great.

There are, in fact, three well-marked and broadly distinguished forest regions, corresponding to and dependent
upon the three geographical sub-divisions, Eastern, Middle
and Western. And while the first section is characterized
by a growth common in its prominent features to that in
the Gulf States, as the long-leaf pine, cypress, &c.; the
western or mountain section contains many species familiar
in the White Mountains, and in New York. Among the
most distinctive, abundant and valuable species are the
pines, oaks, hickories, cypress and juniper.

Pines are the predominant growth of the eastern section.
there are eight species in the State, the most important
being the long-leaf (*pinus australis*), the yellow, (*pinus
mitis*), and the white (*pinus strobus*). The long-leaf pine
is found only in the eastern or sea-coast region; the yellow
pine abounds throughout the State ; the white pine is
limited to the higher mountain regions.

The long-leaf pine is the predominant growth of the
eastern section of the State, and occupies almost exclusively
a broad belt quite across the State, and extending from
near the coast more than a hundred miles into the interior,
covering a territory of near 15,000 square miles. This is
one of the most valuable of all trees, on account of the
number and importance of the uses it subserves. It is
shipped in the form of lumber for civil and naval architecture to all parts of the world, and is unequalled for these
purposes, on account of its strength and durability. It
furnishes the naval stores of commerce, known in all parts
of the world ; the forests of this State furnishing twice as
much as all the other States together. From the rosin of
this tree is made the rosin-oil of commerce, and this substance also supplies the Southern towns with gas.

The yellow pine furnishes an important building timber
in all parts of the State.

The white pine is confined to the spurs and plateaus
of the mountain and Piedmont regions, being found in

great abundance in some counties, and of great size, three feet and more in diameter, and one hundred to one hundred and fifty feet high.

The other species are less widely distributed and less valuable, except the *Pinus tæda*, which, in the Eastern section, sometimes attains a great size, and furnishes an excellent building and ship timber.

The oaks rank with the pines in value, and excel them in variety of uses, number of species and extent of distribution. While the pine, (a single species,) gives character to about one-third of the forest area of the State, the oaks dominate not less than two-thirds. There are twenty species in the United States, all of them found in North Carolina, with possibly one insignificant exception; Among these the most important are :

The white oaks, of which there are several species, (the most valuable), *Quercus alba*, *Q. obtusiloba*, (post oak and *Q. prinus*,) forming extensive forests in all sections of the State. On account of its strength and durability and great abundance, its uses are important and manifold, both for domestic purposes and for export in the form of staves and ship timber. The ship-yards of Liverpool are already seeking their material in the forests of middle North Carolina.

Several other species of oak are also of wide and varied use, chiefly the red oak (*Q. rubra*), black oak (*Q. tinctoria*), and willow oak (*Q. phellos*), which are abundant throughout the middle and western district, and often grow to a very great size. Live oak (*Q. virens*) is found only in the seaboard region, whose value in ship-building is well-known.

Hickory.—Of this tree there are nine species in North America, and seven of them are found in this State, and three species in all parts of it, and in abundance, and often of great size. But little use has hitherto been made of this tree, except as fuel and for wagons and handles; but being one of the most dense, rigid, heavy and iron-like of our woods, it has recently come into great demand, and many large handle and spoke factories have been erected within a few years, whose products are shipped by millions to Europe, California, Australia and all mining countries especially. The forests of North Carolina will supply this world-wide demand for many years.

Walnut exists in two species, one, the common black walnut (*Juglans nigra*), throughout the State, but most abundantly in the middle district. It is a most valuable wood, being very compact, durable, free from attacks of insects, of a very fine dark brown color, and capable of a high polish. It is the most popular and universally used cabinet wood in the United States, but is so common in the middle and western sections of this State that large farms are fenced with it.

The Chestnut (*Castanea vesca*) is one of our largest forest trees, sometimes 10 feet in diameter and 80 to 90 feet high, found mostly and abundantly in the Piedmont and mountain regions of the State, where it is much esteemed and used for fencing, on account of its great durability and facility of working. It is also valued for its abundant crop of fruit, which, with the acorns of the oaks, is the principal dependence of the hog-raisers of the mountain counties.

Poplar (*Liriodendron tulipifera*) is one of the largest and handsomest of our forest trees, and occurs in all parts of the State, attaining its greatest size in the mountains. It is much used for building and other domestic purposes as a substitute for pine, combining lightness and facility of working with rigidity and durability.

Cypress (*Taxodium distichum*) abounds in the swamps and lowlands of the east, forming the almost exclusive growth of several thousand square miles of territory. It grows to a great size, the wood is very light, durable and much used for the manufacture of shingles, which are exported in immense numbers to all the Northern Atlantic ports. It is also used for building purposes, and for staves and telegraph poles, water vessels, etc.

Juniper, or white cedar (*Cupressus thyoides*) is found in the same region, though not so abundant, and is used for the same purposes as the cypress, especially for shingles and cooper work, for which it is even preferred to the latter.

Besides these are the maple (6 species), birch (3 species), beech, ash (4 species), poplar (3 species), elm (3 species), mulberry, sassafras, gum (4 species) dogwood, persimmon, holly, locust (2 species), sycamore, linn, linden or lime (3 species), buckeye (2 species), wild cherry, red cedar, white cedar, magnolia (7 species), willow (4 species), and others, of various uses in domestic economy ; many of them valued as shade and ornamental trees, a number of them much prized as cabinet woods ; among which may be mentioned the black walnut, already described, the red cedar, sometimes nearly equalling the mahogany in beauty of color and grain, free from insects and aromatic ; the black birch, or mountain mahogany, and wild cherry, both of very ornamental grain, taking a high polish ; and so also the curly and bird's eye maple ; the holly, a beautiful, close-grained, white wood, taking a brilliant polish. It will readily be imagined what variety, richness and beauty these numerous species, belonging to so many and widely differing families of plants, must impart to the forests of this State, and what a vast mine of wealth they must become in the near future.

Of the twenty kinds of timber used in the ship-yards in New York, nearly all are found in the forests of this State."

With reference to this important and interesting subject Messrs. E. J. Hale & Son, publishers, New York, have just issued a most valuable work by Mr. P. M. Hale, of Raleigh, entitled "Woods and Timbers of North Carolina," from which much profitable information may be gathered.

Having already quoted at greater length his authority on "*Pinus Australis*," I have only to add Mr. Hale's estimate, for North Carolina, of the long-leaved pine supply, which he gives as follows :

Bladen	288,000,000	feet.
Brunswick	141,000,000	"
Chatham	448,000,000	"
Columbus	288,000,000	"
Cumberland	800,000,000	"
Duplin	21,000,000	"
Harnett	486,000,000	"
Johnston	563,000,000	"
Moore	504,000,000	"
New Hanover	96,000,000	"
Onslow	34,000,000	"
Robeson	864,000,000	"
Sampson	602,000,000	"
Wake	48,000,000	"
Wayne	40,000,000	"
Total	5,229,000,000	"

STEAM SAW MILLS.

The first steam Saw Mill established in Wilmington, so far as can be ascertained, was erected on the western side of the Cape Fear River, on the site now occupied by the Guano Warehouse of the Champion Compress Company, by a person named Mazerretti, in the year 1818.

Sometime afterwards Mr. Henry Howard purchased the lot and built a larger and more valuable mill. Hutchinson and Milan (the latter subsequently British Vice Consul at this port) were also engaged in the milling business between 1820-'25.

Edward B. Dudley and P. K. Dickinson, constituting the firm of Dudley & Dickinson, and two of the most prominent citizens of Wilmington, the one first Governor of the State, elected by the direct vote of the people, and the other identified with the material prosperity of the town, erected a mill at the southern extremity of the settlement about the year 1828.

In 1833–'34 Mr. Aaron Lazarus established the first planing mill in North Carolina upon the site now occupied by Messrs. Northrop & Cumming, and which was destroyed by fire a few months after its erection. Mr. J. K. McIlhenny also owned a mill at or near the locality of Messrs. Dudley & Dickinson's, which he afterwards sold to Capt. Gilbert Potter, who operated it successfully, first under his own name, afterwards under the firm name of Potter & Kidder ; and it is still continued by Messrs. Edward Kidder & Son, and is well known in all lumber markets as one of the most successful mills in the country.

It is worthy of notice, and should be put upon record, that the credit of utilizing the saw-dust for fuel, by which a heavy expense in running steam saw mills has been saved, is due to Mr. Edward Kidder of this city. He was the first to carry the idea, which had long baffled operators, into successful application, and is entitled to the honor which is justly his due.

Mr. P. K. Dickinson, after disposing of his interest in his mill below the town, built another, with planing mill attached, where the depot of the Carolina Central Railroad is now, which was taken down when the Company came into possession of the property.

Some years ago a small mill stood at the foot of Walnut street, put up by a Mr. Nickerson. About the year 1840 Col. John McRae erected the Harrison mill very near that of Nickerson's, and on this site, also, the recently destroyed mill of Mr. J. W. Taylor lately stood. Messrs. Dickinson and Morris owned a mill located on Point Peter, and Mr. Henry R. Savage built one on the south side of the western terminus of Brunswick ferry, which bore the name of Steam Saw Mill No. 5, it being the fifth one then in operation. Later on, Mr. O. G. Parsley erected one at Hilton, which is now operated by Messrs. Parsley & Wiggins.

In the early days of this industry in Wilmington, the sawed lumber was generally shipped to the West Indies, and return cargoes of molasses and sugar imported. It was at that time a very profitable business, as many as 50 lumber vessels having loaded here at the same time, but of late years the over-production in Georgia and in other Southern States has greatly depressed this important industry.

At the present time there are five steam saw mills in active operation in this city. Their average capacity, under favorable circumstances, is about 25,000 feet of lumber per day, each. The amount of sawed lumber exported from this port for the year 1882 from the mills in this city and from those in adjoining counties contiguous to railroads, amounts to 40,291,146 feet.

Of this amount, 9,074,085 feet was foreign shipment, 5,523,400 feet shipped to Baltimore, 9,362,827 feet to New York, and the remainder to other coastwise ports. The home consumption is estimated at between five and six million feet. By local demand is not meant the amount sold in Wilmington only, but in the adjoining country also. By comparing the amount of lumber manufactured and received here from other points by rail, with the receipts for the preceding year, 1881, it will be found that there is a decrease of 5,207,334 feet, which decrease is due to the cause mentioned above.

For a great many years after the erection of steam saw mills here the "gang saws" were the only ones used, but of late years they have been generally superseded by the circular saw, experience having shown that the latter are much more desirable, as well as economical, and they are now used by most of the mills in the city and vicinity.

The quality of the lumber manufactured here is as good

as any made elsewhere, and much better for ship-building than that of any-place farther South. While the lumber of Georgia and Florida has a finer grain, and also a thinner sap, which makes it more desirable in some cases, still it is not as tough or as lasting as our own, and considering the variety of uses to which it is put, we can confidently say that there is no better lumber in the world than our pitch pine.

The mills now in operation here are as follows : Messrs. Edward Kidder & Son, Mr. A. G. Wilson, Messrs. Northrop & Cumming, Messrs. J. H. Chadbourn & Co., and Messrs. Parsley & Wiggins. Mr. J. W. Taylor's mill, which was located at the foot of Walnut street, was destroyed by fire a short time since, but is now being rebuilt.

The power used in these mills is from 75 to 100 horse power, and they are capable of supplying any demand that may be made upon them.

PEANUTS.

Dr. Porcher,—in his Medical Botany of the Southern States, published in Charleston, in 1869,—refers to this product as ground-nut ; pindar ; peanut ; goober-nut ; (*Arachis hypogoea*), brought by the negroes from Africa ; and continues :

The peanut preserves its germinative powers for 40 years. Large quantities were exported from Senegal, on account of the oil which was expressed from them, and which was then, as now, much valued.

According to the analysis of Pagen, and Henry, it is very difficult for the oil to become rancid. In a letter from Mr. W. G. Simms, in 1863, he writes as follows:

"You speak of the ground-nut as a substitute for coffee. But as coffiee it is a very inferior thing to its use as chocolate. The manufacture of chocolate cakes out of the ground-nut alone, and without a particle of cocoa, is an immense and most profitable part of Northern manufacture.

We make it in my family, of a quality not inferior to any you buy. To prepare it for the table, it is beaten in a mortar. At the North, I have been told that the hulls are ground up with the nut, and I do not doubt that this is an improvement, as qualifying the exceeding richness of the nut, which I have usually found too rich prepared as chocolate in our way."

The ground-nut and *bené* make rich and nutricious soup, and act as substitutes for meat. They are often parched and beaten up with sugar, and served as a condiment or dessert. The ground-nut is cultivated to some extent in the Southern States, and great use is made of it on the plantations as an article of food, and for various domestic purposes; it is exported with profit, but troublesome to prepare. I am not aware of any use being made in the Carolinas, of the oil which it affords on expression.

The above was published in Dr. Porcher's report on Medical Botany of the South, 1849. Since the war it is largely employed. The superintendent of the Rockfish Factory, in North Carolina, writes that he has "used the peanut oil by the side of the sperm, and that it works fully as well."

The North Carolina Advertiser published the following:

"The vine, when the pea is removed, makes an excellent forage for cattle, and is said to be equal to the best Northern hay. From the nut is expressed a valuable oil. During the war this oil was extensively used in our machine shops, and its lubricatory properties are pronounced by competent authority to be superior to those of whale oil, for the reason that it does not gum at all. One quality of the oil is extensively employed in the composition of medicines; another is used for burning purposes, and possesses the virtue of not smoking, while a third makes a really excellent salad condiment.

Such, and so varied and important, are the uses to which this simple product can be devoted—uses which the uninformed, who have, perhaps, regarded it only in the light of

an indigestible bulb, would never suspect to proceed from
its cultivation.''

The oil was expressed, by screw pressure, by parties
near Manning, S. C. Mr. Dyson obtained three quarts of
oil from a bushel of the nuts.

Dr. Wood states that it is a non-drying oil, and will not
do for painting, but is used for various purposes in the
arts, for lubricating machinery, and in the manufacture of
woolen cloth ; and would serve, adds Dr. Wood, for burning in lamps, giving even a better light than sperm oil.
Am. J. Pharm., July, 1860.   U. S. Disp., 12th Ed.

In 1862, Messrs. T. C. and B. G. Worth established a
peanut oil mill in Wilmington, and manufactured from the
peanuts grown in this vicinity, a superior article of oil,
(but not fully equal to sperm oil,) which they sold to
nearly all the cotton mills and other manufactories throughout the South, during the remaining period of the war.   It
was found an excellent substitute for machine oil, having
little tendency to gum.

The entire necessary machinery for hulling the nut and
expressing the oil, was improvised by the late Mr. Thomas
L. Colville, of this place, who bore a high reputation as an
ingenious mechanic.

The oil sold during the war at from $3 to $30 per gallon,
in the depreciating currency. The cake was considered
most valuable as fattening food for stock, and brought
correspondingly high prices.

The North Carolina peanut crop is grown on the hum-
mock lands, upon the immediate coast, between the South
Carolina line and Beaufort, N. C. The average yield per acre
is about 30 bushels, and it is considered a fairly remunerative
crop, as the same lands in corn, cotton, or any other crop
usually grown in this section, would likely not produce, in
value, one-half the amount. The average crop for the last
ten years is 125,000 bushels, and the price $1.25 per bushel
of 28 lbs.   The estimate of this year's crop is 150,000

bushels ; but, on account of low prices and bad weather since the harvest, not more than one-fourth of it has yet been marketed.

Wilmington being the most central point, almost the entire crop (and much of it in a very crude and unsalable condition) is marketed here, and by the dealers put in merchantable order, and dealt out to the trade,—the markets being mostly Northwestern and Southern cities.

RICE.

" Rice,* for which we are indebted to the Island of Madagascar, was introduced into Carolina and America at once, toward the close of the seventeenth century. A few grains were sown in the garden of Landgrave Smith, the site of which is now entirely covered by houses and modern improvements, in the city of Charleston. Those few grains produced many ears, which, being disseminated for seed, succeeded in adaptation to the climate ; and the low country of South Carolina since has become the centre of the rice-growing region. The first seed was white, such as is grown in China and Guiana to this day, and such as may still be seen produced on the uplands and inlands of America.

Sometime before the Revolutionary War the " gold seed " rice was introduced, which, owing to its superiority, soon entirely superseded the white. It is now the rice of commerce, and the only grain referred to herein, when rice is mentioned, without being distinguished by some peculiar name or characteristic.

This "gold seed" has undergone improvement in latter years. Hence has resulted the production of a variety longer in the grain, but not perceptibly larger otherwise, which is highly esteemed by foreign consumers, when it is produced in perfection, commanding the highest prices in market. It is called "long-grain" rice, and was obtained from the sowing of part of a single head on the plantation

---

* " Resources of the Southern Fields and Forests," by F. P. Porcher, M. D.

of the late Hon. Joshua John Ward, of Waccamaw. The white rice of the present day measures three-eighths of an inch in length, the same in circumference around its shorter axis, the grain being in shape an irregular elipsoid, and in weight numbers nine hundred and sixty grains to the ounce (Troy). The "gold seed," the rice of commerce, measures three-eighths of an inch in length, the same in circumference, and in weight numbers eight hundred and ninety-six grains to the ounce. The "long grain" rice measures five-twelfths of an inch in length, three-eighths of an inch in circumference, and in weight numbers eight hundred and forty grains to the ounce.

The system of culture for one is suitable for any of these varieties. The first, it is said, will bear upland culture better. The last (long-grain), it is supposed, will bear water better. It does not tiller as much, shoots up a taller stock and longer head, but does not bear as many grains to the head as the other, and more commonly approved kind of "gold seed."

We begin the preparation for a new crop by (clearing out the ditches every third year; the drains are cleaned out every year after plowing) plowing the land as soon after the harvest as the fields can be gleaned, and the scattered rice left on the surface be sprouted. The stubble is turned under by running a deep furrow, say eight inches. This may be continued until the end of January. The sods should have the benefit of the entire winter frosts, if possible, the influence of which disintegrates and prepares them duly for the levelling. Both plowing and harrowing are performed, ordinarily, by oxen—two yoke being required if we go deeper than six to eight inches; and two yoke get on badly in the swamp. The Tuscany breed furnishes the best oxen for our climate.

In March, or when about preparing to plant, the harrows will be made to pass over the plowed ground. After deep plowing, the "plow turns" should be broken up with the spade, sinking the spade as deep as the plow has gone, say eight inches; an able-bodied man will break up in this way, and thoroughly, a surface of fifteen hundred square feet in a day. The field should be well drained, however. The hoe follows to cut up and break the remaining clods and level the surface. The more the soil is comminuted, and the surface brought to a common level, the better. The trenchers then come in with hoes made for the purpose, and trace out with great accuracy the drills in which to sow the seed, fourteen, thirteen or twelve inches apart from centre to centre. They will average (some drawing stake-rows and others filling up the panels) three-quarters of an acre to the hand in a day's work.

When the land is new the trench should be broad, say five inches, and the rice may be scattered in the trench; but for old land, and most of rice land is now old, narrow trenching hoes are preferred, opening a drill three inches wide. Infected with grass-seed and volunteer rice, old land requires close hoeing, and every seed that vegetates outside the drill is cut up and destroyed.

The field is now in high tilth, and resembling somewhat a garden spot, is ready for the seed. The sowers, with great care, yet with wonderful facility and precision, string the seed in the drills, putting two and a half or two and a quarter bushels to the acre. The labor of sowing depends so much upon the state of the weather, whether windy or moist, or otherwise, it is better not to require any given task. Generally each woman will accomplish two or three tasks and do it well—it should never be done otherwise, for the seed cannot be recovered if too thick, nor if too thin can the sowing be repeated without needless waste and increased irregularity.

The best hands are chosen to sow rice. When rice is to be covered with water, without a previous covering of earth, the seed must first be prepared by rolling it in clayed water. There are many planters who still prefer the old system, covering the seed with earth. In this case, after the seed is covered, the water is taken on the field for five or six days to sprout the grain, when it is drawn off, and is returned only when the sprout, "in the needle state," is seen fairly above the ground.

This, "the point flow," is held about four days and then drawn off; after which the culture is the same as above described throughout. The sowing done, water is forth-with admitted (two tides are better than one), and the field remains covered until the sprout becomes green and begins to fork. The water must then be withdrawn, else the plants will be forced to the surface by any slight agitation and float away from their position. The reasoning for a successful substitution of a covering of water for a cover-ing of earth in planting rice, and also for the requisition of sound and perfectly full seed, will be found in the law of germination and growth.

Professor Johnston thus expresses it: "When a seed is committed to the earth, if the warmth and moisture are favorable it begins to sprout. It pushes a shoot upwards, it thrusts a root downwards; but until the leaf expands and the root has fairly entered the soil, the young plant derives no nourishment other than water, either from the earth or from the air. It lives on the starch and gluten contained in the seed."

In the case of rice covered with water, the first shoot is radical and tends downwards but it does not take root until the air is admitted to the leaf, the lungs of the plant, then it becomes rooted instantly. If the water be not reduced when the sprout becomes green, (until the sprout is green it cannot bear the rays of the sun,) the expanding of the leaf in the water will draw up the unfixed root and the whole will rise and float upon the surface.

The water, after floating the trash to the banks, should at no time be over deep, lest the process of germination be delayed, and with any imperfect or defective grains, be prevented altogether.

In Georgia, on one of Dr. Daniels' plantations, near Savannah, the Italian method has been pursued with a good degree of success, namely : The seed is first sprouted, then sown broadcast over the field and covered up by the harrow, which, being reversed, is drawn over the surface. The culture there is with water chiefly.

In twenty days after, or thereabouts, the rice is hoed and flowed deep, the water over-topping the plant for two or three days, in order to destroy the young grass just springing up among the plants, and also the insects that may have lodged upon the blades, or which may have been generated among the stumps or roots, or stubble. At the end of two or three days, the water is slacked down to about half the height of the plant, now somewhat stretched. At this depth it is held until the plants grow strong enough to stand erect, and will admit the laborers to walk between the trenches and pull out the long grass which shows itself, and which will now yield to very slight effort. If any rushes appear, they will now be plucked up by the root and borne out to the banks.

Two days after this weeding, the long water will gradually be drawn off. In Georgia, and elsewhere perhaps, this is called the 'stretch flow.' In that State, as well as in some parts of Carolina, the practice is common to continue the point flow into the 'stretch' or long flow, without drawing the water until the latter be over. This free use of water, as it may be made to substitute one hoeing, may enable the planter to cultivate seven or eight acres to the hand, instead of five and six as of old. But, the proprietor who suffers this method to be practiced in his culture, year by year, if his young crop be not often troubled by the maggot or root-worm, will probably find his land so polluted with water grasses after several years, and so packed as to require rest and change of system to ameliorate it.

A succeeding tide will be taken in and let off immediately, in order to wash out the ditches. Two men, furnished, each with a long-handled rake of curved iron teeth, are put to rake from the ditches all the water-growth which impedes the draining, placing it on the side of the bank. In eight days (the land by that time should be dry) the smaller hoes are used, and the soil is stirred as deep as it can be with them.

The hoe now used has been reduced, latterly, to four inches in breadth. The plant just recovering from the effects of long water, and taking a dry growth, is putting forth new green blades and fresh roots, which, not long enough yet to be interfered with by the deep hoeing, very soon yield to the grateful influence of the air admitted, shoot vigorously into the loosened earth, and nourish a "good stalk."

In the course of fifteen or eighteen days, the field is hoed again and weeded. This last hoeing is also done with the small hoes, but very lightly, to avoid disturbing the roots which are now extended nearly midway between the trenches. As the plant is now beginning to joint, the laborers will step about with care, for if one be broken at the joint it cannot be restored.

A day or two after this third hoeing, the water is put on again, as deep as the last long flow, and is gradually increased in depth, after the rice heads have fairly shot out.

This is called the 'lay-by' flow. Some planters have this flow very shallow, insisting that a deep flow breeds worms, to the injury of the plant before it has shot out, in which case the only remedy is to dry. Up to the time of this flow, is about ninety days for rice sown the first week in April. After this, to the period of maturity, is from sixty to seventy days, during which the water is often changed, and kept fresh, but is never entirely withdrawn until the grain be ripe for the harvest. The improved and best means of keeping the water fresh, is to furnish the field with two trunks—one to admit fresh

water at every flood tide, and the other to void it with the
ebb, so that twice in every twenty-four hours there is
obtained a slight current through the field. This, besides
lessening the infection of the atmosphere (*miasmata*) by
stagnant water, keeps the roots of the plant cool and
healthy, though it postpones the ripening of the rice some
five or eight days.

Meantime, should any grass have escaped the previous
hoeings and weedings, it will show its crest before the rice
matures and be plucked up by the roots. All white rice
will be stripped off by hand.

HARVEST.—And now the grain is ripe for the sickle. The
rice is cut a day before you will say it is fully ripe. For
rice sown April first, the harvest begins usually from the
first to the tenth of September. The water is drawn off
over-night. Soon after the rising of a bright autumn sun,
the reapers are seen amid the thick hanging grain, shoulder
high, mowing it down with the old-fashioned sickle.
Before the dew is all gone, the rice is laid prostrate, even
and orderly across the porous stubble. The next day,
when quite dry of dew, it is tied up in sheaves, and borne
away to the threshing yard, where it is well stacked before
the night dew falls heavy. This last heavy but gleeful
labor completes the field culture of the rice plant."

During the last few years, the reclamation of old rice
lands on the Cape Fear, many of which have been restored
to a high and profitable state of cultivation, has been one
of our principal industries—the present acreage in the
vicinity of Wilmington on river lands being about 2,000
acres, which will be increased next season about 700 acres.
The receipts have, however, fallen much below those of
last year, as will be seen from the table appended : ·

Receipts last year upland rice..66,313 bushels at this date.
    "   this "   "   " ..37,382 ."   "   "

    Decrease.......... .... 28,931 "   "   "

Receipts tide-water rice last year 51,000 bushels at this date.
"   "   " this " 41,191 "   "   "

Decrease................. 9,809   "   "   "

The cause of this decrease is variously accounted for, but it is most likely owing to the risk consequent upon a threatened or possible change in the tariff laws, planters being indisposed to prepare new lands with prospective foreign competition, which would inevitably render the cultivation of American rice hopelessly unprofitable.

Prices for paddy have been ruling lower by 15 to 20 cents per bushel of 45 pounds, than last crop, and clean rice from 1 to 1½ cents per pound decline.

Washington, North Carolina, has sent to this market 10,000 bushels, as compared with 33,000 last year. These receipts naturally belong to Washington, where there is a a large rice mill, and would leave us with 27,000 bushels white rice. The majority of these receipts have come from Eastern Carolina, and principally from Newbern and Beaufort.

Goldsboro has sent to this market 4,000 bushels; Warsaw, Wilson and Mt. Olive have shipped about 5,000 bushels. Some of our receipts have been sent to Northern mills, but not over 9,000 bushels. Five thousand bushels have been shipped into South Carolina, and the remainder milled in our city.

The clean rice from this port is chiefly shipped to New York, Boston and Philadelphia, where it receives an appreciative market, and is well known as the best rice milled in this country. The erection of a mill in Wilmington has made a market for all grades, and planters are not compelled to ship their goods to other cities, and undergo the many losses already known to consignments. Should Congress allow the present duty to remain, it is probable that nearly all the old rice land in this section will be reclaimed and the Cape Fear regain its ancient reputation

with reference to this most profitable and respectable
industry.

I append herewith a carefully prepared table with reference to the Cape Fear plantations and product, and probable increase for next year.

NAME OF PLANTATION.	Acreage.	Bushels Rice Raised.	Next Year's Increase Acreage.	PLANTERS.
Orton	200	12,000	60	K. M. Murchison & Co.
Navassa	230	8,700		Navassa Guano Co.
Hanaper	)			)
Sans Souci	250	7,600		} Jno. F. Garrell.
Trapente	)			)
Fair Oaks	120	5,000	50	Francis M. Moore.
Kendal and Lilliput	130	5,000	70	Fred. Kidder.
Clarendon	155	5,000		S. L. Fremont.
Point Peter and Forks	190	6,500	125	J. W. Atkinson.
Fells	200	4,500		Geo. W. Kidder.
Belvidere	90	2,500		J. D. McRae.
Green Island	90	2,500	25	Wm. Larkins.
Mallory	75	2,200		Wm. Hankins.
Dudleys	80	2,800	20	B. A. Hallett.
Old Town Creek	250	2,000		
Hilton	53	1,255		T. A. Watson and —
Woodburn	75	2,500		R. B. Wood. [Dennis.
Lyrias			25	D. D. Barber.
Thornberry			130	H. M. Bowden.
Bellville	100	2,800		D. L. Russel.
Beau Choix	)	100	2,000		A. W. Reiger.
Glassonbary	)			

*2,300 bushels lost by freshet.
*1,400 bushels burnt.
Scattering lots planted by negroes.

PROVISIONS.

In former years the trade in provisions was done by and through wholesale grocers in this market, who not only supplied the retail demand of the city, but who furnished the planters and distillers in our country section for a radius of several hundred miles. Of late years the trade has fallen into the channel of provision brokers, who, at a small rate of commission, sell to the city dealers, and at times to the outside trade, their daily requirements of corn, meat, hay, flour, oats, and other staple articles, at current prices in Chicago, Louisville and other supply markets, plus the bare expense of freight and charges.

The present annual consumption of provisions in this market is estimated, upon actual receipts, as follows :

Corn................................. 500,000 bushels.
Meat....................... .... 15,000 boxes.
Hay............... .... 1,500 tons.
Flour................................ 50,000 barrels.
Oats.... .... 75,000 bushels.

This enormous trade shows that the farmers and other consumers of provisions in and around Wilmington pay annually to the Chicago, New York and other remote markets, the sum of one million five hundred thousand dollars a year for provisions which ought to be raised by our farmers themselves. Is it a wonder that North Carolina remains poor, or that our farmers who persist in planting cotton and working turpentine, to the utter neglect of provisions and provender, are always behind ? Perhaps the current low prices of cotton this year, compared with the unreasonably high cost of provisions, will teach our people an important lesson, which they have hitherto been slow to learn.

FISHERIES.

There are about fifty fisheries between New River and Federal Point, the proceeds of nearly all of which find a market in Wilmington, though a portion is carried to Beaufort and Morehead City; the bulk of the catch is, however, brought here, and nearly all of the fisheries on this side of New River, deal entirely with this place. Eight or ten years ago, from 4,000 to 6,000 barrels of mullets were brought to this port from these fisheries, but of late years the amount has been greatly reduced.

A fishery near the mouth of New River, which formerly yielded during the season, from 2,000 to 3,000 barrels, is now worthless, owing principally to a change in the channel, which has become so filled up with sand that it cannot be used,—consequently the fish have been diverted from it entirely.

In speaking of barrels of fish, it is to be understood that though they are termed or called barrels, yet they are very small, averaging generally not more than 80 lbs. net, and and bringing in the market, from $3 to $4 a barrel.

The fisheries of Messrs. W. E. Davis & Son are located at Zeke's Island, adjoining the works at New Inlet, where they have three seines at work, and a trap, ingeniously contrived for the purpose, in which many fish are taken.

The fishery is carried on outside the bar and not in the river, and the quantity caught during the last season amounted to about 1,500 barrels of mullets, exclusive of other kinds of fish taken in the seines. These mullets are salted and barrelled, and are worth from $3.50 to $4.25 a barrel, as per quality and size.

All other varieties are shipped fresh, on ice, to the North and to points in the interior of the State, and during the season about 300,000 pounds of fresh fish are shipped by this firm to nine different States, the bulk, however, going to the cities of New York, Philadelphia and Baltimore; and as this industry is not yet fully developed, what results may we not expect when increased experience is brought to the assistance of energy and capital.

In addition to their fisheries, the firm of Davis & Son have erected at Zeke's Island, works for the manufacture Oil and Fish-scrap, the latter said to be an admirable fertilizer.

The season for mullets is during the months of August September, October and November; and for shad, during those of February, March and April. About 11,000 shad are brought here during the season, value about $4,000; however, not more than one third of the catch is disposed of here, the remainder being shipped in every direction, chiefly North, and always by rail. The waters of the Cape Fear produce as fine shad as can be found anywhere, and they are eagerly sought after in the Northern markets.

The sturgeon fishery is also getting to be an important industry. During the season, from the middle of March to the last of October, an average of 2,000 pounds a week of that fish is shipped from this port to New York, where there is a constant demand for it at remunerative prices.

It is but recently that this fish has become an article of commerce. Formerly it was regarded as worthless and was a great annoyance to fishermen, getting entangled in their nets, and breaking them, and it was considered as a nuisance only. A year or two ago, however, a shipment was made to New York as an experiment; the fish attracted attention, and the aggregate of the business since is remarkable,—amounting now to more than 90,000 pounds during the season,—a most profitable industry, as it is derived from a source hitherto regarded as worthless. They are shipped in ice, like other fish, and by rail.

It is said that the Cape Fear sturgeon is fully equal to that taken elsewhere, and prized especially for the roe, which is carefully cleansed and rubbed to a pulp, and having been mixed with salt, it is then sold at a high price as Caviare, a food highly prized by Continental people, particularly the Russians, who monopolize the trade. The flesh of the sturgeon is also dried and smoked in small strips, and commands a ready sale, not unfrequently under the name of smoked salmon.

The sturgeon is spoken of in England, to this day, as a royal fish, having in olden times been served with great pomp, and esteemed most delicate in flesh and flavor. It was also given a conspicuous place in the feasts of the ancient Greeks and Romans. Among our Cape Fear people, however, it is considered the coarsest and most vulgar dish our market affords.

Our waters furnish nearly every variety of fish ; among which are shad, mullets, blue fish or skipjack, speckled trout, pig fish, (one of the most delicate that swims), red and black drum, black fish, rock or bass, Spanish mackerel sun fish, spots, croakers, sheephead, flounders, whiting, sera, boneto, (three varieties), tarpin, (king of the shad), tautog, (weighing from 20 to 40 lbs.), catfish, &c., and also various kinds of fresh water fish,—trout, perch, &c.

In 1714, Lawson gave the names of fish in North Carolina as follows :

"Whales, several sorts, thrashers, devil fish, sword fish, crampois, bottle noses, porpoises, sharks, (two sorts), dog fish, Spanish mackerel, cavallies, bonetos, blue fish, drum, (red), drum, (black), angel fish, bass, or rock fish, sheep head, plaice, flounder, soles, mullets, shad, fat backs, guard,(white),guard,(green),scate, or sting ray, thornback, congar eels, lamprey eels, eels, sun fish, toad fish, sea tench, trout of the salt water,croakers,herring,smelts,shad,breams, taylors. The fresh water fish are : Sturgeon, pike, trouts, gudgeon, perch, English perch, white perch, brown, or Welchmen perch, flat, and mottled, or Irishmen perch, small and flat, with red spots, called round robbins, carp, roach, dace, loaches, sucking fish, catfish, grindals, old wives, fountain fish, white fish. The shell fish are : Large crabs, called stone crabs, smaller flat crabs, oysters, great and small, cockles, clams, muscles, conchs, scallops, man of noses, perriwinkles, or wilks, sea snail horns, fiddlers, runners, Spanish, or pearl oysters, flattings, tortoise and terebin, finger fish, shrimps. Those of the fresh water are crawfish and muscles."

The extent of the oyster business is also worthy of consideration. Our best oysters come from New River, adjoining the county of Onslow. The beds are said to be inexhaustible, and there are no better oysters in the country. Myrtle Grove oysters are smaller than the New River, yet compare favorably in flavor with the bulk of those grown elsewhere.

From 350 to 400 gallons of oysters are received here during a week of seven days ; about 50 gallons a day, and during the months of October, November, December and

January, from 1,200 to 1,500 gallons a month are shipped to other points; after that time the demand gradually falls off, and not more than a fourth of that amount is sold. The price varies as to quality, from 65 cents to $1.00 per gallon ; there are none shipped in the shell.

The terrapin is caught in our waters, and has become almost indispensable to the epicure. The diamond back terrapin is the most valuable of the species. They are caught at the mouth of the river and in all the bays of our Sounds. It is safe to say that the flesh is worth $1.00 a pound—their scarcity makes them so valuable ; not more than 60 dozen were caught here last season for market. They are kept in water pens for propagation, and can be domesticated as easily as a pig or fowl. Though not abundant as yet, with proper care and attention they can be greatly increased, and will be a source of profit in the future to those who undertake their propagation. It is a matter of surprise to many that the trade in terrapins and soft-shelled crabs is so much neglected by our fishermen. A small investment of capital, backed by careful industry in the propagation of oysters, terrapins and crabs on our sea-coast, would undoubtedly yield large returns.

THE DRY GOODS BUSINESS.

It would astonish the old-time citizens, say those who flourished here about fifty years ago, could they return to the scene of their labors and see, not only the vast increase in the dry goods trade of Wilmington, in which many of them were engaged, but also the entirely different manner in which the business is conducted. Then, at all the retail dry goods stores, credit, generally for twelve months, was the rule and cash the exception. Now, the reverse is true, or if credit is given it is for so short a time (scarcely ever more than thirty days) that it is regarded as equivalent to cash. The manner in which the business was then con-

ducted would not be tolerated by the merchants of this progressive age at this time.

To mention but one custom which was universally practiced: whenever a lady customer was not disposed to do her own shopping, a servant was despatched to the proprietors of different stores, with instructions to send by said servant, certain articles of merchandise which she desired to see, and, as was frequently the case, the costliest goods, such as laces, silks, piece goods, etc., could be seen at almost any hour of the day in huge bundles deftly balanced upon the heads of colored servants, passing to and fro upon the streets. It was the universal custom, and though of course a great annoyance at times to the proprietors, could not well be avoided; it is to be borne in mind, however, that that was prior to the era here of railroads and telegraphs; and besides, what could be done then with impunity and without fear of loss, from the smallness of the population of the town, could not now be attempted, even if our merchants were so inclined, owing to the changed condition of our social affairs. It is estimated that the yearly business of the town in those days did not amount to more than two hundred and fifty thousand dollars, including all classes of goods that were usually kept in stores in those days. The principal dealers of that time were Alexander Anderson, John Wooster, Kyle & Dawson, Wright & Savage, W. & Z. Latimer, W. A. Williams, Samuel Shuter; and the business was confined to a retail local trade and to the plantations adjoining the town. Such an institution as a wholesale establishment for dry goods was not only unknown, but never dreamed of. As evidencing the wonderful improvement in that business between the Wilmington of the past and the Wilmington of the present, it is only necessary to mention the following:

The annual sales of dry goods in Wilmington at the present time will not fall short of a million and a half of dollars, including sales at wholesale and retail. There are one or two jobbing houses, one particularly, whose sole business is jobbing goods. The facilities here for buying at wholesale are equally as good as in Richmond or Baltimore, and the prices will compare favorably with either of those points. It should be borne in mind that the jobbing business, which was formerly carried on almost entirely in New York and other Northern cities, is now conducted by houses located in Southern cities. They are familiar with the wants of the surrounding country, are known to the people of the neighborhood, sell upon as good terms as can be obtained in Northern markets, and hence control the trade, for our people are becoming more disposed every year to trade at home, other things being equal, than abroad. There are jobbing houses in Richmond, in Charleston and in Savannah, two or three in each city, and these command the trade from numerous points in the South, and in consequence the immense business heretofore done in New York, which formerly had been the centre of that trade, has greatly declined. It must not be supposed, however, that there has been any decrease in the volume of business transacted in that city. Those houses which formerly did a jobbing business, now confine themselves to packages, that is, selling by package, and not by piece.

In estimating the extent of the dry goods business of Wilmington it is to be understood that a comparatively new business, that of ready-made clothing, is included. Goods of as fine quality as can be found elsewhere can always be obtained in our city, and it may be as well to state that the custom of the surrounding country which seeks its supplies at this point is not only desirable, but eagerly sought after by other places. Nearly every variety of goods known to the trade is kept in stock, and it may surprise some to learn that last season nearly, if not quite, five thousand bales (not pieces) of domestic and plaids, the products of the factories of our own State, were disposed of in this market alone. This fact is extremely gratifying, as it shows that our own fabrics are in greater demand than those manufactured elsewhere ; and it follows, as a natural sequence, that the quality must be better, or there would not be so great a demand for them. There is another and distinct branch of business which has grown to large dimensions, and deserves special notice—the shoe trade. For many years there was but one shoe store in Wilmington, and that was wholly confined to the retail trade. The business has so rapidly increased within the past few years that it amounts to at least half a million dollars annually. In former years there was simply a local demand, now a large amount of capital is required to meet the increasing demands of the business, and wholesale buyers find in our market large and well selected stocks from which to make selections. It is increasing every year, and as new avenues of trade are opened up around us, converging towards this point, we have every reason to anticipate a large increase in that particular branch of business, and a very valuable adjunct to the prosperity of our city.

These evidences of the prosperity of Wilmington must surely be gratifying to all who feel an interest in her future. Though they have been gradual, they are none the less remarkable, and we have every reason to believe that they will continue to increase. Revolutions do not go backward, old things have long since passed away, and if all things have not yet become new, they are certainly undergoing a rapid transformation. The tide of prosperity is sweeping around us on every side. Be it our care to take advantage of the flood that leads to fortune, and place our old town full breast high in the front rank of commercial success.

FERTILIZERS.

The movement of guano from Wilmington, during the year 1882, is shown by the accompanying tables, which indicate a business aggregating about 321,786 bags, valued at $1,287,144. These statistics have not hitherto been recorded, and the figures have been ascertained after much research and carefulness.   The value is estimated as nearly as possible from prices quoted for the several brands and classes of fertilizers referred to.   It will be seen that the Carolina Central Railroad carries largely in excess of any other means of transportation from this market.

FERTILIZERS:

Per Carolina Central Rail Road, 1882.

Guano	124,320	Bags.
Kainit	34,348	"
Phosphate	16,760	"
Dissolved Bone	11,341	"
Chemical Fertilizers	1,912	"
Cotton Fertilizers	2,002	"
Lime	678	"
Stone	50	"
Eureka	100	"
Acid	450	"
Sulphate	1	"
Total	191,962	"

Per Wilmington, Columbia & Augusta Rail Road, 1882.

January	13,092	Bags.
February	35,638	"
March	38,783	"
April	6,908	"
May	192	"
October	20	"
November	80	"
December	2,550	"
Total	97,263	"

Per Wilmington & Weldon Rail Road, 1882.

January	1,320	Bags.
February	2,152	"
March	3,750	"
April	2,085	"
May	120	"
June	20	"
August	957	"
September	827	"
October	200	"
November	137	"
December	9,377	"
Total	20,945	"

PER STEAMERS UP THE CAPE FEAR RIVER, 1882.

Guano	8,409	Bags.
Chemicals	881	"
Kainit	1,232	"
Phosphate	679	"
Fertilizers	288	"
Bones	127	"
Total	11,616	"
Lime	825	Bbls.

TURPENTINE PRODUCTS.

F. Andrew Michaux, in his treatise on the resinous trees of North America, published in Paris, in 1819, says : · "The resinous product of the pine is of six sorts, viz : turpentine, *scrapings*, spirit of turpentine, rosin, tar and pitch. The two last are delivered in their natural state; the others are modified by the agency of fire in certain modes of preparation. More particularly : turpentine is the sap of the tree obtained by making incisions in its trunk. It begins to distil about the middle of March, when the circulation commences, and flows with increasing abundance as the weather becomes warmer, so that July and August are the most productive months. When the circulation is slackened by the chills of autumn, the operation is discontinued, and the remainder of the year is occupied in preparatory labours for the following season, which consist—first, in making the *boxes*. This is done in January and February : in the base of each tree, about 3 or 4 inches from the ground, and of preference, on the south side, a cavity is formed, commonly of the capacity of three pints, but proportioned to the size of the trunk, of which it should occupy a quarter of the diameter ; on stocks more than 6 feet in circumference, two, and sometimes four *boxes* are made on opposite sides. Next comes the *raking*, or the clearing of the ground at the foot of the trees from leaves and herbage, by which means they are secured against the fires that are often kindled in the woods by the carelessness of travellers and wagoners.

If the flames gain the *boxes* already impregnated with turpentine, they are rendered useless, and others must be made. *Notching* is merely making at the sides of the box two oblique gutters, about 3 inches long, to conduct into it the sap that exudes from the edges of the wound. In the interval of a fortnight, which is employed in this operation, the first boxes become filled with sap. A wooden shovel is used to transfer it to pails, which in turn are emptied into casks placed at convenient distances. To increase the product, the upper edge of the box is *chipped* once a week, the bark and a portion of the alburnum being removed to the depth of four concentric circles. The boxes fill every three weeks. The turpentine thus procured is the best, and is called *pure dipping*.

The *chippings* extend the first year a foot above the box, and as the distance increases, the operation is more frequently repeated, to remove the sap coagulated on the surface of the wound. The closing of the pores, occasioned by continued rains, exacts the same remedy ; and it is remarked that the produce is less abundant in moist and cool seasons. After 5 or 6 years the tree is abandoned ; the upper edge of the wound becomes cicatrized, but the bark is never restored sufficiently for the renewal of the process.

It is reckoned that 250 boxes yield a barrel containing 320 lbs. Some persons charge a single negro with the care of 4,000 or 4,500 trees of one box ; others, of only 3,000, which is an easy task. In general, 3,000 trees yield, in ordinary years, 75 barrels of turpentine and 25 of *scraping*, which supposes the boxes to be emptied five or six times in the season. The *scraping* is a coating of sap which becomes solid before it reaches the boxes, and which is taken off in the fall and added to the last runnings. In November, 1807, the *pure dipping* was sold at Wilmington at $3 a barrel, and the scraping a quarter less.

In 1804, the exportation to the Northern States, and to

the English possessions, amounted to 77,827 barrels.
During peace it comes even to Paris, where it is called
Boston turpentine. Throughout the United States it is
used to make yellow soap of a good quality. The consumption in England is great, and, in the official statements, the value imported in 1807 is $465,828 ; in 1805,
Liverpool alone received 40,294 barrels, and in 1807, 18,924
barrels. It was sold there in August, 1807, at $3 a hundred
pounds, and after the American embargo, in 1808, at $8 or
$9. Oddy omits, in his list of articles exported from
Archangel and Stockholm to Great Britain, the resinous ·
product of the pine, which has amounted to 100,000 barrels
of tar in a year. ·

' A great deal of spirits of turpentine is made in North
Carolina : it is obtained by distilling the turpentine in
large copper retorts, which are of an imperfect shape, being
so narrow at the mouth as to retard the operation. Six barrels of turpentine are said to afford one cask or 122 quarts
of the spirit. It is sent to all parts of the United States
even to the Western Country, by way of Philadelphia, to
England, and to France, where it is preferred as less odor-
ous, to that made near Bordeaux. In 1804, 19,526 gallons
were exported from North Carolina. The residuum of the
distillation is *rosin*, which is sold at one-third of the price
of turpentine. The exportation of this substance, in 1804,
was 4,675 barrels.

All the tar of the Southern States is made from dead
wood of the long-leaved pine, consisting of trees prostrated
by time or by the fire kindled annually in the forests, of
the summits of those that are felled for timber, and of limbs
broken off by the ice, which sometimes overloads the
leaves.

It is worthy of remark that the branches of resinous
trees consist almost wholly of *wood*, of which the organization is even more perfect than in the body of the tree ;
the reverse is observed in trees with deciduous leaves : the

explanation of the phenomenon I leave to persons skilled in vegetable physiology.

As soon as vegetation ceases in any part of the tree, its consistence speedily changes; the sap decays, and the heart, already impregnated with resinous juice, becomes surcharged to such a degree as to double its weight in a year: the accumulation is said to be much greater after 4 or 5 years: the general fact may be proved by comparing the wood of trees recently felled, and of others long since dead.

To procure the tar, a *kiln* is formed in a part of the forest abounding in dead wood : this is first collected, stript of the sap, and cut into billets two or three feet long and about three inches thick ; a task which is rendered long and difficult by the knots. The next step is to prepare a place for piling it: for this purpose a circular mound is raised, slightly declining from the circumference to the centre, and surrounded with a shallow ditch. The diameter of the pile is proportioned to the quantity of wood which it is to receive : to obtain 100 barrels of tar, it should be 18 or 20 feet wide. In the middle is a hole with a conduct leading to the ditch, in which is formed a receptacle for the tar as it flows out. Upon the surface of the mound, beaten hard and coated with clay, the wood is laid round in a circle like rays.

The pile, when finished, may be compared to a cone truncated at two-thirds of its height, and reversed, being 20 feet in diameter below, 25 or 30 feet above, and 10 or 12 feet high. It is then strewed with pine leaves, covered with earth, and contained at the sides with a slight cincture of wood. This covering is necessary in order that the fire kindled at the top may penetrate to the bottom with a slow and gradual combustion : if the whole mass was rapidly inflamed, the operation would fail and the labour in part be lost : in fine, nearly the same precautions are exacted in this process as are observed in Europe in making charcoal. A kiln which is to afford 100 or 130 barrels of tar, is 8 or 9 days in burning.

As the tar flows off into the ditch, it is emptied into casks of 30 gallons, which are made of the same species of wood.

Pitch is tar reduced by evaporation : it should not be diminished beyond half its bulk to be of a good quality.

In 1807, tar and pitch were exported to England from the United States, to the amount of $265,000 ; the tar was sold in Liverpool, in August of the same year, at $4.67 a barrel, and when the embargo became known, at $5.56 ; from which inferences may be drawn to the advantage of the United States. At Wilmington the ordinary price is from $1.75 to $2.20 a barrel. Oddy informs us that the tar brought to England between 1786 and 1799, came in equal proportions from Russia, Sweden and the United States ; only a very small quantity was drawn from Denmark. The Swedish tar is the most highly esteemed in commerce, and next that of Archangel ; that of the United States is considered inferior to both, which is owing to its being made from dead wood, while that of Europe is extracted from trees recently felled.   The tar of Carolina is said also to contain earth ; this can be attributable only to the want of care in preparing the receptacles ; if the same pains were taken in the fabrication, it would probably equal that of Europe, though it must be considered that the tar of Russia and Sweden is produced by a different tree, a native of the north of Europe. It has already been remarked that in the United States this manufacture is confined to the maritime part of North Carolina, and to a small tract of Vir-ginia ; but according to the rate of consumption in America and Great Britain, the product would not long suffice if all the extensive regions covered with the long-leaved pine were made to contribute to this object, for the dead wood is said not to be renewed upon a tract that has been cleared, in less than ten or twelve years. It might be advantageous to

make use of green wood, or purposely to strip the trees of
their bark ; and perhaps in this way supplies might be
obtained equivalent to the demand of commerce. Great
benefit would result from stripping the pines of a certain
diameter of their bark ; they would pass completely into
the resinous state in fifteen months, and would be proper
for posts and many other uses which require strong and
lasting wood.   This experiment, which I should have tried
when I was last in South Carolina if the season had not
been too far advanced, should be made in April or the
beginning of May, while the sap is in active circulation,
and the *liber* or inner bark should be exactly removed."

Since Michaux wrote the foregoing treatise three-quarters
of a century ago, there has been but little change in the
preparation for market of these far-famed products of our
State. The cavity or box is now made to hold two pints.
The *notching* of his day is now called cornering, and instead
of a wooden shovel for the removal of sap, an iron imple-
ment, called a dipper, is used.   The *pure dipping* referred
to is now known as virgin turpentine ; and instead of a
negro being "charged with the care of 4,000 to 4,500
boxes," a good hand is now expected to chip 10,000 to
12,000 trees throughout the season, while the dipping is
delegated to other laborers.

(The price of "scrape" is now only three-fifths of the
value of "dip."   Eight barrels of crude turpentine (pure
dipping) now yield one cask of 48 gallons spirits ; and
while the exports of spirits turpentine from North Carolina
in 1804 were 19,526 gallons, they now amount to over
5,300,000 gallons. The exports of rosin in 1804 (4,675 barrels) have since been increased to 554,000 barrels.) .

For the information of those who imagine that our influence as a market for naval stores is waning, and that the
trade is rapidly moving southward to the new districts in
Georgia, I append the following official statistics by way
of comparison :

Comparative Statement of Receipts of Naval Stores for the crop years to
March 10th of 1882 and 1883, at Wilmington, Charleston and Savannah.

1883.

MARCH 10th.	Spirits.	Rosin.	Tar.	Crude.	Total Bbls.
Wilmington......................	85,035	406,519	65,250	65,206	622,010
Charleston...................... ..	70,943	285,149	....	....	356,092
Savannah........................	86,573	378,244	....	....	464,817

1882.

MARCH 10th.	Spirits.	Rosin.	Tar.	Crude.	Total. Bbls.
Wilmington.............	83,148	419,995	59,511	85,118	647,772
Charleston......	51,123	215,725	....	....	266,848
Savannah.........................	52.695	244,589	....	....	297,284

In an old book containing the private correspondence of
Daniel Webster, I find a letter dated Wilmington, May 6,
1847, as follows :

"At 1 o'clock yesterday, ten miles from this city, we met
a special train, with a large deputation, headed by ex-
Governor Dudley. The weather was bad, and the wind
east, and I was rather easily persuaded to stay over a day.
The Governor brought us to his own house, where we are
grandly lodged. I go to the hotel to meet the citizens at
11 o'clock, and go off at half-past 2 this P. M., if the wind
goes down. At present it blows rather hard. This is an
active little city, built on the east side of the river, on sand
hills. The good people are Whigs, but out of the city,
and all round for fifty miles, it is a region whose politics
are personified by Mr. McKay. * * * 'There is a thing,
Harry, which thou hast often heard of, and it is known to
many in this land by the name of pitch,' etc., etc. We
are here in the midst of this very thing, at the very centre
of the tar and turpentine region. The pines are long-leaved
pines. In one of these, a foot from the bottom, a notch is
cut, and its capacity enlarged and its shape fashioned a

little, so as to hold the liquid, by chiseling, and then it is called the 'box.' Above the box the bark is cut off, for a foot or so, and the turpentine oozes out of the tree on to this smooth surface, and then runs slowly into the box. The box holds about a quart. In a good large tree it will fill five times a season. Sometimes there are two boxes in one tree, so that some trees will yield ten quarts a year. But the greatest yield is the first year; after that it is gradually diminished, and in seven or eight years the tree dies, or will yield no more turpentine. Tar is made by bringing together wood, full of turpentine, either trees or knots, and pieces picked up in the woods, and burning it in a pit, just as charcoal is made, then running it off into a hole prepared for it, in the ground. At the present price of the article, this is said to be the best business now doing in the State. I am told good, fresh, well-timbered pine lands can be bought for $1.25 to $1.50 per acre. * * * One barrel of turpentine distilled makes six gallons spirits. The residuum, or resin, is not of much value, say twenty-five cents a barrel. Tar and turpentine are now high, and the business good."

ADULTERATION OF SPIRITS TURPENTINE.

Some months ago our Exchange received a visit from Mr. Ingall, of England, the senior partner of Messrs. Ingall, Phillips & Co., proprietors of the principal tanks in London, where spirits turpentine and petroleum are stored. Mr. Ingall subsequently made a careful tour of our entire turpentine-producing country, including South Carolina, Georgia and Florida, his object being not only to ascertain the probable future product of turpentine by judging himself of our resources, but to investigate alleged or suspected attempts at adulteration, which the high prices current for spirits turpentine naturally encouraged in a country where petroleum and rosin oil, in a refined state, offered so many profitable inducements for adaptation.

Mr. Ingall informed me that until recently, no regular chemical tests had been applied to cargoes of spirits turpentine sent them for storage or tanking, and that various attempts had been made to pass a spurious article upon the London market, which led to the engagement by them of the services of Prof. Henry E. Armstrong, Ph. D., F. R. S., a well-known chemical expert of London, who now analyzes with great care every shipment received at the tanks for that market.

From these gentlemen I have before me, and subject to the inspection of any members of the Exchange, six samples, labelled as follows : (1) Average sample turpentine (spirits). (2) Average sample petroleum. (3) Turpentine (spirits) and 10 per cent. benzine. (4) Turpentine (spirits) and 10 per cent. petroleum. (5.) Turpentine (spirits) and 5 per cent. petroleum. (6) Turpentine (spirits) and $2\frac{1}{2}$ per cent. petroleum.

Adulteration No. 3 seems to be the most successful; comparing the pure spirits turpentine and its mixture with 10 per cent. petroleum spirit (benzine), no variation whatever in color is perceptible to the eye, and no difference can be detected in the odor. The other mixed samples show more or less dissimilarity in color and odor, but would easily deceive a casual observer.

One of the methods of analysis is by the polarimeter. Polarimetry has been employed in the examination of all those substances having the property of polarizing light. For instance, the rays of light falling upon a sample of spirits of turpentine, give to the surface of the fluid a bluish, opalescent hue, because of polarized light. The polarimeter, or polariscope, is an instrument devised to estimate the polarity of a given fluid, and the amount of polarity is expressed in degrees. Therefore a standard of polarization being ascertained for a pure spirit, all deviations would indicate adulteration, or determine the origin of the spirit, whether it be Russian, French or American.

With reference to this beautiful test, Dr. Witthaus gives the following :

"*Polarimetry.*—A ray of light passing from one medium into another of different density, at an angle other than 90° to the plane of separation of the two media, is deflected from its course or *refracted.* Certain substances have the power, not only of deflecting a ray falling upon them in certain directions, but also of dividing it into two rays, which are peculiarly modified. The splitting of the ray is termed *double refraction*, and the altered rays are said to be *polarized.* When a ray of such polarized light meets a mirror held at a certain angle, or a crystal of Iceland spar peculiarly cut (a Nichols' prism), also at a certain angle, it is extinguished. The crystal which produces the polarization, is called the *polarizer*, and that which produces the extinction the *analyzer*. If, when the polarizer and analyzer are so adjusted, as to extinguish a ray passing through the former, certain substances are brought between them, light again passes through the analyzer, and in order again to produce extinction, the analyzer must be rotated upon the axis of the ray to the right or to the left. Substances capable of thus influencing polarized light, are said to be *optically active.* If, to produce extinction, the analyzer is turned in the direction of the hands of a watch, the substance is said to be *dextrogyrous ;* if in the opposite direction, *loevogyrous.* The distance through which the analyzer must be turned, depends upon the peculiar power of the optically active substance, the length of the column interposed, the concentration, if in solution, and the wave-length of the original ray of light. The *specific rotary power* of a substance is the rotation produced, in degrees and tenths, by one gram of the substance dissolved in one cubic centimetre of a non-active solvent, and examined in a column one decimetre long. The specific rotary power is determined by dissolving a known weight of the substance in a given volume of solvent, and observing the angle of rotation produced by a column of given length. Then let $p=$ weight in grams of the substance contained in 1 c. c. of solution ; l the length of the column in decimetres ; a the angle of rotation observed ; and $[a]$ the specific rotary power sought, we have

$$[a] = \frac{a}{pl}$$

In most instruments monochromatic light, corresponding to the D line of the solar spectrum, is used, and the specific rotary power for that ray, is expressed by the sign $[a]_D$. The fact that the rotation is right-handed is expressed by the sign $+$, and that it is left-handed by the sign $-$.

It will be seen from the above formula that, knowing the value of $[a]_D$ for any given substance, we can determine the weight of that substance in a solution by the formula

$$p = \frac{a}{[a]_D + l}$$

Another form of analysis is by ordinary distillation, and still another by treatment with sulphuric acid, and by other chemical tests.*

In the *American Journal of Pharmacy* for March, 1883, appears a paper on the subject of "Turpentine—Its Nature and adulterations," by Professor Armstrong, copied from the *Journal of the Society of Chemical Industry*, which is so replete with interesting matter, that at the risk of appearing tedious with reference to its technicalities, I reproduce it in full.

TURPENTINE: ITS NATURE AND ADULTERATIONS.1

BY PROFESSOR HENRY E. ARMSTRONG, PH.D., F.R.S.

In the course of investigations on the terpenes, camphor and allied compounds, in which I have been engaged during the several years past, the opportunity has occurred of gradually collecting a number of

---

*Attempts at adulteration in the country have been foiled even after passing the Wilmington inspection, by the custom of some shippers, of marking the original brand on the end of the bung stave, in addition to the shipping brand on the head, which serves as a trace in case of need.—

1 From the "Journal of the Society of Chemical Industry," December 29, 1882.

data which probably are of sufficient technical value to find a place in the "Journal of the Society of Chemical Industry."

Thanks to the kindness of my friend, Mr. E. Phillips, of Messrs. Iugall, Phillips & Co., I was enabled to examine average samples of most of the cargoes of turpentine landed by his firm during the years 1877 to 1880, and thus to obtain a clear insight into the character of the commercial article. The high price of turpentine during the past few seasons has undoubtedly led dealers here to adulterate it, and it was to be feared that shippers might not uniformly resist temptation; therefore, at the request of the above-mentioned firm, since the beginning of last year, I have regularly tested all cargoes landed at their wharves.

The crude resinous exudation, formerly known as "turpentine" is no longer an article of commerce in this country, the obviously rational course being nowadays adopted of separating it into its constituents, "spirits of turpentine," or turpentine oil" and resin. On this account the name "turpentine"—*vulgare* "turps"—is now commonly employed as synonymous with the longer appellation, spirits or oil of turpentine, and it is in this sense that the term is employed in the paper.

The commercial varieties of turpentine mainly consist of hydrocarbons of the formula $C_{10}H_{16}$, of which certainly *three* distinct classes may be distinguished, viz.: *terpenes*, *citrenes*, and a third of which *sylvestrene*, the characteristic constituent of Russian turpentine, is the type. Under *terpenes*, I include those varieties which boil at about 156° C.; under *citrenes*, those which boil at about 176° to 178°, such as are the chief constituents of the oils derived from various species of *citrus*.

French Turpentine.—It is generally stated that French turpentine is the produce of a single species of conifer, *Pinus maritima*. It certainly is of remarkably uniform quality, judging from the almost constant rotatory power of samples which I have had occasion to examine at various times, and probably the properties of the terpene of which the French oil mainly consists are not very different from those of the commercial article. Using any form of polarimeter which admits of the observation being made in monochromatic light—it is, perhaps, well to note that the Soleil form cannot be employed for the examination of turpentine—and operating with a 200 mm. column, the value of a_D is on the average about —60° to —61°.

American Turpentine.—American turpentine is said by Hanbury and Flückiger ("Pharmacographia," 1st ed.) to be chiefly the produce of the swamp pine (*Pinus australis*), this and the loblolly pine (*Pinus tœda*) being, they say, the most important sources of turpentine.

The following particulars regarding the separation of the hydrocarbon from the crude resinous exudation will probably be of interest. I

am indebted for them to Dr. Thomas F. Wood, of Wilmington, N. C. ;
they were written at the request of Mr. Charles Rice, American editor
of the "Pharmacographia :"

"Turpentine is distilled in copper stills now. Formerly iron stills
were used. All crude turpentine is distilled with water. A fifteen-
barrel still (barrel weighs two hundred and eighty pounds) is charged
early in the morning. Gentle heat is first applied until the mass is
liquefied, and a coarse wire skimmer is used to remove the chips, bark,
leaves and such other foreign substances as rise to the surface, the temperature meanwhile rising until 316° F. is reached. All the accidental
water (that contained in the crude turpentine as it comes from the
forest) having been distilled off, a small stream of cold water is now
let in, so that the heat is kept at or below 316° F., the boiling point of
oil of turpentine. The oil of turpentine and water now come over,
and the mixture is caught in a wooden tub. The distiller tests the
quality of the flow from time to time in a proof-glass, and the distillation is continued until the proportion of water coming over is 9 of
water to 1 of oil of turpentine. At this stage the heat is withdrawn,
the still-cap is taken off, and the hot resin is drawn off by a valvular
cock at the side of the still near the bottom. This resin passes through
a strainer before it reaches the vat, to rid it of foreign substances,
which may not have been previously removed by the skimmer. The
yield of oil of turpentine from 'virgin dip' (the first exudation from a
newly boxed tree) is about 5 gallons to the barrel, about 20 per cent.
being left in the resin,[1] since the removal of a larger proportion would
darken the color, and consequently depreciate its value. The yield
from 'yellow dip' (the runnings of the second and subsequent years) is
about four gallons to a barrel. The yield from 'scrapings' (the inspis-
sated gum from the tree facings) is about 2 to 3½ gallons, according to
age, and also to the proportion of trash which it contains."

The separation of turpentine, by what is practically a steam distillation process, serves to explain the fact which, until I received the
above information, had often surprised me, that the commercial
article is uniformly free from products of the decomposition of resin by
heat.

Some idea of the importance of the turpentine industry will be
gathered by inspection of the following table representing the number
of barrels imported into London since 1872 :

1873	44,495	1878	56,221
1874	57,720	1879	42,960
1875	57,093	1880	39,649
1876	57,371	1881	63,724
1877	49,500	1882	57,489

---

[1] The fact that the whole of the hydrocarbon is not removed accounts for the
statement sometimes made, that "resin spirit" is optically active, that made from
pure resin, according to my experiments, being inactive.

Probably about two-thirds of the entire quantity sent to this country is landed in London.

In so far as general properties are concerned, there is no practically distinguishable difference, other than in color, I believe, between various samples of the commercial article, but tested by the polarimeter they vary considerably.

The chief port of shipment is Wilmington, and most of the turpentine from this port, like that from Bordeaux, is of remarkably uniform quality. Thus out of thirty-five samples representing in all cases bulks of several hundred barrels, and in a number of cases bulks of from 1000 to 2000 or more barrels, no less than twenty-eight samples varied in rotatory power (value of a_D per 200 mm.), only within the very narrow limits of $27° 6'$ to $28° 35'$; four samples had an inferior rotatory power of $24° 29'$ to $26° 40'$, and only three had a superior rotatory power of respectively $29° 31'$, $31° 21'$, and $32° 38'$.

That shipped from Savannah, on the other hand, is, as a rule, characterized by a relatively low rotatory power, e. g. :

Ex. 1569 barrels......$a_D = 22° 21'$	Ex. 1696 barrels......$a_D = 19°$
Ex. 1000 " ......$a_D = 24° 9'$	Ex. 1870 " ......$a_D = 20° 33'$
Ex. 1383 " ......$a_D = 20° 22'$	Ex. 1200 " ......$a_D = 21° 21'$
Ex. 1571 " ......$a_D = 19° 39'$	Ex. 1595 " ......$a_D = 19° 12'$

In the case of the last of these shipments, I had the opportunity of taking five samples, each representing about one-sixth of the bulk, which gave the following values: $21° 4'$, $21° 19'$, $18° 13'$, $17° 38'$, and $20° 6'$. I have not been able to ascertain whether the turpentine shipped from Savannah is the product of a different tree, or whether the difference in climate between the two districts, of which Wilmington and Savannah are "centres," is the cause of the marked variation from what may be termed the Wilmington type. I trust that the publication of this paper may, as one result, lead to my being favored with information on this point.

Judging from the opportunities which have presented themselves for examining turpentine shipped from Charleston, the deliveries from this port would appear to comprise turpentine of somewhat high rotatory power, as well as those of the Wilmington and Savannah types :

Ex. 1000 barrels......$a_D = 30° 24'$	Ex. 2179 barrels......$a_D = 24° 15'$
Ex. —— " ......$a_D = 30° 38''$	Ex. —— " ......$a_D = 19°$
Ex. 250 " ......$a_D = 33° 33'$	Ex. 1874 " ......$a_D = 26° 42'$
Ex. 1689 " ......$a_D = 28° 15'$	Ex. 1886 " ......$a_D = 29° 39'$
Ex. 200 " ......$a_D = 24°$	

Other parts also furnish a somewhat irregular product ; the values, however, always lie within those already given, and in the majority of cases belong to the Wilmington type, Brunswick alone exhibiting a marked tendency to furnish a product of the Savannah type.

Commercially, I believe, no distinction is made between the turpentine shipped from various American ports; nor indeed is French turpentine, which is now a comparative rarity in the English market, regarded as having distinctive qualities. My observations on the whole justify this practice: French turpentine is slightly less readily oxidized, absorbing oxygen somewhat less rapidly than American turpentine, but the difference is probably insufficient to make itself felt in practice.

Russian Turpentine.—Commercially, this variety is of no importance, as it cannot well be used in paint or varnish-making, both on account of its unpleasant odor and of the extreme readiness in comparison with French or American turpentine with which it absorbs oxygen, forming a viscid oil; its vapor appears also to produce far more marked physiological effects than either of the ordinary oils, inciting violent headache in many individuals.

It is the product of *Pinus sylvestris*, but I have not been able to ascertain whether the turpentine is specially collected, or is a mere by-product. According to one account which I have received, the waste timber is piled into heaps and a fire lighted; the resinous matter which drains away is then collected and the turpentine extracted from it by distillation.

Different samples are remarkably different in their optical character, as the following numbers show:

a_o(per 200 mm.)$=36°$ 29′	44° 11′	40° 42′
56° 7′	41° 0′	46° 45′
34° 18′	35° 28′	36° 4′
38° 58′	30° 42′	37° 5′
32° 27′	35° 20′	42° 10′
31° 20′	38° 6′	39° 52′
34° 8′	45° 10′	30° 10′
39° 58′	38° 4′	

Excepting the first four, all these samples were drawn from single barrels, and were obligingly furnished to me by Mr. Kingzett.

Russian turpentine has been shown by Tilden, "Chem. Soc. Trans," 1878-80, to consist of a peculiar $C_{10}H_{16}$ hydrocarbon, the so-called *Sylvestrene* of Atterberg (Ber. 10, 1202), and of an isomeride possessing the character of American turpentine. Sylvestrene, according to these authors, has a *specific* rotatory power of $(a_o)=19\cdot5°$ (Atterberg), 19·6° (Tilden), that of the associated hydrocarbon being 36·3° (Atterberg). In conformation of the assumption that one of the constituents of Russian turpentine is probably identical with the main constituent of

American turpentine, I may mention that I have separated from the latter by fractional distillation a portion having a rotatory power per 200 mm. of no less than 49° 34′, and that on several occasions, by submitting American turpentine to air oxidation, and afterwards distilling off the unaltered hydrocarbon by steam, I have obtained products of considerably higher rotatory power than the original oils. I have also examined several samples received from Mr. Kingzett of the hydrocarbon carried over by the air current during the air oxidation of Russian turpentine. In most cases these have been almost free from sylvestrene, and have exhibited a higher rotatory power than the original crude turpentine from which they were derived.

The numbers above given fluctuate within wide limits, and are of interest as indicating that the proportions in which the two recognized constituents of Russian turpentine are present probably vary considerably, and also that other perhaps isomeric hydrocarbons are mixed with them; they serve to confirm the idea that American turpentine is also a mixture of isomeric hydrocarbons. I may add that certain observations even lead me to think it not unlikely that the low dextro-rotatory power of American turpentine is due to the presence of a lævo-rotatory terpene; this would serve to explain the difference in optical character of products from different localities. The comparative study of American turpentine—and indeed generally of oils containing $C_{10}H_{16}$ hydrocarbons—from this point of view, I think deserves attention; variations in climatic and other conditions may have led to a gradual differentiation both in botanical and physiological character of a single parent stock.

Method of Analysis.—The terms "petroleum spirit" and "petroleum oil" as commercially used do not admit of very precise definition; for the purpose of this paper, I would therefore define petroleum spirit as being that portion of crude petroleum which may be volatilized by means of steam from water boiling at atmospheric pressure, and petroleum oil as being the non-volatile portion. Judged of by this definition, commercial spirit and oil are, as a rule, more or less mixtures; the amount of spirit in the best burning oil is, however, small.

The presence of petroleum oil in turpentine is readily detected and the amount estimated by steam distilling. Unless it has been freely exposed to the air for a long time, but a mere trace of viscid matter remains on steam-distilling turpentine; on one or two occasions only have I met with samples containing a small amount of resin, which was left as a solid on distilling off the turpentine by a steam current. Should more than a few tenths of a per cent. of non-volatile matter remain, it is probable that petroleum is present. This usually betrays itself by the more or less marked blue fluorescence of the residue; but should this criterion fail, the behavior of petroleum and of the non-

volatile product of the air oxidation of turpentine on digestion with
dilute nitric acid will serve to differentiate them. The latter is readily
oxidized and dissolved; the former does not alter much in bulk, but
apparently undergoes more or less complete nitration. I have never
yet met with a sample containing resin oil, but it would not be difficult
to detect it, as it is oxidized by nitric acid, and behaves in a most
characteristic manner when triturated with a paste of slaked lime,
forming the well-known grease.

The detection and estimation of petroleum spirit is less readily
effected. The method which I employ is based on the different behavior of turpentine and paraffins with sulphuric acid. The paraffins, it
is well known, are almost unaffected, whereas turpentine is polymer-
ized and for the most part converted into substances of high boiling
point which do not volatilize in a current of steam. I say for the most
part, because, as I have elsewhere stated, a certain amount of cymene
and of a paraffinoid hydrocarbon is always produced. Inasmuch as
the amount of cymene so produced varies with the strength of the acid
and the temperature, being larger the more concentrated the acid and
the higher the temperature, it is important always to work under
uniform conditions, at as low a temperature as convenient, and to use
diluted acid. I employ two strengths of acid, a mixture of 2 vols. acid
and 1 vol. water (2:1 acid) and a mixture of 4 vols. acid and 1 vol.
water (4:1 acid). The turpentine—500 c.c. is a convenient quantity—
is placed with about one-fourth to one-third of its bulk of 2:1 acid in
a well-stopped bottle, and the mixture is somewhat cautiously agitated.
It soon becomes more or less heated, and as it is important to effect the
polymerization at a temperature not much above the ordinary atmospheric temperature, the bottle is placed in cold water for a short time.
After repeated agitation with the acid, the turpentine is converted into
a viscid oil, and when this is the case, and no more heat is developed
on continued agitation, the contents of the bottle is transferred to a
separating funnel, the acid layer is run off and the oil poured into a
flask; the latter having been connected with a condenser and a steam-
pot—an ordinary tin can answers admirably—all that is volatile is distilled off. The distillate is mixed with about half its bulk of 4:1 acid,
and treated in a precisely similar manner.

The product from this second operation should only consist of a mixture of cymene and the paraffinoid hydrocarbon; in bulk it should not
be more than 4 to 5 per cent. of the original hydrocarbon. This is the
result of a very large number of estimations; as little as 3 per cent.,
however, has been obtained in experiments conducted with special
care. If much more than about 5 per cent. be obtained, it is desirable
to repeat the treatment with 4:1 acid.

If, from the result of this treatment, it appears probable that petroleum spirit is present, the product is placed in a well-stoppered bottle, together with several times its volume of concentrated sulphuric acid, heated to 50° to 60°, with which it is violently agitated. This treatment is repeated if desirable (weak Nordhausen acid being with advantage substituted for the concentrated sulphuric acid), and the residual hydrocarbon is separated, steam distilled, and then measured. The amount thus obtained should not exceed from ½ to 1 per cent. of the original bulk of turpentine. This treatment with concentrated acid affords a check on the previous determination.

If American petroleum spirit be thus treated it suffers comparatively little loss, so that the amount of hydrocarbon above 1 per cent. represents the *minimum* amount of petroleum spirit in the turpentine. The spirit from Scotch petroleum contains a very much higher proportion of hydrocarbons alterable by sulphuric acid, and therefore cannot be satisfactorily estimated.

To confirm the presence of petroleum spirit, the turpentine should be distilled. Petroleum spirit commences to distill at a temperature which may be above or below that at which turpentine boils, according to its quality, but always distills within comparatively wide limits of temperature; turpentine commences to boil near 160°, and almost entirely passes over below 180.°

The presence of resin spirit also affects the boiling-point in a similar manner. Evidence of the presence of this adulterant is also afforded by the increased yield of hydrocarbons on treatment both with 4:1 and concentrated sulphuric acid, as resin spirit also yields a cymene and paraffinoid hydrocarbon on treatment with 4:1 acid. The cymene from resin spirit being isomeric with that from turpentine, proof of the presence of resin spirit can be obtained by the detection of its cymene, but this is a somewhat delicate operation.

Addendum.—The method above described is also available for the analysis of solvent naphtha from coal tar and similar products; it is, in fact, the only method which is capable of affording results which approach exactness. The problem is by no means so simple, however, as the coal tar product itself contains, besides benzene and its homologues, basic bodies, hydrocarbons alterable by diluted sulphuric acid and paraffins. Until, therefore, a considerable number of genuine samples have been examined, the method is chiefly of value as a qualitative test.—*The Pharm. Jour. and Trans.*, Jan. 20, 1883.

CRUDE TURPENTINE.

The decrease in receipts of Crude Turpentine, this season, is due mainly to the fact, that country distillers have bought and distilled a much larger proportion of the supply than in former years, for which, of course, they had to pay prices, at times, fully equal to the Wilmington quotations.

The Black River, Long Creek and Coharie country, supplies this market principally, and the average price of the year will compare favorably with that of former seasons.

The estimated capacity of the Wilmington Distilleries is about ten times in excess of the supply: it being a matter of fact, that the Union stills alone, ran several years ago, more crude stuff in twenty-four hours, than the present entire average daily receipts, which are divided among ten times the capacity of the Union Distillery.

Within the last two years, much complaint has been made among buyers, respecting the quality of Crude brought to this market, which has greatly deteriorated, in consequence of the habit by many producers, of mixing the face or scrape product, with the dip turpentine, and which has resulted in reducing the average yield in the distillation of soft Turpentine, to five gallons Spirits from a barrel of 280 pounds, while from a better article, one gallon more was formerly obtained.

The yearly receipts of Crude Turpentine in this market for the years ending 31st March were as follows :

1875-76................................. 86,833 Barrels.
1876-77 143,826   "
1877-78...............................142,360   "
1878-79...............................154,985   "
1879-80......................... 132,375   "
1880-81................................. 92,101   "
1881-82................................. 87,486   "
1882-83................................. 68,574   "

The average monthly price for the same time is given below :

For Month of	1873	1874	1875	1876	1877	1878	1879	1880	1881	1882	1883
January			2 50	2 57½	3 12½	2 20	1 77½	2 50	2 90	3 87½	3 50
February			2 37½	2 37½	2 85	2 20	1 82½	2 47½	1 82½	3 50	4 00
March			2 30	2 37½	2 62½	2 05	1 67½	2 77½	2 72½	3 50	3 00
April			2 50	2 55	2 30	1 87½	1 60	2 25	2 60	4 00	
May		2 85	2 25	2 07½	2 17½	1 75	1 00	1 75	2 25	3 00	
June		2 50	1 72½	1 87½	2 10	1 80	1 60	2 55	2 50	2 75	
July		2 25	2 15	1 82½	2 05	1 80	1 62½	1 87½	2 90	3 00	
August		2 25	2 02½	1 75	2 27½	1 80	1 62½	1 62½	2 85	2 75	
September		2 32½	2 15	1 97½	2 37½	1 85	1 75	2 00	2 80	2 50	
October		2 00	2 55	2 22½	2 37½	1 92½	2 25	2 52½	3 02½	2 75	
November		2 60	2 67½	2 47½	2 22½	1 82½	2 50	2 80	3 62½	3 00	
December		2 50	2 55	3 00	2 15	1 85	2 67½	2 80	3 50	3 00	

SPIRITS TURPENTINE.

From the tables appended it will be observed that while our receipts of spirits have materially increased, the demand, as indicated by the average price obtained for the crop, has also grown in larger proportion. The domestic consumption has steadily gained upon an uncertain production, which has hitherto barely supplied a general market, for some time past singularly free from organized speculation.

It was thought in the early part of this season, that reliable indications of a much larger supply than last year's crop, would result in a lower range of prices; but notwithstanding the fact that the combined receipts of Wilmington, Charleston, Savannah and Brunswick alone showed an increase over last year's crop of about 56,000 casks, the value has steadily maintained a close comparison with the average of last season, which was generally admitted to have produced a short crop.

The preparations for the incoming season, indicate a crop under favorable auspices, of about ten per cent. above last year's supply. It is estimated by some intelligent operators, that Georgia may show an increase of perhaps 20 per cent. The reports from North Carolina and South Carolina, indicate no increase.

There is no doubt with reference to a late crop. Some distillers estimate it five weeks later than usual, others four weeks. None, who are informed on the South Carolina and Georgia crop, consider it less than four weeks late. This is owing to unusually cold weather. On the 22nd of March we had a heavy fall of snow in Wilmington, which is almost unprecedented—and cold weather still continues at this date, (5th April). which may curtail the estimate of any in crease in the production.

The supply in London, on the 1st of April, was unusually low but the stock in the United States shows an increase over last year's figures, of 3,508 casks.

The annual receipts of spirits turpentine for ten years past were as follows :

1873-74	138,103	Casks
1874-75	121,198	"
1875-76	97,197	"
1876-77	97,409	"
1877-78	109,707	"
1878-79	109,574	"
1879-80	103,671	"
1880-81	87,107	"
1881-82	85,997	"
1882-83	88,186	"

The average monthly price for ten years has been as follows :

For Month of	1873	1874	1875	1876	1877	1878	1879	1880	1881	1882	1883
January	59½	41½	34⅞	31	43	29⅜	26¼	40½	44	51¾	49¼
February	63½	45	33½	32	38¾	30¾	26¾	40½	42¼	49¾	49¼
March	57	41	32¼	35	35	28⅜	26⅜	44¼	40¾	52½	47¾
April	49	....	31	32	30¾	26¾	28⅜	35¼	35½	56½	....
May	43¾	35	30¾	29	29	27	25⅝	26¾	33¾	45½	....
June	41	33¾	30½	27	28¾	27½	25⅛	25½	37½	41	....
July	39¾	32¼	29½	27⅝	28⅞	27½	25⅞	25¼	39¼	41¾	....
August	39	32	28⅛	27¼	31¾	26⅞	24⅝	29¾	43¼	41	....
September	38	33¾	30¾	30½	32½	26¼	26	34¾	50	41¾	....
October	39½	35½	36¾	31	32	26⅜	37	40¾	48¾	47½	....
November	36	32¾	36	35	31	26⅞	39¼	42⅜	51½	48¾	....
December	37¾	32¾	33¾	42½	29⅜	26½	39¾	42¾	51½	47	....

ROSIN.

The receipts and business in rosin for a year past, have measurably decreased. This is probably owing to the abandonment of many old trees in the interior which failed to yield a profitable return, and to the limited number of new boxes cut at the beginning of the season, as well as to the fact, that notwithstanding the falling off in production, prices current throughout the crop year have ruled unusually low. Comparing last year with that of 1873, a decrease of nearly 40 per cent. in receipts is apparent, but a comparison with the years 1880 to 1882 shows a more favorable record.

The receipts of rosin in Wilmington during the years ending 31st March, for ten years past, were as follows:

1873 and 1874	707,349	barrels.
1874 and 1875	605,521	"
1875 and 1876	540,730	"
1876 and 1877	524,967	"
1877 and 1878	538,259	"
1878 and 1879	581,739	"
1870 and 1880	568,188	"
1880 and 1881	444,552	"
1881 and 1882	454,917	"
1882 and 1883	433,200	"

The average monthly prices current for strained and good strained rosin for ten years past, are given in the following table:

For Month of	1873	1874	1875	1876	1877	1878
January	3 07½	2 12½	1 72½	1 50 @1 54	1 95 @1 97½	1 41¼@1 43¼
February	3 07½	2 12½	1 67½	1 46½@1 48½	1 69 @1 72½	1 35 @1 38¾
March	2 50	1 90	1 67½	1 52½@1 50	1 72½@1 77½	1 32½@1 36¼
April	2 62½	....	1 67½	1 60 @1 63	1 55 @1 60	1 30 @1 33¾
May	2 52½	2 25	1 55	1 50 @1 55	1 42½@1 47½	1 20¾@1 23¾
June	2 35	2 37½	1 47½	1 30 @1 37½	1 42½@1 47½	1 17½@1 20
July	2 37½	1 65	1 42½	1 22½@1 27½	1 37½@1 41¼	1 17½@1 20
August	2 50	1 77½	1 35	1 18¾@1 20	1 45 @1 50	1 13¾@1 15
September	2 45	1 95	1 35	1 36¼@1 40	1 47½@1 52½	1 20 @1 25
October	2 50	2 07½	1 47½	1 52½@1 57	1 42½@1 47½	1 20 @1 25
November	2 32½	2 00	1 52½	1 65 @1 70	1 43¾@1 48½	1 17½@1 20
December	2 20	1 85	1 40	2 10	1 41¼@1 46¼	1 17½@1 20

For Month of	1879	1880	1881	1882	1883
January	1 16¼@1 18¾	1 25 @1 28¾	1 41¼@1 45	1 97½@2 02½	1 32½@1 35
February	1 12½@1 17½	1 18¾@1 22½	1 37½	1 88¾@1 93¾	1 33¾@1 38
March	1 11¼@1 15	1 16¾@1 20	1 47½@1 51¼	1 88¾@1 93¾	1 35 @1 40
April	1 02½@1 06¼	1 07½@1 10	1 46¼@1 50	1 88¾@1 93¾	....
May	1 03¾@1 07½	1 02½@1 07½	1 50 @1 55	1 75 @1 80	....
June	1 07½@1 12½	1 05 @1 10	1 70 @1 75	1 57½@1 67½	....
July	1 05 @1 10	1 03¾@1 07½	1 74¾@1 80	1 47½@1 56¼	....
August	98¾@1 05¾	1 05 @1 10	1 85 @2 06¼	1 35 @1 47½	....
September	92½@ 97½	1 15 @1 20	1 98½@2 07½	1 32½@1 47½	....
October	1 17½@1 12½	1 32½@1 40	2 02½@2 11	1 38¼@1 48¾	....
November	1 40 @1 45	1 35 @1 40	1 90 @1 95	1 33¾@1 43¾	....
December	1 25	1 40 @1 45	1 92½@1 97½	1 32½@1 38¾	....

It is probable that four-fifths of the rosin sold in this market, is of the common and medium grades. In the early part of the crop year, some very handsome rosin, grading N, and W G, and W W, is sold, but as the season advances, these grades become scarce, and the major part of business during the remainder of the year is in strained and good strained, with a small proportion of E F G H I K M. The standard adopted, is the same as was established several years ago by the New York Exchange, with Messrs. Beling, Nemeyer & Co. as supervising inspectors; but frequent complaint has been made of irregularity in their type samples, which is a matter of serious importance to foreign shippers. A universal standard in glass types, would be of great benefit to the trade, and effectually settle the much vexed question of quality, which is so often raised in the fulfilment of sales for future delivery, or shipments upon contracts. An attempt was made some years ago, by a member of this Exchange, to procure standard samples of this character; but the expense was ascertained to be too great for any practical benefit. The volume of business has since increased to such proportions, however, that a united effort by the New York, Wilmington, Charleston and Savannah Exchanges, would easily accomplish the desired result, at a small proportionate cost.

About a year ago, the character of Wilmington shipments of common rosin suffered seriously in foreign markets, in consequence of the careless and sometimes criminal preparation for market; a large proportion of "strained rosin" being mixed with sand and dross, rendering it quite unfit for the purposes of export to Europe, where it is distilled into common oil. So great had this prejudice against Wilmington rosin become, that several importers refused to take our rosin at any price, preferring ✓ that of Charleston and Savannah at greater cost, rather than risk an uncertain quality where only 10 per cent. was inspected. This important matter was then brought to the notice of Wilmington receivers, who at once instituted means of stopping the fraudulent practice referred to, and who have since effectually overcome the difficulty, by closer inspection, and by the entire rejection of doubtful rosin.

The same complaint has been made to us recently, of Charleston rosin, and it behooves the Exchanges, both North and South, to make more stringent rules of inspection for the protection of consumers.

TAR.

The receipts of tar for the past season, have exceeded those of former years; the increase for this year being about seven per cent. above the receipts of last season.

The domestic export of this article is steadily increasing, a considerable trade being done in *cans*, which are shipped for the convenience of Western markets, and which seem to be in good demand from all quarters. The condition of the barrels, is somewhat better than in former years, but there is still great room for improvement. The large falling off in our foreign demand, is in a measure attributable to this long-continued neglect in preparing suitable packages for market; although it is also stated, that the Russian tar of Archangel, in the White Sea, is much preferred for its quality, as well as for its superior packages, which are made of very thick, heavy wood, and seldom leak at all.

A Glasgow broker informed me two years ago, that they then received about thirty cargoes of Archangel tar to one of Wilmington shipment, although there was still a fair request for our product in Liverpool and Hull.

The average monthly prices for the two last years, have been uncommonly good, as may be seen from the table appended with the receipts of this market for a number of years past; and to this fact is no doubt owing the increased supply.

The receipts in Wilmington since 1874, prior to which no record was made, were as follows:

1875 and 1876	53,010	barrels.
1876 and 1877	71,211	"
1877 and 1878	61,674	"
1878 and 1879	78,116	"
1879 and 1880	45,623	"
1880 and 1881	56,460	"
1881 and 1882	68,653	"
1882 and 1883	73,598	"

The prevailing custom of buying tar by weight and selling it by tale barrel for export, is most unsatisfactory to dealers, and it is hoped by many, that the terms of this trade will be more equitably adjusted by the Exchange.

Average prices of Tar in Wilmington each month for ten years.

For Month of	1873	1874	1875	1876	1877	1878	1879	1880	1881	1882	1883
January..............	2 65	2 47½	1 70	1 50	1 75	1 57½	1 37½	1 25	1 45	2 07½	1 85
February	2 82½	2 45	1 65	1 50	1 65	1 52½	1 32½	1 15	1 77½	1 80	1 80
March................	2 92½	2 25	1 35	1 62½	1 65	1 42½	1 20	1 22½	1 62½	1 80	1 60
April..................	3 00	....	1 60	1 57½	1 57½	1 47½	90	1 32½	1 72½	1 92½	....
May....................	2 95	2 30	1 45	1 37½	1 62½	1 37½	77½	1 25	1 90	1 75	....
June...................	3 17½	2 00	1 50	1 52½	1 70	1 37½	75	1 62½	1 52½	1 90	....
July....................	3 50	1 92½	1 77½	1 92½	1 80	1 50	88¾	1 97½	2 57½	1 95	....
August...............	3 37½	2 40	1 80	1 82½	1 82½	1 80	1 11¼	1 47½	2 42½	1 90	....
September..........	2 82½	1 82½	1 45	1 42½	1 77½	1 67½	97½	1 85	2 27½	1 75	....
October..............	2 47½	1 92½	1 45	1 57½	1 65	1 65	1 31¼	2 25	2 17½	1 91¼	....
November..........	2 32½	1 87½	1 50	1 87½	1 55	1 55	1 67½	2 40	2 32½	1 97½	....
December...........	2 37½	1 75	1 65	1 80	1 47½	1 47½	1 07½	1 90	2 15	1 92½	....

COTTON.

It will be seen by an inspection of the table, for ten years, appended, that there has been a large and almost steady increase in the receipts of cotton at this port, from 39,737 bales in 1873-4 to 131,669 bales in 1881-2. The falling off in the receipts this year, is not a fair criterion of the business of this market. During the early part of the season, from the 1st of September to the middle of November, there were no freight vessels offering by sail, so that nearly all our receipts, up to that time, were forwarded by steamer, via New York, at rates which greatly hampered the trade—especially in direct Liverpool business. This unusual scarcity of shipping facilities not only established an unattractive market, but led to the ultimate refusal of over 10,000 bales of through cotton, from Augusta and other interior points, which formerly obtained an outlet by this port.

The receipts from Augusta and other interior points for foreign shipment, were, last season, to the Champion Compress, 4,189 bales—this year they were only 2,650 bales. To the Wilmington Compress last season they were 976 bales —this year there was not a bale received—showing a net decrease of 2,515 bales fom this source alone. It is therefore fair to presume, that, under more favorable circumstances, our business this season would have equalled that of last year.

Cotton receipts in Wilmington for the years ending 31st March 1873-1883 :

1873-74. .... 43,070 Bales.
1874-75.................................. 81,854 "
1875-76.........................:........ 91,589 "
1876-77..................................121,929 "
1877-78..................................120,975 "
1878-79..................................111,798 "
1979-80.................................. 78,345 "

1880-81 .... 116,876 Bales.
1881-82 137,732   "
1882-83 128,466   "

During the year 1873-74 there was no record kept of the daily prices current in our market, but the following table shows the average price for each month, from January, 1875, to the present time, April 1st, 1883.

For Month of	1875	1876	1877	1878	1879	1880	1881	1882	1883
January	14	12 7-16	12 5-16	10 7-16	8 15-16	12¼	11¼	11¾	9⅞
February	14 3-16	12½	11 15-16	10½	9¼	12⅝	11	11 5-16	9¼
March	15 3-16	12 3-16	11 7-16	10½	9 9-16	11⅜	10⅝	11 9-16	9⅝
April	15¼	12¼	10¾	9½	10 11-16	11 15-16	10⅞	11 11-16	....
May	....	11¾	10½	9 15-16	12	11¼	9 9-16	11½	....
June	....	10⅞	10½	10⅝	12¼	11	10¾	11 13-16	....
July	....	10 11-16	11¾	10½	11⅞	10 15-16	10⅝	12½	....
August	....	11¼	10⅝	11½	11⅞	11	11½	12½	....
September	....	11 7-16	10 5-16	10 7-16	10½	11 13-16	11 7-16	11 7-16	....
October	12¾	10¼	10 11-16	9 3-16	10 3-16	10⅝	11	10¾	....
November	12 7-16	10 3-16	10 7-16	8 13-16	11¼	10 15-16	11¼	10¾	....
December	12 3-16	11½	10⅝	8⅝	12¼	11 5-16	11¾	9 13-16	....

DOMESTIC EXPORTS.

For the Year Ended Dec. 31st.	Bales Cotton.	Casks Spirits.	Bbls. Rosin.	Bbls. Tar.	Bbls. Crude.	Feet Lumber.	Bbls. Pitch.	Bushels Peanuts.	Bales C. Goods	Bales Yarns.	Paper Stock.	M Shingles.	Cases Spirits	Cases Tar.
1873	55,016	42,283	312,499	41,030	14,520	12,507,507	8,244	......	2,356	497	......	3,960,560	......	717
1874	52,635	42,708	307,758	47,820	14,945	2,998,295	7,316	35,562	2,375	1,005	......	5,143,408	376	770
1875	52,123	22,259	222,930	30,540	7,955	3,916,046	3,994	41,138	1,984	1,260	......	3,430,200	225	1,515
1876	60,682	29,433	110,970	31,106	3,900	7,575,772	5,762	44,405	3,511	4,076	......	2,963,225	453	1,972
1877	63,508	23,227	86,422	34,933	4,945	8,132,043	4,746	70,570	3,488	5,254	126	4,639,631	49	3,162
1878	54,224	11,021	65,679	32,008	3,087	9,151,894	4,383	104,281	2,417	6,405	308	4,440,425	7	3,106
1879	46,252	22,212	44,881	44,651	2,905	11,451,978	8,492	50,681	1,390	982	47	4,912,350	48	4,918
1880	40,348	33,272	48,361	29,409	3,356	22,819,065	7,993	71,813	683	120	100	3,266,825	125	3,523
1881	67,765	29,161	40,479	45,562	2,235	29,314,987	9,187	77,042	883	341	310	3,680,730	50	6,341
1882	72,624	34,620	165,411	55,036	2,479	31,207,061	7,965	58,885	1,376	576	741	4,748,951	116	

FOREIGN EXPORTS.

For the Year	Bales Cotton.	Casks Spirits.	Bbls. Rosin.	Bbls. Tar.	Bbls. Crude.	Feet Lumber.	Bbls. Pitch.	M Shingles.	Cases Spirits	Cases Tar.
1873	4,634	88,953	347,652	4,296	735	6,920,171	180	2,578,256	......	......
1874	11,927	83,129	248,424	20,709	650	4,231,030	167	3,057,805	......	......
1875	18,140	85,181	300,400	16,419	389	5,904,541	182	1,859,000	......	......
1876	33,202	62,150	379,565	27,785	1,535	7,122,860	316	1,926,555	270	......
1877	50,135	78,605	451,282	35,048	1,087	8,892,018	537	3,412,655	202	10
1878	76,232	107,152	516,279	31,176	1,449	8,916,949	331	2,394,383	6	23
1879	37,486	68,962	468,010	22,721	......	9,435,715	167	2,748,400	......	......
1880	65,718	69,453	389,380	14,032	......	10,452,010	71	3,354,212	......	......
1881	57,664	36,177	445,650	14,969	102	16,184,583	791	3,177,453	......	......
1882	44,634	53,276	338,904	15,507	130	9,074,077	17	1,886,900	......	......

TOTAL EXPORTS.

For the Year Ended Dec. 31st.	Bales Cotton.	Casks Spirits.	Bbls. Rosin.	Bbls. Tar.	Bbls. Crude.	Feet Lumber.	Bbls. Pitch.	Bushels Peanuts.	Bales C. Goods.	Bales Yarn.	Bales P. Stock.	M Shingles.	Cases. Spirits	Cases. Tar.
1873	79,650	131,236	690,151	45,326	15,255	19,517,768	8,421		2,356	497		6,388,896		
1874	64,502	125,837	556,182	68,619	15,565	7,229,325	7,483	33,362	2,375	1,085		8,501,213	376	717
1875	71,263	107,429	525,330	47,159	8,291	9,820,607	4,176	41,138	1,984	1,260		5,189,200	225	770
1876	102,884	91,592	490,555	61,891	5,435	14,688,692	6,078	41,405	3,511	4,076		4,980,740	457	1,515
1877	113,733	101,832	537,704	69,981	6,032	17,024,061	5,293	70,570	3,468	5,254	126	8,052,286	419	1,982
1878	130,456	118,176	581,936	63,184	4,596	18,068,843	4,723	104,281	2,417	6,405	368	6,834,908	209	3,185
1879	83,738	91,224	512,891	67,372	2,905	23,887,693	8,659	59,681	1,390	982	47	7,060,750	51	3,106
1880	106,066	102,725	417,750	53,411	3,356	34,271,675	8,054	71,813	683	191	109	6,627,537	125	4,948
1881	125,429	87,658	486,138	60,491	2,487	45,496,480	9,266	77,012	898	341	340	6,987,183	50	3,923
1882	117,258	87,890	444,318	71,445	2,309	40,281,138	7,982	58,885	1,376	576	741	6,685,851	116	6,341

DESTINATION OF EXPORTS.

Years Ended 31st March	1878-'79			1879-'80			1880-'81			1881-'82			1882-'83		
	Cotton	Spirits	Rosin	Cotton	Spirits	Rosin	Cotton	Spirits	Rosin	Cotton	Spirits	Rosin	Cotton	Spirits	Rosin
Amsterdam	5,379	16,752	51,689	3,451	8,477	42,829	1,209	1,100	1,283		7,202	25,524		7,712	27,232
Antwerp	900							7,394	28,681						
Barcelona		550	1,070		745	5,023		1,900	6,840		825	4,700		1,006	2,963
Belfast		2,700	1,012		1,760	3,460				1,530					
Bremen	7,479	11,923	20,659	4,547	2,970	27,089	7,219	4,320	36,778	7,289	5,544	20,021	2,140	3,610	29,716
Bristol									3,044						
Cardiff															
Cette															
Channel f.o.	5,775	5,771	2,250	2,020	21,376	1,991	9,065	3,702	1,241		6,471	1,253	4,800	7,625	3,697
Cronstadt			8,477						3,145			10,761	950		5,741
Dantzic															
Dordrecht															
Elsinor f.o.															
Fiume	1,365														7,076
Genoa	2,068						1,047	500	11,551			2,650	1,500		
Ghent					2,330										
Gibraltar		6,590						1,790			592			1,730	
Glasgow			43,333			61,974			43,931			27,299			8,353
Granton and Leith			12,697						22,133			11,429			33,488
Havre	2,050	9,354	2,456	1,526	2,934	96,711	2,621	812	8,716	1,430	8,391	98,295		8,690	12,990
Hamburg and Harbourg	1,398	1,797	87,689		2,951		1,753	3,021	72,603		1,163	6,038		1,731	50,725
Hull			5,318			5,176		450	7,267						3,650
Konigsberg									1,941						
Lisbon												800			
Liverpool	39,871	6,257	41,424	22,668	7,774	65,416	49,268	514	17,321	63,584	3,317	13,614	11,314	2,650	17,372
London		27,602	80,434		19,217	64,421		31,148	50,888		21,278	53,040		12,946	54,508
Marseilles			4,000												3,000
Naples															
New Castle		1,130	13,759		1,010	15,599		420	8,460			12,331		75	11,300
Riga			15,283			16,050			7,384			7,161			22,950
Reval															
Rotterdam		4,976	43,192		550	57,333		5,675	32,635		3,165	31,370		4,602	10,767
Rostock			1,734									2,587			4,602
Stettin			29,328			31,920			3,300			28,320			29,107
Sunderland												2,722		50	2,184
Trieste			20,558		100	33,458		550	23,961		400	17,330		750	29,868
Other Ports	2	5	1,045	2	102	2,683		3	52		4	13		2	145
Total Foreign	66,265	95,307	490,337	34,214	72,599	531,663	72,182	63,199	392,318	63,833	58,615	380,278	53,704	54,483	384,534
Total Domestic	45,651	12,860	70,495	41,463	26,302	39,611	46,271	33,121	52,793	71,694	29,752	45,645	70,749	32,567	98,918
Grand Total	111,886	108,257	560,682	75,677	98,901	571,494	118,453	96,320	415,111	135,527	88,367	425,923	124,453	87,050	483,452

DESTINATION OF EXPORTS.

Years Ended 31st March.	1873-74 Cotton	Spirits	Rosin	1874-75 Cotton	Spirits	Rosin	1875-76 Cotton	Spirits	Rosin	1876-77 Cotton	Spirits	Rosin	1877-78 Cotton	Spirits	Rosin
Amsterdam		4,000	350		10,019	18,093	1,075		5,672	7,963			9,197		29,546
Antwerp		11,522	30,679					8,701	24,007	775	1,331	22,060	3,299	8,175	1,770
Barcelona		450	4,905						1,075		6,211				7,131
Belfast	368	2,845	25,178		100	2,275		400	5,565	1,988	300	1,530		980	
Bremen		8,433	25,435		2,672	8,688		500	2,000		1,365	500	2,870		19,219
Bristol					4,530	20,891		9,741	26,350		4,127	20,785		7,714	
Cardiff												1,700			
Cette		19,660	43,761		27,544	13,325	3,038		510	2,773	28,157	9,863	5,923	13,455	5,775
Channel f. o.			7,717			2,461			5,326						3,762
Cronstadt			1,824												
Dantzic															
Dordrecht			1,450						2,500						
Elsinor f. o.															
Fiume															4,750
Genoa		3,251	16,447												
Ghent			3,482												
Glasgow		2,575	62,028		4,250	10,172		5,600	10,722	2,511	2,100	44,664		6,905	40,050
Granton and Leith			3,200			3,973			18,225		1,375	1,015			1,910
Havre					1,650	63,326	1,228	1,550	45,500		1,480	80,325	1,780	6,091	100,797
Hamburg and Harbourg					200	200		300	4,182		780	7,382	1,066	5,657	11,691
Hull															
Konigsberg															
Lisbon	5,518	5,490	32,652		5,738	32,846	23,585	7,688	70,851	21,058	127	29,084	28,583	5,715	24,409
Liverpool		20,553	49,012		17,180	22,477		33,075	57,112		17,803	61,463		30,788	82,297
London															8,357
Marseilles															2,280
Naples															7,051
New Castle					600	3,851		550	3,476		300	9,851		304	
Riga			8,779			4,000									
Reval															
Rotterdam		12,618	76,704		4,556	45,871		6,455	50,904		590	43,005	1,493	1,306	45,775
Rostock						2,018							1,965		
Stettin			53,267		100	32,219			17,256			38,457			19,307
Sunderland					100	1,045									
Trieste		2,500	2,500			2,000			3,001		92	8,172		58	18,648
Other Ports		29	49		9	1,061		38	265			846			1,146
Total Foreign	61,012	97,871	448,639	11,311	78,848	289,772	25,986	80,024	389,482	36,948	66,498	381,100	56,576	87,675	433,821
Total Domestic	36,457	42,162	282,072	61,040	37,670	330,442	58,103	24,766	190,914	77,858	27,127	113,927	66,098	19,573	77,486
Grand Total	42,869	140,033	730,702	72,351	116,478	620,214	82,989	104,790	580,396	114,780	93,625	495,027	121,974	107,248	513,307

APPENDIX.

With reference to the remarks upon our honored and distinguished dead in "Oakdale," the following "copy" was inadvertently omitted, and is appended herewith as a proof of what Wilmington people have done, and will yet do, in time of sore trial :

Among those who, by services during the yellow fever season, have imposed upon the city of Wilmington a debt that can never be repaid, were Phineas W. Fanning and Isaac Northrop.

The former held the post of Secretary and Treasurer—or an office with duties akin—in the Howard Association. He was the dispenser of such charity as a sorely impoverished people could place at his disposal. At any hour of the day or night, he gladly heeded the call to relieve the suffering. The scourge at last laid him on a bed which might prove the bed of death. Even then, he would refuse no one a hearing, and from his chamber there issued orders to feed the starving, or to supply with nurses and with medicine the sick and dying.

Mr. Isaac Northrop accompanied his family to a place of security, and then returned to the city in pursuance of a noble resolve to devote his energies, his life, if need be, to the friendless and the poor. It was a purpose in which self had no place—deliberate, well-considered and intelligently formed. He sought every opportunity for doing

good. From his own stores the poor were furnished till
abundant supplies were exhausted. All his thoughts, all
his physical powers, were given to the work in hand. When
he was compelled to cease from his labors to confront death
itself, he was not taken by surprise. He had contemplated
such a termination of his duties, and made full preparation
for the event. His name deserves to be written high a mong
the unselfish ones of earth.

www.ingramcontent.com/pod-product-compliance
Lightning Source LLC
Chambersburg PA
CBHW020848270326
41928CB00006B/607